WEST-E English Language, Literature, and Composition
0041
Teacher Certification Exam

By: Sharon Wynne, M.S.
Southern Connecticut State University

"And, while there's no reason yet to panic, I think it's only prudent that we make preparations to panic."

XAMonline, INC.
Boston

Copyright © 2008 XAMonline, Inc.
All rights reserved. No part of the material protected by this copyright notice may be reproduced or utilized in any form or by any means, electronic or mechanical, including photocopying, recording or by any information storage and retrievable system, without written permission from the copyright holder.

To obtain permission(s) to use the material from this work for any purpose including workshops or seminars, please submit a written request to:

XAMonline, Inc.
21 Orient Ave.
Melrose, MA 02176
Toll Free 1-800-509-4128
Email: info@xamonline.com
Web www.xamonline.com
Fax: 1-781-662-9268

Library of Congress Cataloging-in-Publication Data

Wynne, Sharon A.
    English Language, Literature, and Composition 10041: Teacher Certification / Sharon A. Wynne. -2nd ed. ISBN 978-1-58197-636-6
    1. English Language Literature and Composition 10041.
    2. Study Guides.   3. Praxis
    4. Teachers' Certification & Licensure.   5. Careers

Disclaimer:
The opinions expressed in this publication are the sole works of XAMonline and were created independently from the National Education Association, Educational Testing Service, or any State Department of Education, National Evaluation Systems or other testing affiliates.

Between the time of publication and printing, state specific standards as well as testing formats and website information may change that is not included in part or in whole within this product. Sample test questions are developed by XAMonline and reflect similar content as on real tests; however, they are not former tests. XAMonline assembles content that aligns with state standards but makes no claims nor guarantees teacher candidates a passing score. Numerical scores are determined by testing companies such as NES or ETS and then are compared with individual state standards. A passing score varies from state to state.

Printed in the United States of America   œ-1

West-E: English Language, Literature, and Composition 0041
ISBN: 978-1-58197-636-6

About the WEST-E/Praxis II Examination in English Language, Literature, and Composition

The Praxis Examination in English is broken down into three sections:

Content Knowledge
2 hours—120 Multiple choice questions

Categories
1.0 Reading and Understanding Text
    66 questions—55% of the exam
2.0 Language and Linguistics
    18 questions—15% of the exam
3.0 Composition and Rhetoric
    36 questions—30% of the exam

Essays
2 hours—4 Essay questions

Categories
4.0 Interpreting Literature: Poetry
    1 question—25% of the exam
5.0 Interpreting Literature: Prose
    1 question—25% of the exam
6.0 Issues in English: Understanding Literary Issues
    1 question—25% of the exam
7.0 Issues in English: Literary Issues and Literary Texts
    1 question—25% of the exam

Pedagogy
1 hour—2 Constructed Response questions

Categories
8.0 Teaching Literature
    1 question—50% of the exam
9.0 Responding to Student Writing
    1 question—50% of the exam

Essay Scoring

For **Competencies 4.0-7.0**, responses are graded holistically. The score range is 0 to 3.

A score of 3:
- Analyzes the specified literary element/central idea/literary issue in the selection accurately and with some depth.
- Paraphrases or summarizes the central idea fully and accurately.
- Shows a sound understanding of the selection.
- Supports points with appropriate examples from the selection and explains how the examples support those points.
- Is coherent and demonstrates control of language, including diction and syntax.
- Demonstrates facility with the conventions of standard written English.
- For the Literary Issues question: Develops a thesis according to the demands of the question and uses appropriate examples from two literary works to support the thesis.

A score of 2:
- Analyzes the specified literary elements/central idea/literary issue in the selection with overall accuracy but may overlook or misinterpret some elements.
- Demonstrates understanding of the selection but may contain some misreadings.
- Supports points with appropriate examples from the selection but may fail to explain how the examples support those points.
- Is coherent and demonstrates control of language, including diction and syntax.
- Displays control of the conventions of standard written English but may have some flaws.

A score of 1:
Demonstrates some ability to engage with the selection/issue statement but is flawed in one or more of the following ways:
- Incorrectly identifies literary elements in the selection or provides a superficial analysis of those elements.
- Inaccurately paraphrases or summarizes the central idea.
- Demonstrates an insufficient or inaccurate understanding of the selection.
- Fails to support points with appropriate examples from the selection.
- Lacks coherence or has serious problems with the control of language, including diction and syntax.
- Contains serious and persistent writing errors.

A score of 0:
> A zero is given for blank papers, off-topic responses, responses containing severely inaccurate or incoherent observations, or responses that merely rephrase the question.

Pedagogy Scoring

Competency 8.0 Teaching Literature

The question consists of three parts. The score range is 0 to 6. Points are distributed as follows:

Part A—2 points
> 1 point for each appropriate literary feature central to the work of literature. Each literary feature must be specific to the work chosen and appropriate for the grade level.

Part B—2 points
> 1 point for each appropriate obstacle to understanding, including the explanation for why the obstacle is likely. Each obstacle must be specific to the work chosen and appropriate for the grade level.

Part C—2 points
> 1 point for the discussion of each appropriate instructional activity designed to help students understand the literary features and/or overcome obstacles to understanding. Each instructional activity must be specific to the work chosen and appropriate for the grade level.

If the response contains a significant number of errors in the conventions of standard written English, one point will be subtracted from the total points earned for the question. Responses on a literary work other than one chosen from the list provided in the question will receive a score of 0.

The criteria for evaluating whether a literary feature, obstacle, or instructional activity is "appropriate" are established through a "model answers" methodology. This methodology is described as follows.

The "Model Answers" Methodology

For each question, experienced English teachers are asked to write representative responses that, in their estimation, are consistent with the knowledge that prospective beginning English teachers should have. These teachers are carefully chosen to represent the diverse perspectives and situations relevant to the testing population.

The question writer uses these "model answers" to develop a question-specific scoring guide for the question, creating a list of specific examples that would receive full credit. This list is considered to contain *examples* of correct answers, not all the possible correct answers.

The question-specific scoring guides based on model answers provide the basis for choosing the papers that will serve as benchmark and sample papers for the purpose of training the scorers at the scoring session for the question.

During the scoring session while reading student papers, scorers can add new answers to the scoring guide as they see fit.

Training at the scoring session is aimed to ensure that scorers do not score papers on the basis of their opinions or their own preferences but rather make judgments based on the carefully established criteria in the scoring guide.

Competency 9.0 Responding to Student Writing

The question consists of four parts. The score range is 0 to 6. Points are distributed as follows.

Part A—1 point for the identification of one significant strength and explanation of how it contributes to the paper's effectiveness.

Part B—1 point for the identification of one significant weakness and explanation of how it interferes with the paper's effectiveness.

Part C—2 points: 1 point for the correct identification of each of the two specific errors.

Part D—2 points for the discussion of the follow-up assignment that is connected to the strengths or weaknesses of the student's paper and that contributes to the development of the student as a writer.

If the response contains a significant number of errors in the conventions of standard written English, one point will be subtracted from the total points earned for the question. Responses on a literary work other than one chosen from the list provided in the question will receive a score of 0.

The criteria for evaluating whether a strength, weakness, error, or follow-up assignment is awarded the point or points are established through the "Model Answers" methodology. See the above description.

TEACHER CERTIFICATION STUDY GUIDE

TABLE OF CONTENTS

COMPETENCY 1.0   READING AND UNDERSTANDING TEXT 1

Skill 1.1 Paraphrasing, comparing, and interpreting (literally and inferentially) various types of texts, including fiction, poetry, essays, and other nonfiction 1

Skill 1.2 Identifying and interpreting figurative language and other literary elements, e.g., metaphor, simile, voice, point of view, tone, style, setting, diction, mood, allusions, irony, clichés, analogy, hyperbole, personification, alliteration, and foreshadowing 4

Skill 1.3 Identifying patterns, structures, and characteristics of literary forms and genres, e.g., elements of fiction and features of different poetic and prose forms and understanding how these patterns, structures, and characteristics may influence the meaning and effect of a work. 14

Skill 1.4 Identifying major works and authors of American, British, and World literature from various cultures, genres, and periods, including literature for young adults 24

Skill 1.5 Situating and interpreting texts within their historical and cultural contexts 46

Skill 1.6 Recognizing and identifying various instructional approaches to and elements of teaching reading and textual interpretation, e.g., cueing systems, activating prior knowledge, constructing meaning through context, and metacognitive strategies 50

COMPETENCY 2.0   Language and Linguistics 61

Skill 2.1 Understanding the principles of language acquisition and development, including social, cultural, and historical influences and the role and nature of dialects 61

Skill 2.2 Understanding elements of the history and development of the English language and American English, including linguistic change, etymology, and processes of word formation 66

Skill 2.3 Understanding and applying the elements of traditional grammar, e.g., syntax, sentence types, sentence structure, parts of speech, modifiers, sentence combining, phrases and clauses, capitalization, and punctuation 72

ENG. LANGUAGE LIT. & COMP.

Skill 2.4 Understanding the elements of semantics, including ambiguity, euphemism, doublespeak, connotation, and jargon and how these elements affect meaning 95

COMPETENCY 3.0 COMPOSITION AND RHETORIC 102

Skill 3.1 Understanding and applying elements of teaching writing, including:
- Individual and collaborative approaches to teaching writing, e.g., stages of the writing process (prewriting, drafting, revising, editing, publishing, evaluating) and how those stages work recursively.
- Tools and response strategies for assessing student writing, e.g., peer review, portfolios, holistic scoring, scoring rubrics, self-assessment, and conferencing.
- Common research and documentation techniques, e.g., gathering and evaluating data, using electronic and print media, and MLA and APA citations 102

Skill 3.2 Understanding and evaluating rhetorical features in writing, including:
- Purposes for writing and speaking and the role of the audience within varying contexts.
- Organization in a piece of writing and the creation and preservation of coherence.
- Strategies for the organization, development, and presentation of print, electronic, and visual media.
- Discourse aims, e.g., creative, expository, persuasive.
- Methods of argument and types of appeals, e.g., argumentative strategies, analogy, extended metaphor, allusion.
- Style, tone, voice, and point of view as part of rhetorical strategy.
- Recognition of bias, distinguishing between fact and opinion, and identifying stereotypes, inferences, and assumptions 115

COMPETENCY 4.0 INTERPRETING LITERATURE: POETRY 140

Skill 4.1 Interpret a poetry selection from English, American, or world literature of any period 140

COMPETENCY 5.0 INTERPRETING LITERATURE: PROSE 140

Skill 5.1 Interpret a prose selection from English, American, or world literature of any period 140

TEACHER CERTIFICATION STUDY GUIDE

COMPETENCY 6.0   **ISSUES IN ENGLISH: UNDERSTANDING LITERARY ISSUES** 150

Skill 6.1   Evaluate the argument and rhetorical features of a passage that addresses an issue in the study of English.................. 150

COMPETENCY 7.0   **ISSUES IN ENGLISH: LITERARY ISSUES AND LITERARY TEXTS** 154

Skill 7.1   Take and defend a position on an issue in the study of English, using references to works of literature to support that position.... 154

COMPETENCY 8.0   **TEACHING LITERATURE** 155

Skill 8.1   Choose from a list of literary works provided:
- Identify two literary features of the work that are central to teaching it. Cite specific examples from the work.
- Identify two obstacles to understanding that students might experience when encountering the work. They should be specific to the work selected, not just a general discussion of problems students could face with any piece of literature.
- Describe two instructional activities that would help students understand the literary features and/or overcome obstacles to understanding 155

COMPETENCY 9.0   **RESPONDING TO STUDENT WRITING** 160

Skill 9.1   Read an authentic piece of student writing and then assess the strengths and weaknesses of the writing. Identify errors in the conventions of standard written English and create a follow-up assignment that addresses the strengths or weaknesses of the student's writing 160

Resources 162

Sample Test 168

Answer Key 210

Rigor Table 211

Rationales with Sample Questions 212

TEACHER CERTIFICATION STUDY GUIDE

GREAT STUDY AND TESTING TIPS!

What to study in order to prepare for the subject assessments is the focus of this study guide but equally important is *how* you study.

You can increase your chances of truly mastering the information by taking some simple but effective steps.

Study Tips:

1. **Some foods aid the learning process.** Foods such as milk, nuts, seeds, rice, and oats help your study efforts by releasing natural memory enhancers called CCKs (*cholecystokinin*) composed of *tryptophan*, *choline*, and *phenylalanine*. All of these chemicals enhance the neurotransmitters associated with memory. Before studying, try a light, protein-rich meal of eggs, turkey, and fish. All of these foods release the memory-enhancing chemicals. The better the connections, the more you comprehend.

    Likewise, before you take a test, stick to a light snack of energy boosting and relaxing foods. A glass of milk, a piece of fruit, or some peanuts all release various memory-boosting chemicals and help you to relax and focus on the subject at hand.

2. **Learn to take great notes.** A by-product of our modern culture is that we have grown accustomed to getting our information in short doses (i.e. TV news sound bites or *USA Today*-style newspaper articles.)

    Consequently, we've subconsciously trained ourselves to assimilate information better in **neat little packages**. If you scrawl notes all over the paper, you fragment the flow of the information. Strive for clarity.

    Newspapers use a standard format to achieve clarity. Your notes can be much clearer through use of proper formatting. A very effective format is called the Cornell Method.

    - Take a sheet of loose-leaf lined notebook paper and draw a line all the way down the paper about 1-2" from the left-hand edge.

    - Draw another line across the width of the paper about 1-2" up from the bottom. Repeat this process on the reverse side of the page.

    Look at the highly effective result. You have ample room for notes, a left-hand margin for special emphasis items or inserting supplementary data from the textbook, a large area at the bottom for a brief summary, and a little rectangular space for just about anything you want.

ENG. LANGUAGE LIT. & COMP.

3. **Get the concept, and then the details.** Too often we focus on the details and don't gather an understanding of the concept. However, if you simply memorize only dates, places, or names, you may well miss the whole point of the subject.

   A key way to understand things is to put them in your own words. If you are working from a textbook, automatically summarize each paragraph in your mind. If you are outlining text, don't simply copy the author's words.

   Rephrase them in your own words. You remember your own thoughts and words much better than someone else's, and you subconsciously tend to associate the important details to the core concepts.

4. **Ask Why.** Pull apart written material paragraph by paragraph and don't forget the captions under the illustrations.

   Example: If the heading is "Stream Erosion," flip it around to read "Why do streams erode?" Then answer the questions.

   If you train your mind to think in a series of questions and answers, not only will you learn more but you will also lessen the test anxiety because you are used to answering questions.

5. **Read for reinforcement and future needs.** Even if you only have 10 minutes, put your notes or a book in your hand. Your mind is similar to a computer; you have to input data in order to have it processed. *By reading, you are creating the neural connections for future retrieval.* The more times you read something, the more you reinforce the learning of ideas.

   Even if you don't fully understand something on the first pass, *your mind stores much of the material for later recall.*

6. **Relax to learn so go into exile.** Our bodies respond to an inner clock called biorhythms. Burning the midnight oil works well for some people, but not everyone.

   If possible, set aside a particular place to study that is free of distractions. Shut off the television, cell phone, and pager and exile your friends and family during your study period.

   If you really are bothered by silence, try background music. Light classical music at a low volume has been shown to aid in concentration.

   Music that evokes pleasant emotions without lyrics are highly suggested. Try just about anything by Mozart. It relaxes you.

7. **Use arrows, not highlighters.** At best, it's difficult to read a page full of yellow, pink, blue, and green streaks.

   Try staring at a neon sign for a while and you'll soon see my point; the horde of colors obscures the message.

   A quick note: a brief dash of color, an underline, and an arrow pointing to a particular passage are much clearer than a horde of highlighted words.

8. **Budget your study time.** Although you shouldn't ignore any of the material, *allocate your available study time in the same ratio that topics may appear on the test.*

Testing Tips:

1. **Get smart, play dumb. Don't read anything into the question.** Don't assume that the test writer is looking for something other than what is asked. Stick to the question as written and don't read extra things into it.

2. **Read the question and all the choices *twice* before answering the question.** You may miss something by not carefully reading and then rereading both the question and the answers.

   If you really don't have a clue as to the right answer, leave it blank on the first time through. Go on to the other questions as they may provide a clue on how to answer the skipped questions.

   If later on, you still can't answer the skipped ones . . . ***Guess.*** The only penalty for guessing is that you *might* get it wrong. Only one thing is certain; if you don't put anything down, you will get it wrong!

3. **Turn the question into a statement.** Look at the way the questions are worded. The syntax of the question usually provides a clue. Does it seem more familiar as a statement rather than as a question? Does it sound strange?

   By turning a question into a statement, you may be able to spot if an answer sounds right, and it may also trigger memories of material you have read.

4. **Look for hidden clues.** It's actually very difficult to compose multiple-foil (choice) questions without giving away part of the answer in the options presented.

TEACHER CERTIFICATION STUDY GUIDE

In most multiple-choice questions you can often readily eliminate one or two of the potential answers. This leaves you with only two real possibilities and automatically your odds go to fifty-fifty for very little work.

5. **Trust your instincts.** For every fact that you have read, you subconsciously retain something of that knowledge. On questions that you aren't certain about, go with your basic instincts. *Your first impression on how to answer a question is usually correct.*

6. **Mark your answers directly on the test booklet.** Don't bother trying to fill in the optical scan sheet on the first pass through the test. *Just be very careful not to mismark your answers when you eventually transcribe them to the scan sheet.*

7. **Watch the clock!** You have a set amount of time to answer the questions. Don't get bogged down trying to answer a single question at the expense of 10 questions you can more readily answer.

THIS PAGE BLANK

COMPETENCY 1.0 READING AND UNDERSTANDING TEXT

Skill 1.1 Paraphrasing, comparing, and interpreting (literally and inferentially) various types of texts, including fiction, poetry, essays, and other nonfiction.

In general, readers will attempt to construct meaning from a text if they believe the text has something important to convey to them. Establishing a general frame of relevance and conveying enthusiasm about it then are important considerations in deciding how to present a text.

The purpose of any given text is to communicate some type of information. For communication to occur, there has to be an interaction between a sender (the text) and a receiver (the audience). The best case scenario would be for the text to be internally well-suited to convey its meaning and equally well-suited to the receptive capacities of the audience.

Current learning theory establishes that students have distinct learning styles; some learn better through auditory input; others learn through visuals; others learn kinesthetically. With this learning-style variability in mind, a text incorporating material accessible to students with different learning styles has a better chance of being generally understood than a text presented in one medium only. Pictures, charts, audio clips, and video clips incorporated into print documents enhance the outcomes for the most students possible.

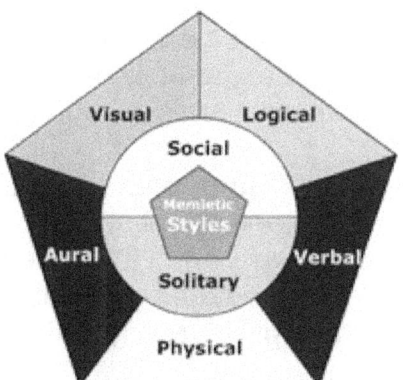

Learn about **Learning Styles** at http://www.learning-styles-online.com/overview/

Aside from considerations of learning style, a text that is presented in a medium that suits the cultural or experiential background of a given audience has a better chance of having its meaning conveyed than one presented without consideration of such audience-background characteristics. For instance, presenting a well-known fairy tale in a rap medium might well result in enhanced communication of relevant information for an audience of inner-city children.

Beyond these issues, a text has a better chance of conveying its message if it is presented in an engaging manner. For instance, if a story is read in a monotone, the outcome is surely less positive than if the same story is read with prosody. Furthermore, today's students are used to much more media stimulation than the adults who typically teach them and present texts to them. Without sufficient stimulation, students may have difficulty maintaining a viable attention span.

Still another way in which medium of text presentation can affect a reader's construction of meaning involves whether the processing routines include opportunities for students to participate in brain-friendly processing routines. Such routines include opportunities for various types of role playing, for discussing ethical dilemmas in pairs with time constraints and role expectations (one person talks, the other listens and then paraphrases), and for dramatizing scenes or issues within the target text.

INTERPRETING TEXT

To *interpret* means essentially to read with understanding and appreciation. It is not as daunting as it is made out to be. Simple techniques for interpreting literature follow.

Inferencing is a process that involves the reader making a reasonable judgment based on the information given and engages readers to literally construct meaning. You can develop and enhance this key skill in by reading an expository book aloud and then demonstrate for them the following reading habits: looking for clues, reflecting on what the reader already knows about the topic, and using the clues to figure out what the author means/intends.

Identifying main ideas in an expository text can be improved when the readers have an explicit strategy for identifying important information. They can make this strategy part of their everyday reading style, "walking" through the following exercises during guided reading sessions. They should read the passage so that the topic is readily identifiable. It will be what most of the information is about.

Next they should be asked to be on the lookout for a sentence within the expository passage that summarizes the key information in the paragraph. Then they should read the rest of the passage or excerpt in light of this information and also note which information in the paragraph is less important. The important information the readers have identified in the paragraph can be used to formulate the author's main idea. The readers may even want to use some of the author's own language in stating that idea.

Monitoring means self-clarifying. As they read, students often realize that what they are reading is not making sense. They then need a plan for making sense out of the excerpt—a stop and think strategy during which they reflect "Does this make sense?" When they conclude that it does not, they can re-read the text, read ahead in the text, look up unknown words or ask for help.

What is important about monitoring is that some readers ask these questions and try these approaches without ever being explicitly taught them in school by a teacher. However, these strategies need to be explicitly modeled and practiced under the guidance of the teacher by most, if not all, readers.

Summarizing engages the reader in pulling together into a cohesive whole the essential bits of information within a longer passage or excerpt of text. Readers can be taught to summarize informational or expository text by following these guidelines. First they should look at the topic sentence of the paragraph or the text and ignore the trivia. Then they should search for information which has been mentioned more than once and make sure it is included only once in their summary. Find related ideas or items and group them under a unifying heading. Search for and identify a main idea sentence. Finally, put the summary together using all these guidelines.

Generating questions can motivate and enhance readers' comprehension of reading in that they are actively involved. The following guidelines will help generate meaningful questions that will trigger constructive reading of expository texts. First readers should preview the text by reading the titles and subheadings. Then they should also look at the illustrations and the pictures. Finally they should read the first paragraph. These first previews should yield an impressive batch of specific questions.

Next, readers should ask themselves a "think" question. After they write down the question, they should read to find important information to answer their "think" question. Ask that they write down the answer they found and copy the sentence or sentences where they found the answer. Also have them consider whether, in light of their further reading through the text, their original question was a good one.

Determining the author's context will examine the author's feelings, beliefs, past experiences, goals, needs, and physical environment. Readers can appreciate and understand how these elements may have affected the writing to enrich an interpretation of it.

Understanding symbols to unearth a meaning the author might have intended but not expressed, or even something the author never intended at all, can help readers interpret text. Referred to as a sign, a **symbol** designates something which stands for something else. In most cases, it is standing for something that has a deeper meaning than its literal denotation. Symbols can have personal, cultural, or universal associations.

TEACHER CERTIFICATION STUDY GUIDE

Skill 1.2 Identifying and interpreting figurative language and other literary elements, e.g., metaphor, simile, voice, point of view, tone, style, setting, diction, mood, allusions, irony, clichés, analogy, hyperbole, personification, alliteration, and foreshadowing.

FIGURATIVE LANGUAGE

Figurative language allows for the statement of truths that more literal language cannot provide. Skillfully used, a figure of speech will help the reader see more clearly and focus upon particulars. Figures of speech add many dimensions of richness to our reading and understanding; they also allow many opportunities for worthwhile analysis.

Essential terminology and literary devices germane to literary analysis include the following.

Alliteration: Alliteration occurs when the initial sounds of a word, beginning either with a consonant or a vowel, are repeated in close succession. Examples include "Athena and Apollo," "Nate never knows," "people who pen poetry."

Note that the words only have to be close to one another: Alliteration that repeats and attempts to connect a number of words is little more than a tongue twister.

The function of alliteration, like rhyme, might be to accentuate the beauty of language in a given context, or to unite words or concepts through a kind of repetition. Alliteration, like rhyme, can follow specific patterns. Sometimes the consonants aren't always the initial ones, but they are generally the stressed syllables. Alliteration is less common than rhyme, but because it is less common, it can call our attention to a word or line in a poem that might not have the same emphasis otherwise.

In its simplest form, it reinforces one or two consonant sounds. An example is from Shakespeare's Sonnet #12:

> When I do **c**ount the **c**lock that **t**ells the **t**ime.

Some poets have used more complex patterns of alliteration by creating consonants both at the beginning of words and at the beginning of stressed syllables within words. An example is from Shelley's "Stanzas Written in Dejection Near Naples"

> The **C**ity's voice it**s**elf is **s**oft like **S**olitude's

ENG. LANGUAGE LIT. & COMP.

Antithesis: Balanced writing about conflicting ideas, usually expressed in sentence form. Some examples are "expanding from the center," "shedding old habits," and "searching never finding."

Aphorism: A focused, succinct expression about life from a sagacious viewpoint. Writings by Ben Franklin, Sir Francis Bacon, and Alexander Pope contain many aphorisms. "Whatever is begun in anger ends in shame" is an aphorism by Benjamin Franklin.

Apostrophe: Literary device of addressing an absent or dead person, an abstract idea, or an inanimate object. Sonneteers, such as Sir Thomas Wyatt, John Keats, and William Wordsworth, address the moon, stars, and the dead Milton.

> For more information, consult **Glossary of Poetry Terms** http://www.infoplease.com/spot/pmglossary1.html

For example, in William Shakespeare's *Julius Caesar*, Mark Antony addresses the corpse of Caesar in the speech that begins: "O, pardon me, thou bleeding piece of earth / That I am meek and gentle with these butchers! / Thou art the ruins of the noblest man / That ever lived in the tide of times. / Woe to the hand that shed this costly blood!"

Assonance: If alliteration occurs at the beginning of a word and rhyme at the end, assonance takes the middle territory. Assonance occurs when the vowel sound within a word matches the same sound in a nearby word, but the surrounding consonant sounds are different. "Tune" and "June" are rhymes; "tune" and "food" are assonant. The function of assonance is frequently the same as end rhyme or alliteration; all serve to give a sense of continuity or fluidity to the verse. Assonance might be especially effective when rhyme is absent: It gives the poet more flexibility, and it is not typically used as part of a predetermined pattern. Like alliteration, it does not so much determine the structure or form of a poem but rather it is more ornamental.

Bathos: A ludicrous attempt to portray pathos—that is, to evoke pity, sympathy, or sorrow. It may result from inappropriately dignifying the commonplace, elevated language to describe something trivial, or greatly exaggerated pathos.

Blank Verse: Poetry written in iambic pentameter but unrhymed. Works by Shakespeare and Milton are epitomes of blank verse. Milton's *Paradise Lost* states, "Illumine, what is low raise and support, / That to the higthh of this great argument I may assert Eternal Providence / And justify the ways of God to men."

Caesura: A pause, usually signaled by punctuation, in a line of poetry. The earliest usage occurs in *Beowulf*, the first English epic dating from the Anglo-Saxon era. "To err is human, // to forgive, divine" (Pope).

ENG. LANGUAGE LIT. & COMP.

Climax: A number of phrases or sentences are arranged in ascending order of rhetorical forcefulness. Example from Melville's *Moby Dick*:

> All that most maddens and torments; all that stirs up the lees of things; all truth with malice in it; all that cracks the sinews and cakes the brain; all the subtle demonisms of life and thought; all evil, to crazy Ahab, were visibly personified and made practically assailable in Moby Dick.

Conceit: A comparison, usually in verse, between seemingly disparate objects or concepts. John Donne's metaphysical poetry contains many clever conceits. For instance, Donne's "The Flea" (1633) compares a flea bite to the act of love; and in "A Valediction: Forbidding Mourning" (1633) separated lovers are likened to the legs of a compass, the leg drawing the circle eventually returning home to "the fixed foot."

Connotation: The ripple effect surrounding the implications and associations of a given word, distinct from the denotative or literal meaning. For example, the word "rest" in *Hamlet's* "Good night, sweet prince, and flights of angels sing thee to thy rest" refers to a burial.

Consonance: The repeated usage of similar consonant sounds, most often used in poetry. "Sally sat sifting seashells by the seashore" is a familiar example.

Couplet: Two rhyming lines of poetry. Shakespeare's sonnets end in heroic couplets written in iambic pentameter. Pope is also a master of the couplet. His *Rape of the Lock* is written entirely in heroic couplets.

Denotation: What a word literally means, as opposed to its connotative meaning.

Diction: The right word in the right place for the right purpose. The hallmark of a great writer is precise, unusual, and memorable diction.

Epiphany: The moment when the something is realized and comprehension sets in. James Joyce used this device in his short story collection *The Dubliners*.

Euphemism: The substitution of an agreeable or inoffensive term for one that might offend or suggest something unpleasant. Many euphemisms are used to refer to death to avoid using the real word such as "passed away," "crossed over," or nowadays "passed."

Exposition: Fill-in or background information about characters meant to clarify and add to the narrative; the initial plot element that precedes the buildup of conflict.

Free Verse: Poetry that does not have any predictable meter or patterning. Margaret Atwood, e. e. cummings, and Ted Hughes write in this form.

Hyperbole: Exaggeration for a specific effect. An example from Shakespeare's *The Merchant of Venice*:

> Why, if two gods should play some heavenly match
> And on the wager lay two earthly women,
> And Portia one, there must be something else
> Pawned with the other, for the poor rude world
> Hath not her fellow.

Iambic Pentameter: The two elements in a set five-foot line of poetry. An iamb is two syllables, unaccented and accented, per foot or measure. Pentameter means five feet of these iambs per line or ten syllables.

Imagery: Imagery can be described as a word or sequence of words that refers to any sensory experience—that is, anything that can be seen, tasted, smelled, heard, or felt on the skin or fingers. While prose writers may also use these images, they are most distinctive of poetry. The poet intends to make an experience available to the reader. In order to do that, the poet must appeal to one of the senses. The most-often-used one, of course, is the visual sense. The poet will deliberately paint a scene in such a way that the reader can see it. However, the purpose is not simply to stir the visceral feeling but also to stir the emotions. A good example is "The Piercing Chill" by Taniguchi Buson (1715-1783):

> The piercing chill I feel:
> My dead wife's comb, in our bedroom,
> Under my heel . . .

In only a few short words, the reader can feel many things: the shock that might come from touching the corpse, a literal sense of death, the contrast between her death and the memories he has of her when she was alive. Imagery might be defined as speaking of the abstract in concrete terms, a powerful device in the hands of a skillful poet.

Inversion: An atypical sentence order to create a given effect or interest. Francis Bacon and Milton's work use inversion successfully. Emily Dickinson was fond of arranging words outside of their familiar order. For example in "Chartless" she writes "Yet know I how the heather looks" and "Yet certain am I of the spot." Instead of saying "Yet I know" and "Yet I am certain" she reverses the usual order and shifts the emphasis to the more important words.

Irony: An unexpected disparity between what is written or stated and what is really meant or implied by the author. Verbal, dramatic and situational are the three literary ironies. Verbal irony is when an author says one thing and means something else. Dramatic irony is when an audience perceives something that a character in the literature does not know. Irony of situation is a discrepancy between the expected result and actual results. Shakespeare's plays contain numerous and highly effective uses of irony. O. Henry's short stories have ironic endings.

In poetry, it is often used as a sophisticated or resigned awareness of contrast between what is and what ought to be and expresses a controlled pathos without sentimentality. It is a form of indirection that avoids overt praise or censure. An early example: the Greek comic character Eiron, a clever underdog who by his wit repeatedly triumphs over the boastful character Alazon.

Kenning: Another way to describe a person, place, or thing so as to avoid prosaic repetition. The earliest examples can be found in Anglo-Saxon literature such as *Beowulf* and "The Seafarer." Instead of writing King Hrothgar, the anonymous monk wrote great Ring-Giver, or Father of his people. A lake becomes the swans' way, and the ocean or sea becomes the great whale's way. In ancient Greek literature, this device was called an "epithet."

Malapropism: A verbal blunder in which one word is replaced by another similar in sound but different in meaning. This derives from Sheridan's Mrs. Malaprop in *The Rivals* (1775). Thinking of the geography of contiguous countries, she spoke of the "geometry" of "contagious countries." Meaning the "pinnacle of perfection," she describes someone as "the pineapple of perfection."

The Pineapple of Perfection!

Metaphor: Indirect comparison between two things. It is the use of a word or phrase denoting one kind of object or action in place of another to suggest a comparison between them. While poets use them extensively, they are also integral to everyday speech. For example, chairs are said to have "legs" and "arms" although we know that humans and other animals have these appendages.

Metaphysical Poetry: Verse characterization by ingenious wit, unparalleled imagery, and clever conceits. The greatest metaphysical poet is John Donne. Henry Vaughn and other 17th century British poets contributed to this movement as in *Words*, "I saw eternity the other night, like a great being of pure and endless light."

Metonymy: Use of an object or idea closely identified with another object or idea to represent the second. "Hit the books" means "go study." Washington, D.C. means the U.S. government and the White House means the U.S. president.

> Share this website with your students
> **NewsHour Extra: Poetry**
> http://www.pbs.org/newshour/extra/poetry/#

Motif: A key, oft-repeated phrase, name, or idea in a literary work. Dorset/Wessex in Hardy's novels and the moors and the harsh weather in the Bronte sisters' novels are effective use of motifs. Shakespeare's *Romeo and Juliet* represents the ill-fated young lovers' motif.

Octava Rima: A specific eight-line stanza of poetry whose rhyme scheme is abababcc. Lord Byron's mock epic, *Don Juan*, is written in this poetic way.

Onomatopoeia: Word used to evoke the sound in its meaning. The early Batman series used "pow," "zap," "whop," "zonk," and "eek" in an onomatopoetic way. The naming of a thing or action by a vocal imitation of the sound associated with it such as buzz or hiss or the use of words whose sound suggests the sense. A good example: from "The Brook" by Tennyson:

> I chatter over stony ways,
> In little sharps and trebles,
> I bubble into eddying bays,
> I babble on the pebbles.

Oxymoron: A contradiction in terms deliberately employed for effect. It is usually seen in a qualifying adjective whose meaning is contrary to that of the noun it modifies such as "wise folly." Other examples include jumbo shrimp, unkindly kind, or singer John Mellencamp's "It hurts so good."

Paradox: Seemingly untrue statement, which when examined more closely proves to be true. John Donne's sonnet "Death Be Not Proud" postulates that death shall die and humans will triumph over death, at first thought not true, but ultimately explained and proven in this sonnet.

Parallelism: A type of close repetition of clauses or phrases that emphasize key topics or ideas in writing. The arrangement of ideas in phrases, sentences, and paragraphs that balance one element with another of equal importance and similar wording.

An example from Francis Bacon's *Of Studies:* "Reading maketh a full man, conference a ready man, and writing an exact man." The psalms in the King James Version of the Bible contain many examples.

Personification: Human characteristics are attributed to an inanimate object, an abstract quality, or animal. Examples: John Bunyan wrote characters named Death, Knowledge, Giant Despair, Sloth, and Piety in his *Pilgrim's Progress*. The metaphor of an arm of a chair is a form of personification. Carl Sandburg, in his poem "Fog," writes "The fog comes / on little cat feet. // It sits looking / over harbor and city / on silent haunches / and then moves on."

Quatrain: A poetic stanza composed of four lines. A Shakespearean or Elizabethan sonnet is made up of three quatrains and ends with a heroic couplet.

Scansion: The two-part analysis of a poetic line. Count the number of syllables per line and determine where the accents fall. Divide the line into metric feet. Name the meter by the type and number of feet. Much is written about scanning poetry. Try not to inundate your students with this jargon; rather allow them to feel the power of the poets' words, ideas, and images instead.

Slant Rhyme: This occurs when the final consonant sounds are the same but the vowels are different. Occurs frequently in Irish, Welsh, and Icelandic verse. Examples include "green and gone," "that and hit," "ill and shell."

Simile: Direct comparison between two things using "like," "as," such as." For example: "My love is like a red-red rose."

Soliloquy: A highlighted speech, in drama, usually delivered by a major character expounding on the author's philosophy or expressing, at times, universal truths. This is done with the character alone on the stage, as in Hamlet's famous "To be or not to be" soliloquy.

Spenserian Stanza: Invented by Sir Edmund Spenser for use in *The Faerie Queene*, his epic poem honoring Queen Elizabeth I. Each stanza consists of nine lines, eight in iambic parameter. The ninth line, called an alexandrine, has two extra syllables or one additional foot.

Sprung Rhythm: Invented and used extensively by the poet, Gerard Manley Hopkins. It consists of variable meter, which combines stressed and unstressed syllables fashioned by the author. See "Pied Beauty" or "God's Grandeur."

Stream of Consciousness: A style of writing which reflects the mental processes of the characters expressing, at times, jumbled memories, feelings, and dreams. James Joyce, Virginia Woolf, and William Faulkner use stream of consciousness in their writings.

Symbolism: A **symbol** is an object or action that can be observed with the senses in addition to its suggesting many other things. The lion is a symbol of courage; the cross a symbol of Christianity; the color green a symbol of envy.

These can almost be defined as metaphors because society agrees on the one-to-one meaning of them. Symbols used in literature are usually of a different sort. They tend to be private and personal; their significance is only evident in the context of the work where they are used. A good example of a symbol is poetry is the mending wall in Frost's poem.

A symbol can certainly have more than one meaning, and the meaning may be as personal as the memories and experiences of the particular reader. In analyzing a poem or a story, students should identify the symbols and their possible meanings.

Looking for symbols is often challenging, especially for novice poetry readers. However, these suggestions may be useful: First, pick out all the references to concrete objects such as a newspaper, black cats, or other nouns. Note any that the poet emphasizes by describing in detail, by repeating, or by placing at the very beginning or ending of a poem.

Ask yourself, what is the poem about? What does it add up to? Paraphrase the poem and determine whether the meaning depends upon certain concrete objects. Then ponder what the concrete object symbolizes in this particular poem.

Look for a character with the name of a prophet who does little but utter prophecy or a trio of women who resemble the Three Fates. A symbol may be a part of a person's body such as the eye of the murder victim in Poe's story "The Tell-Tale Heart" or a look, a voice, or a mannerism.

Some things a symbol is not: an abstraction such as truth, death, and love; in narrative, a well-developed character who is not at all mysterious; the second term in a metaphor. In Emily Dickinson's "The Lightning Is a Yellow Fork," the symbol is the lightning, not the fork.

Synecdoche: A synecdoche is a figure of speech in which the word for part of something is used to mean the whole; for example, "sail" for "boat," or vice versa.

Terza Rima: A series of poetic stanzas use the recurrent rhyme scheme of aba, bcb, cdc, ded, and so forth. The second-generation Romantic poets—Keats, Byron, Shelley, and, to a lesser degree, Yeats—used this Italian verse form, especially in their odes. Dante used this stanza in *The Divine Comedy*.

Tone: The discernible attitude inherent in an author's work regarding the subject, readership, or characters. Jonathan Swift or Pope's tone is satirical. James Boswell's tone toward Samuel Johnson is admiring.

> Read about **Tone and Style**
> http://www.delmar.edu/engl/wrtctr/handouts/ToneStyle.pdf

Wit: Writing of genius, keenness, and sagacity expressed through clever use of language. Alexander Pope and the Augustans wrote about and were said to possess wit.

Poets use figures of speech to sharpen the effect and meaning of their poems and to help readers see things in ways they have never seen them before. Marianne Moore observed that a fir tree has "an emerald turkey-foot at the top." Her poem makes us aware of something we probably had never noticed before. The sudden recognition of the likeness yields pleasure in the reading.

The approach to take in analyzing a poem on the basis of its figures of speech is to ask the question: What does it do for the poem? Does it underscore meaning? Does it intensify understanding? Does it increase the intensity of our response?

LITERARY ELEMENTS

The elements of fiction vary in importance and development from story to story. Some stories are mainly plot-driven while others are character studies. Stories can be so tightly constructed that all elements work together to develop the theme and entertain the reader. Although readers can certainly enjoy a story without an in-depth understanding of these elements, they can develop a deeper appreciation for those works which display the author's talent and writing skill.

Plot is sometimes called action, or the sequence of the events. If the plot does not *move*, the story quickly dies. Therefore, the successful writer of stories uses a wide variety of active verbs in creative and unusual ways. If a reader is kept interested by the movement of the story, the experience of reading it will be pleasurable. That reader will probably want to read more of this author's work. Careful, unique, and unusual choices of active verbs will bring about that effect.

William Faulkner is a good example of a successful writer whose stories are lively and memorable because of his use of unusual active verbs. In analyzing the development of plot, analytical readers will look at the verbs. However, the development of believable conflicts is also vital. If there is no conflict, there is no story. In critical thinking readers should ask: What devices does a writer use to develop the conflicts, and are they real and believable?

Character is portrayed in many ways: description of physical characteristics, dialogue, interior monologue, the thoughts of the character, the attitudes of other characters toward this one, and so on. Descriptive language depends on the ability to recreate a sensory experience for the reader.

If the description of the character's appearance is a visual one, then the reader must be able to *see* the character. What's the shape of the nose? What color are the eyes? How tall or how short is this character? Thin or chubby? How does the character move? How does the character walk? Writers choose terms that will create a picture for the reader. It's not enough to say the eyes are blue, for example. What kind of blue? Often the color of eyes is compared to something else to enhance the readers' ability to visualize the character.

A good test of characterization is the level of emotional involvement of the reader in the character. If the reader is to become involved, the description must provide an actual experience—seeing, smelling, hearing, tasting, or feeling. In the following example, Isaac Asimov deftly describes a character both directly and indirectly.

> Undersecretary Albert Minnim was a small, compact man, ruddy of skin, and graying, with the angles of his body smoothed down and softened. He exuded an air of cleanliness and smelled faintly of tonic. It all spoke of the good things of life that came with the liberal rations obtained by those high in Administration.
>
> Isaac Asimov, *The Robot Series: The Naked Sun*

Dialogue will reflect characteristics. Is it clipped? Is it highly dialectal? Does a character rely on colloquialisms (*dis me*, *bling*)? The ability to portray the speech of a character can make or break a story.

The kind of person the character is in the mind of the reader is dependent on impressions created by description and dialogue. How do other characters feel about this one as revealed by their treatment of him/her, their discussions of him/her with each other, or their overt descriptions of the character? For example, "John, of course, can't be trusted with another person's possessions." In analyzing a story, it's useful to discuss the devices used to produce character.

Setting may be visual, temporal, psychological, or social. Descriptive words are often used here also. In Edgar Allan Poe's description of the house in "The Fall of the House of Usher" as the protagonist/narrator approaches it, the air of dread and gloom that pervades the story is caught in the setting and sets the stage for the story. A setting may also be symbolic, as it is in Poe's story, where the house is a symbol of the family that lives in it. As the house disintegrates, so does the family.

The language used in all of these aspects of a story—plot, character, and setting—work together to create the **mood** of a story. Poe's first sentence establishes the mood of the story:

> During the whole of a dull, dark, and soundless day in the autumn of the year, when the clouds hung oppressively low in the heavens, I had been passing alone, on horseback, through a singularly dreary tract of country; and at length found myself, as the shades of the evening drew on, within view of the melancholy House of Usher.

Why did the author write this story? This question will lead to the **theme**—the underlying main idea. Whether a story is escapist or interpretive, it will have a controlling idea that is integral to its development. This idea is more than a topic (love, anger, guilt, jealousy); it is the author's view of the moral.

Sometimes the title of a story will help reveal the theme. For example, in "The Tell-Tale Heart," Poe tells us a story about guilt and the effect it has on one's conscience. The title foreshadows the outcome and helps the reader understand how all these elements contribute to an effective story.

Skill 1.3   **Identifying patterns, structures, and characteristics of literary forms and genres, e.g., elements of fiction and features of different poetic and prose forms and understanding how these patterns, structures, and characteristics may influence the meaning and effect of a work.**

LITERARY FORMS

Definitions of Selected Genres

The major literary genres include allegory, ballad, drama, epic, epistle, essay, fable, novel, poem, romance, and the short story.

Allegory: A story in verse or prose with characters representing virtues and vices. There are two meanings, symbolic and literal. John Bunyan's *The Pilgrim's Progress* is the most renowned of this genre.

Check out more than 180 items
**allegories, fables, parables
& teaching tales**
http://www.insight-books.com/ALLF

Drama: Plays—comedy, modern, or tragedy—typically in five acts. Traditionalists and neoclassicists adhere to Aristotle's unities of time, place and action. Plot development is advanced through dialogue. Literary devices include asides, soliloquies and the chorus, which represents public opinion. Greatest of all dramatists/playwrights is William Shakespeare. Other dramaturges include Henrik Ibsen, Tennessee Williams, Arthur Miller, George Bernard Shaw, Tom Stoppard, Jean Racine, Moliére (Jean Baptiste de Poquelin), Sophocles, Aeschylus, Euripides, and Aristophanes.

Epic: Long poem usually of book length reflecting values inherent in the generative society. Epic devices include an invocation to a muse for inspiration, purpose for writing, universal setting, a protagonist and antagonist who possess supernatural strength and acumen, and interventions of God or the gods. Understandably, there are very few epics: Homer's *Iliad* and *Odyssey*, Virgil's *Aeneid*, John Milton's *Paradise Lost*, Edmund Spenser's *The Faerie Queene*, Elizabeth Barrett Browning's *Aurora Leigh*, and Alexander Pope's mock-epic, *The Rape of the Lock*.

Epistle: A letter that is not always originally intended for public distribution but, because of the fame of the sender and/or recipient, becomes public domain. Paul wrote epistles that were later placed in the Bible.

Essay: Typically a limited length prose work focusing on a topic and propounding a definite point of view and authoritative tone. Great essayists include Thomas Carlyle, Charles Lamb, Thomas DeQuincy, Ralph Waldo Emerson and Michel de Montaigne, who is credited with defining this genre.

Fable: Terse tale offering up a moral or exemplum. Geoffrey Chaucer's "The Nun's Priest's Tale" is a fine example of a *bete fabliau* or beast fable in which animals speak and act characteristically human, illustrating human foibles.

Legend: A traditional narrative or collection of related narratives, popularly regarded as historically factual but actually a mixture of fact and fiction.

Myth: Stories that are more or less universally shared within a culture to explain its history and traditions.

Novel: The longest form of fictional prose containing a variety of characterizations, settings, local color and regionalism. Most have complex plots, expanded description, and attention to detail. Some of the great novelists include Jane Austin, Charlotte Bronte Emily Bronte, Mark Twain, Leo Tolstoy, Victor Hugo, Thomas Hardy, Charles Dickens, Nathaniel Hawthorne, E.M. Forster, and Gustave Flaubert.

Poem: Verse, whose only requirement is rhythm. Sub-genres include fixed types of literature such as the sonnet, elegy, ode, pastoral, and villanelle. Unfixed types of literature include blank verse and dramatic monologue.

Romance: A highly imaginative tale set in a fantastical realm dealing with the conflicts between heroes, villains and/or monsters. "The Knight's Tale" from Chaucer's *Canterbury Tales*, *Sir Gawain and the Green Knight* and John Keats' "The Eve of St. Agnes" are prime representatives.

Short Story: Typically a terse narrative, with less developmental background about characters. May include description, author's point of view, and tone. Edgar Allen Poe emphasized that a successful short story should create one focused impact. Considered to be great short story writers are Ernest Hemingway, William Faulkner, Mark Twain, James Joyce, Shirley Jackson, Flannery O'Connor, Guy de Maupasssant, Saki (H.H. Munro), Edgar Allen Poe, and Alexander Pushkin.

Types of Drama

Since the days of the Greeks, drama has undergone many permutations. Definitions which were once rigid have softened as theater has become a more accurate picture of the lives it depicts.

Tragedy: The classic definition dating back to Aristotle is that tragedy is a work of drama written in either prose or poetry, telling the story of a brave, noble hero who, because of some tragic character flaw (*hamartia*), brings ruin upon himself. It is characterized by serious, poetic language that evokes pity and fear.

In modern times, dramatists have tried to update drama's image by drawing its main characters from the middle class and showing their nobility through their nature instead of their standing. Sophocles' *Oedipus Rex* is the classic example of tragedy, while works of Henrik Ibsen and Arthur Miller epitomize modern tragedy.

Read more about **Greek Tragedy**
http://depthome.brooklyn.cuny.edu/classics/dunkle/studyguide/tragedy.htm

Comedy: The comedic form of dramatic literature is meant to amuse and often ends happily. It uses techniques such as satire or parody, and can take many forms, from farce to burlesque. Examples include Dante Alighieri's *The Divine Comedy,* Noel Coward's play *Private Lives,* some of Geoffrey Chaucer's *Canterbury Tales,* and some of William Shakespeare's plays, such as *A Midsummer's Night Dream.*

Comic Drama: As the name suggests, this form of theater is a combination of serious and light elements. It originated in the Middle Ages under the auspices of the Catholic Church which tried to reach the common people in mystery and morality plans. The modern equivalent would be the television's "dramedies" that present a serious plot with comic elements.

Melodrama: This is a form of extreme drama that has a somewhat formulaic structure. The hero saves the day from the dastardly villain and wins the heart of the wholesome heroine. The word is a combination of *melody* and *drama* because music was used to heighten the emotions. Although the term is sometimes used as a critical pejorative, it is a true art form with stereotyped characters and plot manipulations. Oftentimes, various operas are melodramatic so it should be no surprise that soap operas are considered part of this genre.

Farce: This is an extreme form of comedy marked by physical humor, unlikely situations, and stereotyped characters. It is often considered a form of low comedy and is represented in movies by the Three Stooges, Charlie Chaplin, Harold Lloyd, and Buster Keaton. Today's students might easily recognize farce with movies like *Dumb and Dumber, There's Something About Mary, Talladega Nights,* and *Monty Python's Spamalot.*

Dramatic Monologue: A dramatic monologue is a speech given by an actor as if talking to himself or herself, but actually intended for the audience. It reveals key aspects of the character's psyche and sheds insight on the situation at hand. The audience takes the part of the silent listener, passing judgment and giving sympathy at the same time. This form was invented and used predominantly by Victorian poet Robert Browning.

Tempo: Interpretation of dialogue must be connected to motivation and detail. During this time, the director is also concerned with pace and seeks a variation of tempo. If the overall pace is too slow, then the action becomes dull and dragging. If the overall pace is too fast, then the audience will not be able to understand what is going on, for they are being hit with too much information to process.

Dramatic Arc: Good drama is built on conflict of some kind—an opposition of forces or desires that must be resolved by the end of the story. The conflict can be internal, involving emotional and psychological pressures, or it can be external, drawing the characters into tumultuous events. These themes are presented to the audience in a narrative arc that looks roughly like this:

Following the Arc: Although any performance may have a series of rising and falling levels of intensity, in general the opening should set in motion the events which will generate an emotional high toward the middle or end of the story. Then, regardless of whether the ending is happy, sad, bittersweet, or despairing, the resolution eases the audience down from those heights and establishes some sense of closure.

Reaching the climax too soon undermines the dramatic impact of the remaining portion of the performance whereas reaching it too late rushes the ending and creates a jarringly abrupt end to events.

Types of Poetry

Narrative Poetry

The greatest difficulty in analyzing narrative poetry is that it partakes of many genres. It can have all the features of poetry: meter, rhyme, verses, and stanzas, but it can have all the features of prose, not only fictional prose but also nonfictional. It can have a protagonist, characters, conflicts, action, plot, climax, theme, and tone. It can also be a persuasive discourse and have a thesis (real or derived) and supporting points. The arrangement of an analysis will depend to a great extent upon the peculiarities of the poem itself.

Narrative poetry has been very much a part of the output of modern American writers totally apart from attempts to write epics. Many of Emily Dickinson's poems are narrative in form and retain the features that we look for in the finest of American poetry. The first two verses of "A Narrow Fellow in the Grass" illustrate the use of narrative in a poem:

> A narrow fellow in the grass
> Occasionally rides;
> You may have met him—did you not?
> His notice sudden is.
>
> The grass divides as with a comb,
> A spotted shaft is seen;
> And then it closes at your feet
> And opens further on. . . .

This is certainly narrative in nature and has many of the aspects of prose narrative. At the same time, it is a poem with rhyme, meter, verses, and stanzas and can be analyzed as such.

> Learn more about
> **Narrative Poetry**
> http://www.poetry-portal.com/styles9.html

Epic Poetry

In an epic, the conflicts take place in the social sphere rather than a personal life, and it will have a historical basis or one that is accepted as historical. The conflict will be between opposed nations or races and will involve diverging views of civilization that are the foundation of the challenge. Often it will involve the pitting of a group that conceives of itself as a higher civilization against a lower civilization and, more often than not, divine will determines that the higher one will win, exerting its force over the lower, barbarous, and profane enemy.

Examples are the conflict of Greece with Troy, the fates of Rome with the Carthaginian and the Italian, the Crusaders with the Saracen, or even of Milton's Omnipotent versus Satan. In analyzing these works, protagonist and antagonist need to be clearly identified, the conflicts established, the climax and an outcome that sets the world right in the mind of the writer clearly shown.

At the same time, the form of the epic as a poem must be considered. What meter, rhyme scheme, verse form, and stanza form have been chosen to tell this story? Is it consistent? If it varies, where does it vary and what does the varying do for the poem/story? What about figures of speech? Is there alliteration or onomatopoeia?

The epic is a major literary form historically although it had begun to fall out of favor by the end of the seventeenth century. There have been notable efforts to produce an American epic, but they always seem to slide over into prose. The short story and the novel began to take over the genre. Even so, some would say that *Moby Dick* is an American epic.

Lyric Poetry

The Greek poets used to sing their poetry and accompany their songs by playing a lyre. This musical quality characterizes the many types of lyric poetry.

Sonnet: The sonnet is a fixed-verse form of Italian origin, which consists of 14 lines that are typically five-foot iambics rhyming according to a prescribed scheme. Popular since its creation in the thirteenth century in Sicily, it spread at first to Tuscany, where Petrarch adopted it. The Petrarchan sonnet generally has a two-part theme. The first eight lines, the octave, state a problem, ask a question, or express an emotional tension. The last six lines, the sestet, resolve the problem, answer the question, or relieve the tension. The rhyme scheme of the octave is abbaabba; that of the sestet varies.

Sir Thomas Wyatt and Henry Howard, Earl of Surrey, introduced this form into England in the sixteenth century. It played an important role in the development of Elizabethan lyric poetry, and a distinctive English sonnet developed, which was composed of three quatrains, each with an independent rhyme-scheme, and it ended with a rhymed couplet.

A form of the English sonnet created by Edmond Spenser combines the English form and the Italian. The Spenserian sonnet follows the English quatrain and couplet pattern but resembles the Italian in its rhyme scheme, which is linked: abab bcbc cdcd ee. Many poets wrote sonnet sequences, where several sonnets were linked together, usually to tell a story. Considered to be the greatest of all sonnet sequences is one of Shakespeare's, which are addressed to a young man and a "dark lady" wherein the love story is overshadowed by the underlying reflections on time and art, growth and decay, and fame and fortune.

The sonnet continued to develop, more in topics than in form. When John Donne in the seventeenth century used the form for religious themes, some of which are almost sermons, or on personal reflections ("When I consider how my light is spent"), there were no longer any boundaries on the themes it could take.

That it is a flexible form is demonstrated in the wide range of themes and purposes it has been used for—all the way from more frivolous concerns to statements about time and death. William Wordsworth, John Keats, and Elizabeth Barrett Browning used the Petrarchan form of the sonnet. A well-known example is Wordsworth's "The World Is Too Much With Us." Rainer Maria Rilke's *Sonnette an Orpheus* (1922) is a well-known twentieth-century sonnet. Analysis of a sonnet should focus on the form—does it fit a traditional pattern or does it break from tradition? If so, why did the poet choose to make that break? Does it reflect the purpose of the poem? What is the theme? What is the purpose? Is it narrative? If so, what story does it tell and is there an underlying meaning? Is the sonnet appropriate for the subject matter?

Ballad: A ballad is a story told or sung, usually in verse and accompanied by music. Literary devices found in ballads include the refrain, or repeated section, and incremental repetition, or anaphora, for effect. Earliest forms were anonymous folk ballads. Later forms include Coleridge's Romantic masterpiece "The Rime of the Ancient Mariner."

Limerick: The limerick probably originated in County Limerick, Ireland, in the 18th century. It is a form of short, humorous verse, often nonsensical, and often ribald. Its five lines rhyme aabbaa with three feet in all lines except the third and fourth, which have only two. Rarely presented as serious poetry, this form is popular because almost anyone can write it.

In the 19th century, Edward Lear popularized the limerick in *A Book of Nonsense*. Here's an example:

>There was an Old Man with a beard,
>Who said, "It is just as I feared!
>Two Owls and a Hen,
>Four Larks and a Wren,
>Have all built their nests in my beard!"

Analysis of a limerick should focus on its form. Does it conform to a traditional pattern or does it break from the tradition? If so, what impact does that have on the meaning? Is the poem serious or frivolous? Is it funny? Does it try to be funny but does not achieve its purpose? Is there a serious meaning underlying the frivolity?

Cinquain: A cinquain is a poem with a five-line stanza. Adelaide Crapsey (1878-1914) called a five-line verse form a cinquain and invented a particular meter for it. Similar to the haiku, there are two syllables in the first and last lines and four, six, and eight in the middle three lines. It has a mostly iambic cadence. Her poem, "November Night," is an example:

>Listen...
>With faint dry sound
>Like steps of passing ghosts,
>the leaves, frost-crisp'd, break from the trees
>And fall.

Haiku: Haiku is a very popular unrhymed form that is limited to seventeen syllables arranged in three lines thus: five, seven, and five syllables. This verse form originated in Japan in the seventeenth century where it is accepted as serious poetry and is Japan's most popular form. Originally, a haiku was to deal with the season, the time of day, and the landscape although as it has come into more common use, the subjects have become less restricted. The imagist poets and other English writers used the form or imitated it. It's a form much used in classrooms to introduce students to the writing of poetry.

Here's an example by Japanese poet Kobaayashi Issa, translated by American poet Robert Haas.

>New Year's morning--
>everything is in blossom!
>I feel about average.

Analysis of a cinquain and a haiku poem should focus on form first. Does the haiku poem conform to the seventeen-syllable requirement and are they arranged in a five, seven, and five pattern? For a cinquain, does it have only five lines? Does the poem distill the words so as much meaning as possible can be conveyed? Does it treat a serious subject? Is the theme discernable?

Short forms like these seem simple to dash off; however, they are not effective unless the words are chosen and pared so the meaning intended is conveyed. The impact should be forceful, and that often takes more effort, skill, and creativity than longer forms. Students should consider all of this in their analyses.

Mythology and Oral Tradition

Literary allusions are drawn from classic mythology, national folklore, and religious writings that are supposed to have such familiarity to the reader that he can recognize the comparison between the subject of the allusion and the person, place, or event in the current reading.

Children and adolescents who have knowledge of proverbs, fables, myths, epics, and the Bible can understand these allusions and thereby appreciate their reading to a greater degree than those who cannot recognize them.

Classical Mythology

Much of the mythology that produces allusions in world literature is a product of ancient Greece and Rome because Greek and Roman myths have been liberally translated. Some Norse myths are also well known.

Children are fond of myths because those ancient people sought explanations for what happened in their lives in a manner accessible and familiar to children. These stories provide insight into the order and ethics of life. In them, ancient heroes overcome the terrors of the unknown, and explanations are given for thunder and lightning, the changing seasons, the origin and function of magical creatures of the forests and seas, and frightening natural phenomena. There is often a childlike directness in the emotions of supernatural beings. Many good translations of myths exist, but Edith Hamilton's *Mythology* is the definitive choice for adolescents.

Fairy Tales

Fairy tales are lively fictional stories involving children or animals that come in contact with super beings via magic. They provide happy solutions to human dilemmas. The fairy tales of many nations are peopled by trolls, elves, dwarfs, and pixies, child-sized beings capable of fantastic accomplishments.

Among the most famous are "Beauty and the Beast," "Cinderella," "Hansel and Gretel," "Snow White and the Seven Dwarfs," "Rumplestiltskin," and "Tom Thumb." In each tale, the protagonist survives prejudice, imprisonment, ridicule, and even death to receive justice in a cruel world.

> Check out
> **Sur La Lune Fairy Tales and Folklore**
> http://www.surlalunefairytales.com/introduction/index.html

Older readers encounter a kind of fairy tale world in Shakespeare's *The Tempest* and *A Midsummer Night's Dream*, which use pixies and fairies as characters. Adolescent readers today are as fascinated by the creations of fantasy realms in the works of Piers Anthony, Ursula LeGuin, and Anne McCaffrey. An extension of interest in the supernatural is the popularity of science fiction that allows us to use current knowledge to predict the possible course of the future.

Angels (or sometimes fairy godmothers) play a role in some fairy tales, and Milton in *Paradise Lost* and *Paradise Regained* also used symbolic angels and devils.

Biblical stories provide many allusions. Parables, moralistic-like fables but with human characters, include the stories of the Good Samaritan and the Prodigal Son. References to the treachery of Cain and the betrayal of Christ by Judas Iscariot are oft-cited examples.

Fables and Folktales

This literary group of stories and legends was originally orally transmitted to the common populace to provide models of exemplary behavior or deeds worthy of recognition and homage.

In fables, animals talk, feel, and behave like human beings. Fables always have a moral, and the animals depict specific people or groups indirectly. For example, in Aesop's *Fables*, the lion represents the King and the wolf represents the cruel, often unfeeling, nobility. In *The Lion and the Mouse, the* moral is that "little friends may prove to be great friends." In *The Lion's Share*, it is "might makes right." British folktales (*How Robin Became an Outlaw* and *St. George Slaying of the Dragon*) investigate the interplay between power and justice.

American Folk Tales

American folktales are divided into two categories: tall tales and legends.

Imaginary tales, also called **tall tales,** are humorous tales based on non-existent, fictional characters developed through blatant exaggeration.

- John Henry is a two-fisted steel driver who beats out a steam drill in competition.

- Rip Van Winkle sleeps for twenty years in the Catskill Mountains and upon awakening cannot understand why no one recognizes him.

- Paul Bunyan, a giant lumberjack, owns a great blue ox named Babe and has extraordinary physical strength. He is said to have plowed the Mississippi River while the impression of Babe's hoof prints created the Great Lakes.

Real tales, also called **legends,** are based on real persons who accomplished the feats that are attributed to them even if they are slightly exaggerated.

- For more than forty years, Johnny Appleseed (John Chapman) roamed Ohio and Indiana planting apple seeds.

- Daniel Boone, - scout, adventurer, and pioneer - blazed the Wilderness Trail and made Kentucky safe for settlers.

- Paul Revere, a colonial patriot, rode through the New England countryside warning of the approach of British troops.

- George Washington cut down a cherry tree, which he could not deny. Or did he?

Skill 1.4   Identifying major works and authors of American, British, and World literature from various cultures, genres, and periods, including literature for young adults.

AMERICAN LITERATURE

When compared to other countries, America has had a relatively brief history and thus a comparatively smaller canon of literature. Nevertheless, its fiction and nonfiction have the depth and breadth to tell the story of its people. To study American literature is to study also American history. Students will discover the interconnectedness of writing as a reflection of the historical, social, ethnic, political and economic environment of the time.

American Literature is defined by a number of clearly identifiable periods.

Native American Works from Various Tribes

These were originally part of a vast oral tradition that spanned most of continental America from as far back as before the 15th century.

Characteristics of native Indian literature include
- Reverence for and awe of nature.
- The interconnectedness of the elements in the life cycle.

Themes of Indian literature often reflect
- The hardiness of the native body and soul.
- Remorse for the destruction of their way of life.
- The genocide of many tribes by the encroaching settlement and Manifest Destiny policies of the U. S. government.

The Colonial Period

Stylistically, early colonists' writings were neo-classical, emphasizing order, balance, clarity, and reason. Because the people had been schooled in England, their writing and speaking was still decidedly British even as their thinking became entirely American.

Early American literature reveals the lives and experiences of the New England expatriates who left England to find religious freedom.

William Bradford's excerpts from *The Mayflower Compact* relate vividly the hardships of crossing the Atlantic in such a tiny vessel, the misery and suffering of the first winter, the approaches of the American Indians, the decimation of their ranks, and the establishment of the Bay Colony of Massachusetts.

Anne Bradstreet's poetry relates colonial New England life. From her journals, modern readers learn of the everyday life of the early settlers, the hardships of travel, and the responsibilities of different groups and individuals in the community, Early American literature also reveals the commercial and political adventures of the Cavaliers who came to the New World with King George's blessing.

> "If ever two were one, then surely we.
> If ever man were loved by wife, then thee."
> Read more about
> **Anne Bradstreet**
> http://www.annebradstreet.com/Default.htm

William Byrd's journal, *A History of the Dividing Line,* concerning his trek into the Dismal Swamp separating the Carolinian territories from Virginia and Maryland makes quite lively reading. A privileged insider to the English Royal Court, Byrd, like other Southern Cavaliers, was given grants to pursue business ventures.

The Revolutionary Period

The Revolutionary Period contains non-fiction genres: essay, pamphlet, speech, famous document, and epistle. Major writers and works of the Revolutionary Period include the following:

Thomas Paine's pamphlet, *Common Sense*, though written by a recently transplanted Englishman, spoke to the American patriots' common sense in dealing with the issues in the cause of freedom.

Other contributions are Benjamin Franklin's essays from *Poor Richard's Almanac* and satires such as "How to Reduce a Great Empire to a Small One" and "A Letter to Madame Gout."

There were great orations such as Patrick Henry's *Speech to the Virginia House of Burgesses* (the "Give me liberty or give me death" speech) and George Washington's *Farewell to the Army of the Potomac.* Less memorable are Washington's inaugural addresses, which strike modern readers as lacking sufficient focus.

The *Declaration of Independence*, the brainchild predominantly of Thomas Jefferson (along with some prudent editing by Ben Franklin), is a prime example of neoclassical writing—balanced, well crafted, and focused.

Epistles include the exquisitely written, moving correspondence between John Adams and Abigail Adams. The poignancy of their separation—she in Boston, he in Philadelphia—is palpable and real.

The Romantic Period

Early American folktales, and the emergence of a distinctly American writing, not just a stepchild to English forms, constitute the next period.

Washington Irving's characters, Icabod Crane and Rip Van Winkle, represent a uniquely American folklore devoid of English influences. The characters are indelibly marked by their environment and the superstitions of the New Englander. The early American writings of James Fenimore Cooper and his *Leatherstocking Tales* allow provide readers a window into their uniquely American world through the stirring accounts of drums along the Mohawk, the French and Indian Wars, the futile British defense of Fort William Henry and the brutalities of this period. Natty Bumppo, Chingachgook, Uncas, and Magua are unforgettable characters who reflect the American spirit in thought and action.

The poetry of Fireside Poets—James Russell Lowell, Oliver Wendell Holmes, Henry Wadsworth Longfellow, and John Greenleaf Whittier— was recited by American families and read in the long New England winters. In "The Courtin'," Lowell used Yankee dialect to tell the story. Spellbinding epics by Longfellow (such as *Hiawatha*, *The Courtship of Miles Standish*, and *Evangeline)* told of adversity, sorrow, and ultimate happiness in a uniquely American fashion. "Snowbound" by Whittier relates the story of a captive family isolated by a blizzard, stressing family closeness.

Nathaniel Hawthorne and Herman Melville are the preeminent early American novelists, writing on subjects definitely regional, specific and American, yet sharing insights about human foibles, fears, loves, doubts, and triumphs.

Hawthorne's writings range from children's stories, like the Cricket on the Hearth series, to adult fare of dark, brooding short stories such as "Dr. Heidegger's Experiment," "The Devil and Tom Walker," and "Rapuccini's Daughter." His masterpiece, *The Scarlet Letter*, takes on the society of hypocritical Puritan New Englanders, who ostensibly left England to establish religious freedom but who have become entrenched in judgmental finger wagging. They ostracize Hester and condemn her child, Pearl, as a child of Satan. Great love, sacrifice, loyalty, suffering, and related epiphanies add universality to this tale. *The House of the Seven Gables* deals with kept secrets, loneliness, societal pariahs, and love ultimately triumphing over horrible wrong.

Herman Melville's great opus, *Moby Dick*, follows a crazed Captain Ahab on his Homeric odyssey to conquer the great white whale that has outwitted him and his whaling crews time and again. The whale has even taken Ahab's leg and, according to Ahab, wants all of him. Melville recreates in painstaking detail and with insider knowledge of the harsh life of a whaler out of New Bedford by way of Nantucket.

The Life and Works of Herman Melville
http://www.melville.org/

For those who don't want to learn about every guy rope or all parts of the whaler's rigging, Melville offers up the succinct tale of *Billy Budd* and his Christ-like sacrifice to the black-and-white maritime laws on the high seas. An accident results in the death of one of the ship's officers, a slug of a fellow, who had taken a dislike to the young, affable, shy Billy. Captain Vere must hang Billy for the death of Claggert but knows that this is not right. However, an example must be given to the rest of the crew so that discipline can be maintained.

Edgar Allan Poe creates a distinctly American version of romanticism with his 16-syllable line in "The Raven," the classical "To Helen," and his Gothic "Annabelle Lee." The horror short story can be said to originate from Poe's pen. "The Tell-Tale Heart," "The Cask of Amontillado," "The Fall of the House of Usher," and "The Masque of the Red Death" are exemplary short stories. In addition, the genre of detective story emerges with Poe's "Murders in the Rue Morgue."

American Romanticism has its own offshoot in the Transcendentalism of Ralph Waldo Emerson and Henry David Thoreau. One wrote about transcending the complexities of life; the other, who wanted to get to the marrow of life, immersed himself in nature at Walden Pond and wrote an inspiring autobiographical account of his sojourn, aptly titled *On Walden Pond*. Thoreau also wrote passionately regarding his objections to the interference of government imposed on the individual in "On the Duty of Civil Disobedience."

Emerson's elegantly-crafted essays and war poetry still validate several important universal truths. Probably most remembered for his address to Thoreau's Harvard graduating class, "The American Scholar," he defined the qualities of hard work and intellectual spirit required of Americans in their growing nation.

The Transition Between Romanticism and Realism

The Civil War period ushers in the poignant poetry of Walt Whitman and his homage to all who suffer from the ripple effects of war and presidential assassination. His "Come up from the Fields, Father" about a Civil War soldier's death and his family's reaction and "When Lilacs Last in the Courtyard Bloom'd" about the effects of Abraham Lincoln's death on the poet and the nation should be required readings in any American literature course. Further, his *Leaves of Grass* gave America its first poetry truly unique in form, structure, and subject matter.

> Find more sites about
> **American Literature**
> http://www.wsu.edu/~campbelld/amlit/sites.htm

Emily Dickinson, like Walt Whitman, leaves her literary fingerprints on a vast array of poems, all but three of which were never published in her lifetime. Her themes of introspection and attention to nature's details and wonders are, by any measurement, world-class works. Her posthumous recognition reveals the timeliness of her work. American writing had most certainly arrived!

Mark Twain also left giant footprints with his unique blend of tall tale and fable. "The Celebrated Jumping Frog of Calaveras County" and "The Man who Stole Hadleyburg" are epitomes of short story writing. Move to novel creation, and Twain again rises above others by his bold, still disputed, oft-banned *The Adventures of Huckleberry Finn*, which examines such taboo subjects as a white person's love of a slave, the issue of leaving children with abusive parents, and the outcomes of family feuds. Written partly in dialect and southern vernacular, *The Adventures of Huckleberry Finn* is touted by some as the greatest American novel.

The Realistic Period

The late nineteenth century saw a reaction against the tendency of romantic writers to look at the world through rose-colored glasses. Writers like Frank Norris (*The Pit*) and Upton Sinclair (*The Jungle*) used their novels to decry conditions for workers in slaughterhouses and wheat mills.

Upton Sinclair
http://www.online-literature.com/upton_sinclair/

In *The Red Badge of Courage*, Stephen Crane wrote of the daily sufferings of the common soldier in the Civil War. Realistic writers wrote of common, ordinary people and events using realistic detail to reveal the harsh realities of life. They broached taboos by creating protagonists whose environments often destroyed them. Romantic writers would have only protagonists whose indomitable wills helped them rise above adversity. Crane's *Maggie: A Girl of the Streets* deals with a young woman forced into prostitution to survive. In "The Occurrence at Owl Creek Bridge," Ambrose Bierce relates the unfortunate hanging of a Confederate soldier.

Short stories, like Bret Harte's "The Outcasts of Poker Flat" and Jack London's "To Build a Fire," deal with unfortunate people whose luck in life has run out. Many writers, sub-classified as naturalists, believed that man was subject to a fate over which he had no control.

Contemporary American Literature

Twentieth century American writing can be divided into the following three genres: drama, fiction, and poetry.

American Drama: The greatest and most prolific of American playwrights include these playwrights:

- Eugene O'Neill, *Long Day's Journey into Night, Mourning Becomes Electra,* and *Desire Under the Elms*
- Arthur Miller, T*he Crucible, All My Sons,* and *Death of a Salesman*
- Tennessee Williams. *Cat on a Hot Tin Roof, The Glass Menagerie, and A Street Car Named Desire*
- Edward Albee, *Who's Afraid of Virginia Woolf? Three Tall Women, and A Delicate Balance*

American Fiction: The renowned American novelists include these authors:

- Eudora Welty, *The Optimist's Daughter*
- John Updike, *Rabbit Run* and *Rabbit Redux*
- Sinclair Lewis, *Babbit* and *Elmer Gantry*
- F. Scott Fitzgerald, *The Great Gatsby* and *Tender Is the Night*
- Ernest Hemingway, *A Farewell to Arms* and *For Whom the Bell Tolls*
- William Faulkner, *The Sound and the Fury* and *Absalom, Absalom*
- Bernard Malamud, *The Fixer* and *The Natural*

American Poetry: The poetry of the twentieth century is multifaceted, as represented by Edna St. Vincent Millay, Marianne Moore, Richard Wilbur, Langston Hughes, Maya Angelou, and Rita Dove. Above all others are the many-layered poems of Robert Frost. His New England motifs of snowy evenings, birches, apple picking, stone wall mending, hired hands, and detailed nature studies relate universal truths in exquisite diction, polysyllabic words, and rare allusions to either mythology or the Bible.

BRITISH LITERATURE

Anglo-Saxon

> Review a
> **Timeline of British Literature**
> http://www.studyguide.org/
> brit_lit_timeline.htm

The Anglo-Saxon period spans six centuries but produced only a smattering of literature. The first British epic is *Beowulf,* anonymously written by Christian monks many years after the events in the narrative supposedly occurred. This Teutonic saga relates the triumph three times over monsters by the hero, Beowulf. "The Seafarer," a shorter poem, some history, and some riddles are the rest of the Anglo-Saxon canon.

Medieval

The Medieval period introduces Geoffrey Chaucer, the father of English literature, whose *Canterbury Tales* are written in the vernacular, or street language of England, not in Latin. Thus, the tales are said to be the first work of British literature.

Next, Thomas Malory's *Le Morte d'Arthur* calls together the extant tales from Europe as well as England concerning the legendary King Arthur, Merlin, Guenevere, and the Knights of the Round Table. This work is the generative work that gave rise to the many Arthurian legends that stir the chivalric imagination.

Renaissance and Elizabethan Periods

The Renaissance, the most important period since it is synonymous with William Shakespeare, begins with importing the idea of the Petrarchan or Italian sonnet into England. Sir Thomas Wyatt and Sir Philip Sydney wrote English versions. Next, Sir Edmund Spenser invented a variation on this Italian sonnet form, aptly called the Spenserian sonnet. His masterpiece is the epic, *The Faerie Queene*, honoring Queen Elizabeth I's reign. He also wrote books on the Red Cross Knight, St. George and the Dragon, and a series of Arthurian adventures. Spencer was dubbed the Poet's Poet. He created a nine-line stanza, eight lines iambic pentameter and an extra-footed ninth line, an alexandrine. Thus, he invented the Spenserian stanza as well.

William Shakespeare, the Bard of Avon, wrote 154 sonnets, 39 plays, and two long narrative poems. The sonnets are justifiably called the greatest sonnet sequence in all literature. Shakespeare dispensed with the octave/sestet format of the Italian sonnet and invented his three quatrains, one heroic couplet format.

His plays are divided into comedies, history plays, and tragedies. Great lines from these plays are more often quoted than from any other author. The Big Four tragedies, *Hamlet*, *Macbeth*, *Othello*, and *King Lear* are acknowledged to be the most brilliant examples of this genre.

Seventeenth Century

John Milton's devout Puritanism was the wellspring of his creative genius that closes the remarkable productivity of the English Renaissance. His social commentary in such works as *Aereopagitica*, *Samson Agonistes*, and his elegant sonnets would be enough to solidify his stature as a great writer. It is his masterpiece based in part on the Book of Genesis that places Milton very near the top of the rung of a handful of the most renowned of all writers. *Paradise Lost*, written in balanced, elegant neoclassic form, truly does justify the ways of God to man.

The greatest allegory about man's journey to the Celestial City (Heaven) was written at the end of the English Renaissance, as was John Bunyan's *The Pilgrim's Progress*, which describes virtues and vices personified. This work is, or was for a long time, second only to the Bible in numbers of copies printed and sold.

The Jacobean Age gave us the marvelously witty and cleverly constructed conceits of John Donne's metaphysical sonnets as well as his insightful meditations and his version of sermons or homilies.

"Ask not for whom the bell tolls" and "No man is an island unto himself" are famous epigrams from Donne's *Meditations*. His most famous conceit is that which compares lovers to a footed compass traveling seemingly separate, but always leaning towards one another and conjoined in "A Valediction: Forbidding Mourning."

Eighteenth Century

Ben Jonson, author of the wickedly droll play *Volpone* and the Cavalier *carpe diem* poets Robert Herrick, Sir John Suckling, and Richard Lovelace also wrote during King James I's reign.

The Restoration and Enlightenment reflect the political turmoil of the regicide of Charles I, the Interregnum Puritan government of Oliver Cromwell, and the restoring of the monarchy to England by the coronation of Charles II, who had been given refuge by the French King Louis. Neoclassicism became the preferred writing style, especially for Alexander Pope. New genres, such as *The Diary of Samuel Pepys*, the novels of Daniel Defoe, the periodical essays and editorials of Joseph Addison and Richard Steele, and Alexander Pope's mock epic *The Rape of the Lock* demonstrate the diversity of expression during this time.

Writers who followed were contemporaries of Dr. Samuel Johnson, the lexicographer of *The Dictionary of the English Language*. Fittingly, this Age of Johnson, which encompasses James Boswell's biography of Dr. Johnson, Robert Burns' Scottish dialect and regionalism in his evocative poetry and the mystical pre-Romantic poetry of William Blake usher in the Romantic Age and its revolution against Neoclassicism.

Romantic Period

The Romantic Age encompasses what is known as the First Generation Romantics, William Wordsworth and Samuel Taylor Coleridge, who collaborated on *Lyrical Ballads,* which defines and exemplifies the tenets of this style of writing. The Second Generation includes George Gordon, Lord Byron, Percy Bysshe Shelley, and John Keats. These poets wrote sonnets, odes, epics, and narrative poems, most dealing with homage to nature.

Read about
The Romantic Period
http://www.wwnorton.com/college/english/nael/romantic/welcome.htm

Wordsworth's most famous other works are "Intimations on Immortality" and "The Prelude." Byron's satirical epic *Don Juan* and his autobiographical *Childe Harold's Pilgrimage* are irreverent, witty, self-deprecating and, in part, cuttingly critical of other writers and critics.

Shelley's odes and sonnets are remarkable for sensory imagery. Keats' sonnets, odes, and longer narrative poem *The Eve of St. Agnes* are remarkable for their introspection and the tender age of the poet, who died when he was only twenty-five.

In fact, all of the Second Generation died before their times. Wordsworth, who lived to be eighty, outlived them all, including Coleridge, his friend and collaborator.

Others who wrote during the Romantic Age are the essayist Charles Lamb and the novelist Jane Austin. The Brontë sisters, Charlotte and Emily, wrote one novel each, which are noted as two of the finest ever written, *Jane Eyre* and *Wuthering Heights*. Mary Anne Evans, also known as George Eliot, wrote several important novels: her masterpiece, *Middlemarch*, and *Silas Marner*, *Adam Bede*, and *Mill on the Floss*.

Nineteenth Century

http://www.victorianweb.org/

The Victorian Period is remarkable for the diversity and proliferation of work in three major areas. Poets who are typified as Victorians include Alfred, Lord Tennyson, who wrote *Idylls of the King*, twelve narrative poems about the Arthurian legend, and Robert Browning, who wrote chilling, dramatic monologues, such as "My Last Duchess," as well as long poetic narratives such as *The Pied Piper of Hamlin*. His wife Elizabeth wrote two major works, the epic feminist poem, *Aurora Leigh*, and her deeply moving and provocative *Sonnets from the Portuguese,* in which she details her deep love for Robert and his startling, to her, reciprocation.

Gerard Manley Hopkins, a Catholic priest, wrote poetry with sprung rhythm. A. E. Housmann, Matthew Arnold, and the Pre-Raphaelites, especially the brother and sister duo, Dante Gabriel Rosetti and Christina Rosetti, contributed much to round out the Victorian Era poetic scene. The Pre-Raphaelites, a group of 19th-century English painters, poets, and critics, reacted against Victorian materialism and the neoclassical conventions of academic art by producing earnest, quasi-religious works. Medieval and early Renaissance painters up to the time of the Italian painter Raphael inspired the group.

Robert Louis Stevenson, the great Scottish novelist, wrote his adventure/history lessons for young adults. Victorian prose ranges from the incomparable, keenly woven plot structures of Charles Dickens to the deeply moving Dorset/Wessex novels of Thomas Hardy, in which women are repressed and life is more struggle than euphoria. Rudyard Kipling wrote about Colonialism in India in works like *Kim* and *The Jungle Book* that create exotic locales and a distinct main point concerning the Raj, the British Colonial government during Queen Victoria's reign. Victorian drama is a product mainly of Oscar Wilde, whose satirical masterpiece *The Importance of Being Earnest* farcically details and lampoons Victorian social mores.

Twentieth Century

The early twentieth century is represented mainly by the towering achievement of George Bernard Shaw's dramas: *St. Joan*, *Man and Superman*, *Major Barbara*, and *Arms and the Man,* to name a few. Novelists are too numerous to list, but

Joseph Conrad, E. M. Forster, Virginia Woolf, James Joyce, Nadine Gordimer, Graham Greene, George Orwell, and D. H. Lawrence comprise some of the century's very best.

Twentieth century poets of renown and merit include W. H. Auden, Robert Graves, T. S. Eliot, Edith Sitwell, Stephen Spender, Dylan Thomas, Philip Larkin, Ted Hughes, Sylvia Plath, and Hugh MacDarmid. This list is by no means complete.

WORLD LITERATURE

North American Literature

North American literature is divided between the United States, Canada, and Mexico. Canadian writers of note include feminist Margaret Atwood, (*The Hand Maiden's Tale*); Alice Munro, a remarkable short story writer; and W. P. Kinsella, another short story writer whose two major subjects are North American Indians and baseball.

Mexican writers include 1990 Nobel Prize winning poet Octavio Paz (*The Labyrinth of Solitude*) and feminist Rosario Castillanos (*The Nine Guardians*).

Central American/Caribbean Literature

The Caribbean and Central America encompass a vast area and cultures that reflect oppression and colonialism by England, Spain, Portugal, France, and The Netherlands. The Caribbean writers

> **The Norton Anthology of World Literature**
> http://www.wwnorton.com/college/english/nawol/

include Samuel Selvon from Trinidad and Armando Valladares of Cuba. Central American authors include dramatist Carlos Solorzano, from Guatemala, whose plays include *Dona Beatriz, The Hapless, The Magician,* and *The Hands of God.*

South American Literature

Chilean Gabriela Mistral was the first Latin American writer to win the Nobel Prize for literature. She is best known for her collections of poetry, *Desolation and Feeling*.

Chile was also home to Pablo Neruda, who, in 1971, also won the Nobel Prize for literature for his poetry. His 29 volumes of poetry have been translated into more than 60 languages, attesting to his universal appeal. *Twenty Love Poems* and *Song of Despair* are justly famous. Isabel Allende is carrying on the Chilean literary standards with her acclaimed novel, *House of Spirits*. Argentine Jorge Luis Borges is considered by many literary critics to be the most important writer of his century from South America. His collections of short stories, *Ficciones*, brought him universal recognition. Also from Argentina, Silvina Ocampo, a collaborator with Borges on a collection of poetry, is famed for her poetry and short story collections, which include *The Fury* and *The Days of the Night*.

Horacio Quiroga represents Uruguay, and Brazil has Joao Guimaraes Rosa, whose novel, *The Devil to Pay*, is considered first-rank world literature.

Continental European Literature

With its long history of great writers, continental European literature expands the world of students and broadens their exposure to different cultures and values. This category as discussed below excludes British literature as it was covered previously.

Germany

German poet and playwright Friedrich von Schiller is best known for his history plays *William Tell* and *The Maid of Orleans*. He is a leading literary figure in Germany's Golden Age of Literature. Also from Germany, Rainer Maria Rilke, the great lyric poet, is one of the poets of the unconscious, or stream of consciousness. Germany also has given the world Herman Hesse, (*Siddartha*), Gunter Grass (*The Tin Drum*), and the greatest of all German writers, Goethe.

Scandinavia

Scandinavian literature includes the work of Hans Christian Andersen of Denmark, who advanced the fairy tale genre with such wistful tales as "The Little Mermaid" and "Thumbelina."

The social commentary of Henrik Ibsen in Norway startled the world through drama exploring such issues as feminism (*The Doll's House* and *Hedda Gabler*) and the effects of sexually-transmitted diseases (*The Wild Duck* and *Ghosts*).

Read more about **Henrik Ibsen**
http://www.hf.uio.no/ibsensenteret/index_eng.html

Sweden's Selma Lagerlof is the first woman to win the Nobel Prize for literature. Her novels include *Gosta Berling's Saga* and the world-renowned *The Wonderful Adventures of Nils*, a children's work.

Russia

Russian literature is vast and monumental. Who has not heard of Fyodor Dostoyevski's *Crime and Punishment* and *The Brothers Karamazov* or of Count Leo Tolstoy's *War and Peace*? These are examples of psychological realism. Dostoyevski's influence on modern writers cannot be over stressed.

Tolstoy's *War and Peace* is the sweeping account of the invasion of Russia and Napoleon's taking of Moscow. This novel is called the national novel of Russia. Further advancing Tolstoy's greatness is his ability to create realistic and unforgettable female characters, especially Natasha in *War and Peace* and Anna in *Anna Karenina*. Pushkin is famous for great short stories; Anton Chekhov for drama (*Uncle Vanya*, *The Three Sisters*, *The Cherry Orchard*); and Yevgeny Yevtushenko for poetry (*Babi Yar*). Boris Pasternak won the Nobel Prize (*Dr. Zhivago*). Aleksandr Solzhenitsyn (*The Gulag Archipelago*) returned to Russia after years of expatriation in Vermont. Ilya Varshavsky, who creates fictional societies that are dystopias, or the opposite of utopias, represents the genre of science fiction.

France

France has a multifaceted canon of great literature that is universal in scope and that almost always champions some social cause. Examples include the poignant short stories of Guy de Maupassant; the fantastic poetry of Charles Baudelaire (*Fleurs du Mal*); the groundbreaking lyrical poetry of Rimbaud and Verlaine; and the existentialism of Jean-Paul Sartre (*No Exit*, *The Flies*, *Nausea*), Andre Malraux (*The Fall*) and Albert Camus (*The Stranger* and *The Plague*), the recipient of the 1957 Nobel Prize for literature.

Learn more about **Jean Paul Sartre**
http://www.users.muohio.edu/shermalw/honors_2001_fall/honors_papers_2001/detwilerj_Sartre.htm

Feminist writings include those of Sidonie-Gabrielle Colette, known for her short stories and novels, as well as Simone de Beauvoir.

Drama in France is best represented by Rostand's *Cyrano de Bergerac* and the neo-classical dramas of Racine and Corneille (*El Cid*). Feminist writers include Simone de Beauvoir and Sidonie-Gabrielle Colette, known for her short stories and novels. The great French novelists include Andre Gide, Honore de Balzac (*Cousin Bette*), Stendel (*The Red and the Black*), and Alexandre Dumas (*The Three Musketeers* and *The Man in the Iron Mask*). Victor Hugo is the Charles Dickens of French literature, having penned the masterpieces *The Hunchback of Notre Dame* and *Les Miserables*. The stream of consciousness of Proust's *Remembrance of Things Past* and the Absurdist theatre of Samuel Beckett and Eugene Ionesco (*The Rhinoceros*) attest to the groundbreaking genius of the French writers.

Slavic Nations

Austrian writer Franz Kafka (*The Metamorphosis, The Trial,* and *The Castle*) is considered by many to be the literary voice of the first-half of the twentieth century. Poet Vaclav Havel represents the Czech Republic. Slovakia has dramatist Karel Capek (*R.U.R.*). Romania is represented by Elie Weisel (*Night*), a Nobel Prize winner.

Spain

Spain's great writers include Miguel de Cervantes (*Don Quixote*) and Juan Ramon Jimenez. The anonymous national epic, *El Cid*, has been translated into many languages.

Italy

Italy's greatest writers include Virgil (*The Aeneid)*, Giovanni Boccaccio (*The Decameron*), Dante Alighieri (*The Divine Comedy*) and the more contemporary Alberto Moravia.

Ancient Greece

Greece will always be foremost in literary stature because of Homer's epics, *The Iliad* and *The Odyssey*. No one except Shakespeare is more often cited. The works of Plato and Aristotle in philosophy; of Aeschylus, Euripides, and Sophocles in tragedy, and of Aristophanes in comedy further solidify Greece's pre-eminence. Greece is the cradle not only of democracy but of literature as well.

African Literature

African literary greats include South Africans Nadine Gordimer (Nobel Prize for literature) and Peter Abrahams (*Tell Freedom: Memories of Africa*), an autobiography of life in Johannesburg. Chinua Achebe (*Things Fall Apart*) and the poet, Wole Soyinka, hail from Nigeria. Mark Mathabane wrote an autobiography *Kaffir Boy* about growing up in South Africa. Egyptian writer Naguib Mahfouz and Doris Lessing from Rhodesia, now Zimbabwe, write about race relations in their respective countries. Lessing won the 2007 Nobel Prize for Literature. Because of her radical politics, Lessing was once banned from her homeland and the Union of South Africa, as was Alan Paton whose seemingly simple story, *Cry, the Beloved Country*, brought the plight of blacks and the whites' fear of blacks under apartheid to the rest of the world.

> Learn more about
> **Postcolonial Literature in English**
> http://www.thecore.nus.edu.sg/post/misc/africov.html

Far East Literature

Asia has many modern writers who are being translated for the western reading public. India's Krishan Chandar has authored more than 300 stories. Rabindranath Tagore won the Nobel Prize for literature in 1913 (*Song Offerings*). R. K. Narayan, India's most famous writer (*The Guide*), is interested in mythology and legends of India. Santha Rama Rau's work *Gifts of Passage* is her true story of life in a British school where she tries to preserve her Indian culture and traditional home.

Revered as Japan's most famous female author, Fumiko Hayashi (*Drifting Clouds*) by the time of her death had written more than 270 literary works.

In 1968 the Nobel Prize for literature was awarded to Yasunari Kawabata (*The Sound of the Mountain, The Snow Country*). His Palm-of-the-Hand Stories take the essentials of Haiku poetry and transform them into the short story genre.

Katai Tayama (*The Quilt*) is touted as the father of the Japanese confessional novel. His works, characterized as naturalism, are definitely not for the squeamish. The "slice of life" psychological writings of Ryunosuke Akutagawa gained him acclaim in the western world. His short stories, especially "Rashamon" and "In a Grove," are greatly praised for style as well as content.

China, too, has given to the literary world. Li Po, the T'ang dynasty poet from the Chinese Golden Age, revealed his interest in folklore by preserving the folk songs and mythology of China. Po further enables his readers to enter into the Chinese philosophy of Taoism and to understand feelings against expansionism during the T'ang dynastic rule. The T'ang dynasty, which was one of great diversity in the arts, saw Jiang Fang help create the Chinese version of a short story. His themes often express love between a man and a woman.

Modern feminist and political concerns are written eloquently by Ting Ling, who used the pseudonym Chiang Ping-Chih. Her stories reflect her concerns about social injustice and her commitment to the women's movement.

LITERATURE FOR ADOLESCENTS

Prior to twentieth century research on child development and child/adolescent literature's relationship to that development, books for adolescents were primarily didactic. They were designed to address history, manners, and morals.

Middle Ages

As early as the eleventh century, Anselm, the Archbishop of Canterbury, wrote an encyclopedia designed to instill in children the beliefs and principles of conduct acceptable to adults in medieval society. Early monastic translations of the Bible and other religious writings were written in Latin for the edification of the upper class.

Fifteenth century hornbooks were designed to teach reading and religious lessons. William Claxton printed English versions of *Aesop's Fables*, Mallory's *Le Morte d'Arthur,* and stories from Greek and Roman mythology. Though printed for adults, tales of adventures of Odysseus and the Arthurian knights were also popular with literate adolescents.

Renaissance

The Renaissance saw the introduction of the inexpensive chapbooks, small in size and 16-64 pages in length. Chapbooks were condensed versions of mythology and fairy tales. Designed for the common people, chapbooks were imperfect grammatically but were immensely popular because of their adventurous contents. Though most of the serious, educated adults frowned on the sometimes vulgar little books, they received praise from Richard Steele of *Tattler* fame for inspiring his grandson's interest in reading and in pursuing his other studies.

Meanwhile, the Puritans' three most popular reads were the Bible, John Foe's *Book of Martyrs*, and John Bunyan's *Pilgrim's Progress*. Though venerating religious martyrs and preaching the moral propriety which was to lead to eternal happiness, the stories of the *Book of Martyrs* were often lurid in their descriptions of the fate of the damned. In contrast, *Pilgrim's Progress*, not written for children and difficult reading even for adults, was as attractive to adolescents for its adventurous plot as for its moral outcome. In Puritan America, the *New England Primer* set forth the prayers, catechisms, Bible verses, and illustrations meant to instruct children in the Puritan ethic. The seventeenth-century French used fables and fairy tales to entertain adults, but children found them enjoyable as well.

Seventeenth Century

The late seventeenth century brought the first concern with providing literature that specifically targeted the young. Pierre Peril's *Fairy Tales*, Jean de la Fontaine's retellings of famous fables, Mme. d'Aulnoy's novels based on old folktales, and Mme. de Beaumont's Beauty and the Beast were written to delight as well as instruct young people. In England, publisher John Newbury was the first to publish a line for children. These included a translation of Perrault's *Tales of Mother Goose; A Little Pretty Pocket-Book*, "intended for instruction and amusement" but decidedly moralistic and bland in comparison to the previous century's chapbooks; and *The Renowned History of Little Goody Two Shoes*, allegedly written by Oliver Goldsmith for a juvenile audience.

Eighteenth Century

Largely, eighteenth century adolescents were finding their reading pleasure in adult books: Daniel Defoe's *Robinson Crusoe*, Jonathan Swift's *Gulliver's Travels*, and Johann Wyss's *Swiss Family Robinson*. More books were being written for children, and moral didacticism, though less religious, was nevertheless ever present.

The short stories of Maria Edgeworth, the four-volume *The History of Sandford and Merton* by Thomas Day, and Martha Farquharson's twenty-six volume *Elsie Dinsmore* series dealt with pious protagonists who learned restraint, repentance, and rehabilitation from sin.

Two bright spots in this period of didacticism were Jean Jacques Rousseau's *Emile* and *The Tales of Shakespeare*, and Charles and Mary Lamb's simplified versions of Shakespeare's plays. Rousseau believed that a child's abilities were enhanced by a free, happy life, and the Lambs subscribed to the notion that children were entitled to entertaining literature written in language comprehensible to them.

Nineteenth Century

Child/adolescent literature truly began its modern rise in nineteenth century Europe. Hans Christian Andersen's *Fairy Tales* were fanciful adaptations of the somber revisions of the Grimm brothers in the previous century. Andrew Lang's series of colorful fairy books contain the folklores of many nations and are still part of the collections of many modern libraries. Clement Moore's "A Visit from St. Nicholas" is a cheery, non-threatening child's view of the night before Christmas. The humor of Lewis Carroll's books about Alice's adventures, Edward Lear's poems with caricatures and Lucretia Nole's stories of the Philadelphia Peterkin family are full of fancy and not a smidgen of morality.

Other popular Victorian novels introduced the modern fantasy and science fiction genres: William Makepeace Thackeray's *The Rose and the Ring*, Charles Dickens' *The Magic Fishbone*, and Jules Verne's *Twenty Thousand Leagues Under the Sea*. Adventure to exotic places became a popular topic: Rudyard Kipling's *Jungle Books*, Verne's *Around the World in Eighty Days*, and Robert Louis Stevenson's *Treasure Island* and *Kidnapped*. In 1884, the first English translation of Johanna Spyri's *Heidi* appeared.

North America was also finding its voices for adolescent readers. American Louisa May Alcott's *Little Women* and Canadian L.M. Montgomery's *Anne of Green Gables* ushered in the modern age of realistic fiction. American youth were enjoying the adventures of Tom Sawyer and Huckleberry Finn. For the first time, children were able to read books about real people just like themselves.

Twentieth Century

The literature of the twentieth century is extensive and diverse and, as in previous centuries, influenced by the adults who write, edit, and select books for youth consumption. In the first third of the century, suitable adolescent literature dealt with children from good homes with large families. These books projected an image of a peaceful, rural existence.

> For more information, read
> **Introductory Lecture on Children's & Adolescent Literature**
> http://homepages.wmich.edu/~tarboxg/Introductory_Lecture_on_Children's_&_Adol_Lit.html

Though the characters and plots were more realistic, the stories maintained focus on topics that were considered emotionally and intellectually proper. Popular at this time were Laura Ingalls Wilder's *Little House on the Prairie* series and Carl Sandburg's biography *Abe Lincoln Grows Up*. English author J.R.R. Tolkein's fantasy, The Hobbit, prefaced modern adolescent readers' fascination with the works of Piers Antony, Madelaine L'Engle, and Anne McCaffery.

For Fifth and Sixth Grades

These classic and contemporary works combine the characteristics of multiple theories. Functioning at the concrete operations stage (Piaget), being of the "good person," orientation (Kohlberg), still highly dependent on external rewards (Bandura), and exhibiting all five needs previously discussed from Maslow's hierarchy, these eleven- to twelve-year-olds should appreciate the following titles, grouped by reading level. These titles are also cited for interest at that grade level and do not reflect high-interest titles for older readers who do not read at grade level. Some high interest titles will be cited later.

Reading Level 6.0 to 6.9
Barrett, William. *Lilies of the Field*
Cormier, Robert. *Other Bells for Us to Ring*
Dahl, Roald. *Danny, Champion of the World; Charlie and the Chocolate Factory*
Lindgren, Astrid. *Pippi Longstocking*
Lindbergh, Anne. *Three Lives to Live*
Lowry, Lois. *Rabble Starkey*
Naylor, Phyllis. *The Year of the Gopher, Reluctantly Alice*
Peck, Robert Newton. *Arly*
Speare, Elizabeth. *The Witch of Blackbird Pond*
Sleator, William. *The Boy Who Reversed Himself*

For Seventh and Eighth Grades

Most seventh and eight grade students, according to learning theory, are still functioning cognitively, psychologically, and morally as sixth graders. As these are not inflexible standards, some twelve- and thirteen-year-olds are much more mature socially, intellectually, and physically than the younger children who share the same school. They are becoming concerned with establishing individual and peer group identities that presents conflicts with breaking from authority and the rigidity of rules. Some at this age are still tied firmly to the family and its expectations while others identify more with those their own age or older.

> Check out these
> **Online Resources for K-12 Teachers:**
> **Children's and Adolescent Literature**
> http://www.indiana.edu/~reading/ieo/digests/d149.html

Enrichment reading for this group must help them cope with life's rapid changes or provide escape and thus must be either realistic or fantastic depending on the child's needs. Adventures and mysteries (the Hardy Boys and Nancy Drew series) are still popular today. These preteens also become more interested in biographies of contemporary figures rather than legendary figures of the past.

Reading Level 7.0 to 7.9
Armstrong, William. *Sounder*
Bagnold, Enid. *National Velvet*
Barrie, James. *Peter Pan*
London, Jack. *White Fang, Call of the Wild*
Lowry, Lois. *Taking Care of Terrific*
McCaffrey, Anne. *The Dragonsinger* series
Montgomery, L. M. *Anne of Green Gables* and sequels
Steinbeck, John. *The Pearl*
Tolkien, J. R. R. *The Hobbit*
Zindel, Paul. *The Pigman*

Reading Level 8.0 to 8.9
Cormier, Robert. *I Am the Cheese*
McCullers, Carson. *The Member of the Wedding*
North, Sterling. *Rascal*
Twain, Mark. *The Adventures of Tom Sawyer*
Zindel, Paul. *My Darling, My Hamburger*

For Ninth Grade

Depending upon the school environment, ninth graders may be the rank the highest in a junior high school or the lowest in a high school. Much of their social development and thus their reading interests become motivated by peer associations. They are technically adolescents operating at the early stages of formal operations in cognitive development. Their perceptions of their own identities are becoming well-defined, and they are fully aware of the ethics required by society. Ninth graders are more receptive to the challenges of classic literature but still enjoy popular teen novels.

Reading Level 9.0 to 9.9
Brown, Dee. *Bury My Heart at Wounded Knee*
Defoe, Daniel. *Robinson Crusoe*
Dickens, Charles. *David Copperfield*
Greenberg, Joanne. *I Never Promised You a Rose Garden*
Kipling, Rudyard. *Captains Courageous*
Mathabane, Mark. *Kaffir Boy*
Nordhoff, Charles. *Mutiny on the Bounty*
Shelley, Mary. *Frankenstein*
Washington, Booker T. *Up From Slavery*

For Tenth to Twelfth Grades

All high school sophomores, juniors and seniors can handle almost all other literature except for a few of the very most difficult titles like *Moby Dick* or *Vanity Fair*. However, since many high school students do not progress to the eleventh or twelfth grade reading level, they will still have their favorites among authors whose writings they can understand. Many will struggle with assigned novels but still read high interest books for pleasure. A few high interest titles are listed below without reading level designations, though most are 6.0 to 7.9.

Bauer, Joan. *Squashed*
Borland, Hal. *When the Legends Die*
Danzinger, Paula. *Remember Me to Harold Square*
Duncan, Lois. *Stranger with My Face*
Hamilton, Virginia. *The Planet of Junior Brown*
Hinton, S. E. *The Outsiders*
Paterson, Katherine. *The Great Gilly Hopkins*

Teachers of students at all levels must be familiar with the materials offered by the libraries in their own schools. Only then can they guide their students into appropriate selections for their social age and reading level development.

Adolescent literature, because of the age range of readers, is extremely diverse. Fiction for the middle group, usually ages ten/eleven to fourteen/fifteen, deals with issues of coping with internal and external changes in their lives. Because children's writers in the twentieth century have produced increasingly realistic fiction, adolescents can now find problems dealt with honestly in novels.

Teachers of middle/junior high school students see the greatest change in interests and reading abilities. Fifth and sixth graders, included in elementary grades in many schools, are viewed as older children while seventh and eighth graders are preadolescent.

Ninth graders included sometimes as upper tier in junior high school and sometimes as underlings in high school, definitely view themselves as teenagers. Their literature choices will often be governed more by interest than by ability - thus, the wealth of high-interest, low readability books that have flooded the market in recent years. Tenth through twelfth graders will still select high-interest books for pleasure reading but are also easily encouraged to stretch their literature muscles by reading more classics.

Because of the rapid social changes, topics that once did not interest young people until they reached their teens—suicide, gangs, and homosexuality—are now subjects of books for even younger readers. The plethora of high-interest books reveals how desperately schools have failed to produce on-level readers and how the market has adapted to that need.

However, these high-interest books are now readable for younger children whose reading levels are at or above normal. No matter how tastefully written, some contents are inappropriate for younger readers. The problem becomes not so much steering them toward books that they have the reading ability to handle but encouraging them toward books whose content is appropriate to their levels of cognitive and social development. A fifth-grader may be able to read V.C. Andrews book *Flowers in the Attic* but not possess the social or moral development to handle the deviant behavior of the characters.

At the same time, because of the complex changes affecting adolescents, the teacher must be well versed in learning theory and child development as well as competent to teach the subject matter of language and literature.

Skill 1.5 Situating and interpreting texts within their historical and cultural contexts.

One way of interpreting literature is to examine the various contexts during which it was written. Here are a few examples.

HISTORICAL AND CULTURAL CONTEXT

Local Color

Local color is defined as the presenting of the peculiarities of a particular locality and its inhabitants. This genre began to be seen primarily after the Civil War although there were certainly precursors such as Washington Irving and his depiction of life in the Catskill Mountains of New York. However, the local colorist movement is generally considered to have begun in 1865, when humor began to permeate the writing of those who were focusing on a particular region of the country.

> Read more about
> **Regional Realism**
> http://www.learner.org/amerpass/
> unit08/usingvideo.html

Samuel L. Clemens (Mark Twain) is best-known for his humorous works about the southwest such as "The Notorious Jumping Frog of Calaveras County." The country had just emerged from its "long night of the soul," a time when death, despair, and disaster had preoccupied the nation for almost five years. It's no wonder that the artists sought to relieve the grief and pain and lift spirits nor is it surprising that their efforts brought such a strong response. Mark Twain is generally considered to be not only one of America's funniest writers but one who also wrote great and enduring fiction.

Other examples of local colorists who used many of the same devices are George Washington Cable, Joel Chandler Harris, Bret Harte, Sarah Orne Jewett, and Harriet Beecher Stowe.

Slavery

The best-known of the early writers who used fiction as a political statement about slavery is Harriet Beecher Stowe, author of *Uncle Tom's Cabin*. This was her first novel, and it was published first as a serial in 1851 then as a book in 1852. This antislavery book infuriated Southerners. However, Stowe herself had been angered by the 1850 Fugitive Slave Law that made it legal to indict those who assisted runaway slaves. It also took away rights not only of the runaways but also of the free slaves. She intended to generate a protest of the law and slavery. It was the first effort to present the lives of slaves from their standpoint.

The novel is about three slaves, Tom, Eliza, and George who are together in Kentucky. Eliza and George are married to each other but have different masters. They successfully escape with their little boy, but Tom does not.

Although he has a wife and children, he is sold, ending up finally with the monstrous Simon Legree, where he dies at last.

Stowe cleverly used depictions of motherhood and Christianity to stir her readers. When President Lincoln finally met her, he told her it was her book that started the war.

Many writers used the printed word to protest slavery:
- Frederick Douglass
- William Lloyd Garrison
- Benjamin Lay, a Quaker
- Jonathan Edwards, Connecticut theologian
- Susan B. Anthony

Immigration

Immigration has been a popular topic for literature from the time of the Louisiana Purchase in 1804. The recent *Undaunted Courage* by Stephen E. Ambrose is ostensibly the autobiography of Meriwether Lewis but is actually a recounting of the Lewis and Clark expedition. Presented as a scientific expedition by President Jefferson, the expedition was actually intended to provide maps and information for the opening up of the west. A well-known novel of the settling of the west by immigrants from other countries is *Giants in the Earth* by Ole Edvart Rolvaag, himself a descendant of immigrants.

As one of the major movements during the 20th century, immigration swelled the population, and literature documented the resultant changes in the American culture.

John Steinbeck's *Cannery Row* and *Tortilla Flats* glorify the lives of Mexican migrants in California. Amy Tan's *The Joy Luck Club* deals with the problems faced by Chinese immigrants.

Leon Uris' *Exodus* deals with the social history that led to the founding of the modern state of Israel. It was published in 1958, only a short time after the Holocaust. It also deals with attempts of concentration camp survivors to get to the land that has become the new Israel. In many ways, it is the quintessential work on immigration—causes and effects.

Civil Rights

Many of the abolitionists were also early crusaders for civil rights. However, the 1960s movement focused attention on the plight of the people who had been "freed" by the Civil War in ways that brought about long overdue changes in the opportunities and rights of African Americans.

David Halberstam, who had been a reporter in Nashville at the time of the sit-ins by eight young black college students that initiated the revolution, wrote *The Children*, published in 1998 by Random House, for the purpose of reminding Americans of their courage, suffering, and achievements. Congressman John Lewis, Fifth District, Georgia, was one of those eight young men who has gone on to a life of public service. Halberstam records that when older black ministers tried to persuade these young people not to pursue their protest, John Lewis responded: "If not us, then who? If not now, then when?"

Some examples of protest literature:
- James Baldwin, *Blues for Mister Charlie*
- Martin Luther King, *Where Do We Go from Here?*
- Langston Hughes, *Fight for Freedom: The Story of the NAACP*
- Eldridge Cleaver, *Soul on Ice*
- Malcolm X, *The Autobiography of Malcolm X*
- Stokely Carmichael and Charles V. Hamilton, *Black Power*
- Leroi Jones, *Home*

Vietnam

An America that was already divided over the Civil Rights movement faced even greater divisions over the war in Vietnam. Those who were in favor of the war and who opposed withdrawal saw it as the major front in the war against communism. Those who opposed the war and who favored withdrawal of the troops believed that it would not serve to defeat communism and was a quagmire.

Though set in the last years of World War II, *Catch-22* by Joseph Heller was a popular antiwar novel that became a successful movie of the time.

Authors Take Sides on Vietnam, edited by Cecil Woolf and John Bagguley is a collection of essays by 168 well-known authors throughout the world. *Where is Vietnam?* edited by Walter Lowenfels consists of 92 poems about the war.

Many writers were publishing works for and against the war, but the genre that had the most impact was rock music. Bob Dylan was an example of the musicians of the time. His music represented the hippie aesthetic and brilliant, swirling colors and hallucinogenic imagery and created a style that came to be called psychedelic. Some other bands that originated during this time and became well-known for their psychedelic music, primarily about the Vietnam War in the early years, are the Grateful Dead, Jefferson Airplane, Big Brother, Sly and the Family Stone. In England, the movement attracted the Beatles and the Rolling Stones.

Another way to examine literature is by understanding the four major time periods of writings: Neoclassicism, Romanticism, Realism, and Naturalism. Certain authors, among these Chaucer, Shakespeare, and Donne, though writing during a particular literary period, are considered to have a style all their own.

NEOCLASSICISM

Patterned after the greatest writings of classical Greece and Rome, this type of writing is characterized by balanced, graceful, well-crafted, refined, elevated style. Major proponents of this style are poet laureates, John Dryden and Alexander Pope. The eras in which they wrote are called the Ages of Dryden and Pope. The self is not exalted and focus is on the group, not the individual, in neoclassic writing.

ROMANTICISM

These writings emphasize the individual. Emotions and feelings are validated. Nature acts as an inspiration for creativity; it is a balm of the spirit. Romantics hearken back to medieval, chivalric themes and ambiance. They also emphasize supernatural, Gothic themes and settings, which are characterized by gloom and darkness. Imagination is stressed. New types of writings include detective and horror stories and autobiographical introspection (William Wordsworth).

There are two generations in British Literature: First Generation includes William Wordsworth and Samuel Taylor Coleridge whose collaboration, *Lyrical Ballads*, defines romanticism and its exponents. Wordsworth maintained that the scenes and events of everyday life and the speech of ordinary people were the raw material of which poetry could and should be made. Romanticism spread to the United States, where Ralph Waldo Emerson and Henry David Thoreau adopted it in their transcendental romanticism, emphasizing reasoning. Further extensions of this style are found in Edgar Allan Poe's Gothic writings.

Second Generation romantics include the ill-fated Englishmen Lord Byron, John Keats, and Percy Bysshe Shelley. Byron and Shelley, who for some most epitomize the romantic poet (in their personal lives as well as in their work), wrote resoundingly in protest against social and political wrongs and in defense of the struggles for liberty in Italy and Greece. The Second Generation romantics stressed personal introspection and the love of beauty and nature as requisites of inspiration.

REALISM

Unlike classical and neoclassical writing which, often deal with aristocracies and nobility or the gods, realistic writers deal with the common man and his socio/economic problems in a non-sentimental way. Muckraking, social injustice, domestic abuse, and inner city conflicts are examples of writings by writers of realism. Realistic writers include Thomas Hardy, George Bernard Shaw, and Henrik Ibsen.

NATURALISM

This is realism pushed to the maximum, writing which exposes the underbelly of society, usually the lower class struggles. This is the world of penury, injustice, abuse, ghetto survival, hungry children, single parenting, and substance abuse. Émile Zola was inspired by his readings in history and medicine and attempted to apply methods of scientific observation to the depiction of pathological human character, notably in his series of novels devoted to several generations of one French family.

Skill 1.6 **Recognizing and identifying various instructional approaches to and elements of teaching reading and textual interpretation, e.g., cueing systems, activating prior knowledge, constructing meaning through context, and meta-cognitive strategies.**

Students can improve their skills at reading and interpreting text by using various techniques to comprehend the text. You can use these various instructional approaches with your students to enhance their comprehension and appreciation of various texts.

Prior knowledge can be defined as all of your prior experiences, learning, and development which precede your entering a specific learning situation or attempting to comprehend a specific text. Sometimes prior knowledge can be erroneous or incomplete. Obviously, if there are misconceptions in a reader's prior knowledge, these must be corrected so that the reader's overall comprehension skills can continue to progress. Prior knowledge includes the accumulated positive and negative experiences that readers have acquired both in and out of school.

These might come from traveling, watching television, visiting museums and libraries to visiting hospitals, prisons, and surviving poverty. Whatever the prior knowledge that students bring to the school setting, the independent reading and writing the students do in school immeasurably expands their prior knowledge and hence broadens their reading comprehension capabilities.

As you prepare to begin any imaginative/literary text, you must consider the following about the students' level of prior knowledge:

1. What prior knowledge needs to be activated for the text, theme or for the writing to be done successfully?
2. How independent are the students in using strategies to activate their prior knowledge?

Comprehension occurs when the reader correctly interprets the print on the page and constructs meaning from it. Comprehension depends on activating prior knowledge, cultural and social background of the reader, and the reader's ability to use comprehension monitoring strategies.

Cues are used to direct and monitor reading comprehension. As they self monitor their reading comprehensions, readers have to integrate various sources of information or cues to help them construct meaning from text and graphic illustrations.

Context clues help readers determine the meaning of words they are not familiar with. The context of a word is the sentence or sentences that surround the word. Read the following sentences and attempt to determine the meanings of the words in bold print.

> The **luminosity** of the room was so incredible that there was no need for lights.

If there was no need for lights, then one must assume that the word luminosity has something to do with giving off light. The definition of "luminosity," therefore, is the emission of light.

> Jamie could not understand Joe's feelings. His mood swings made understanding him somewhat of an **enigma.**

The fact that he could not be understood made him somewhat of a puzzle. The definition of "enigma" is a mystery or puzzle.

Word Forms: Sometimes a very familiar word can appear as a different part of speech.

You may have heard that **fraud** involves a criminal misrepresentation, so when it appears as the adjective form **fraudulent** ("He was suspected of fraudulent activities") you can make an educated guess. You probably know that something out of date is **obsolete**; therefore, when you read about "built-in **obsolescence**," you can detect the meaning of the unfamiliar word.

ENG. LANGUAGE LIT. & COMP.

The context for a word is the written passage that surrounds it. Sometimes the writer offers synonyms—words that have nearly the same meaning. Context clues can appear within the sentence itself, within the preceding and/or following sentence(s), or in the passage as a whole.

Sentence Clues: Often, a writer will actually define a difficult or particularly important word for you the first time it appears in a passage. Phrases like *that is, such as, which is,* or *is called* might announce the writer's intention to give just the definition you need. Occasionally, a writer will simply use a synonym (a word that means the same thing) or near-synonym joined by the word *or*. Look at the following examples:

> The **credibility**, that is to say, the believability, of the witness was called into question by evidence of previous perjury.

> Nothing would **assuage** or lessen the child's grief.

Punctuation: At the sentence level, punctuation is often a clue to the meaning of a word. Commas, parentheses, quotation marks and dashes tell the reader that a definition is being offered by the writer.

> A tendency toward **hyperbole**, extravagant exaggeration, is a common flaw among persuasive writers.

> Political **apathy** - lack of interest - can lead to the death of the state.

A writer might simply give an **explanation** in other words that you can understand in the same sentence:

> The **xenophobic** townspeople were suspicious of every foreigner.

Writers also explain a word in terms of its opposite at the sentence level:

> His **incarceration** was ended, and he was elated to be out of jail.

Adjacent Sentence Clues: The context for a word goes beyond the sentence in which it appears. At times, the writer uses adjacent (adjoining) sentences to present an explanation or definition:

> The $200 for the car repair would have to come out of the **contingency** fund. Fortunately, Angela's father had taught her to keep some money set aside for just such emergencies.

Analysis: The second sentence offers a clue to the definition of *contingency* as used in this sentence: "emergencies." Therefore, a fund for contingencies would be money tucked away for unforeseen and/or urgent events.

Entire Passage Clues: On occasion, you must look at an entire paragraph or passage to figure out the definition of a word or term. In the following paragraph, notice how the word *nostalgia* undergoes a form of extended definition throughout the selection rather than in just one sentence.

> The word **nostalgia** links Greek words for "away from home" and "pain." If you're feeling **nostalgic**, then you are probably in some physical distress or discomfort, suffering from a feeling of alienation and separation from loved ones or loved places. **Nostalgia** is that awful feeling you remember from the first time you went away to camp or spent the weekend with a friend's family—homesickness, or some condition even more painful than that. But in common use, **nostalgia** has come to have more sentimental associations. A few years back, for example, a **nostalgia** craze had to do with the 1950's. We resurrected poodle skirts and saddle shoes, built new restaurants to look like old ones, and tried to make chicken a la king just as mother probably never made it. In TV situation comedies, we recreated a pleasant world that probably never existed and relished our **nostalgia**, longing for a homey, comfortable lost time.

TYPES OF RESPONSES

Reading literature involves a reciprocal interaction between the reader and the text. These responses can be emotional, interpretive, critical, and evaluative.

Emotional: In an emotional response, readers can identify with the characters and situations so as to project themselves into the story. They feel a sense of satisfaction by associating aspects of their own lives with the people, places, and events in the literature. Emotional responses are observed in readers' verbal and non-verbal reactions—laughter, comments on its effects, and retelling or dramatizing the action.

Interpretive: Interpretive responses result in inferences about character development, setting, or plot; analysis of style elements—metaphor, simile, allusion, rhythm, tone; outcomes derivable from information provided in the narrative; and assessment of the author's intent. Interpretive responses are made verbally or in writing.

Critical: Critical responses involve making value judgments about the quality of a piece of literature. Reactions to the effectiveness of the writer's style and language use are observed through discussion and written reactions.

> Learn more about
> **Reading Response Journals**
> http://www.education-world.com/a_curr/profdev/profdev085.shtmlreading%20strategies%20index.htm

Evaluative: Some reading response theorists add a response that considers the readers' considerations of such factors as how well the piece of literature represents its genre, how well it reflects the social/ethical mores of society, and how well the author has approached the subject for freshness and slant.

Middle school readers will exhibit both emotional and interpretive responses. Naturally, making interpretive responses depends on the degree of knowledge the student has of literary elements. Children show critical reactions on a fundamental level when they are able to say why a particular book was boring or why a particular poem was sad. Adolescents in ninth and tenth grades should begin to make critical responses by addressing the specific language and genre characteristics of literature.

Evaluative responses are harder to detect and are rarely made by any but a few advanced high school students. However, a teacher who knows what to listen for can recognize evaluative responses and incorporate them into discussions.

For example, if a student says, "I don't understand why that character is doing that," she is making an interpretive response to character motivation. However, if she goes on to say, "What good is that action?" she is giving an evaluative response that should be explored in terms of "What good should it do and why isn't that positive action happening?"

At the emotional level, another student might say, "I almost broke into a sweat when the author was describing the heat in the burning house." An interpretive response says, "The author used descriptive adjectives to bring his setting to life." Critically, the student adds, "The author's use of descriptive language contributes to the success of the narrative and maintains reader interest through the whole story." If he goes on to wonder why the author allowed the grandmother in the story to die in the fire, he is making an evaluative response.

Levels of Response

The levels of reader response will depend largely on the reader's level of social, psychological, and intellectual development. Most middle school students have progressed beyond merely involving themselves in the story enough to be able to retell the events in some logical sequence or describe the feeling that the story evoked. They are aware to some degree that the feeling evoked was the result of a careful manipulation of good elements of fiction writing. They may not explain that awareness as successfully as a high school student, but they are beginning to grasp the concepts and not just the personal reactions. They are beginning to differentiate between responding to the story itself and responding to a literary creation.

Fostering Self-esteem and Empathy for Others

All-important is the use of literature as bibliotherapy that allows the reader to identify with others and become aware of alternatives while not feeling directly betrayed or threatened. For the high school student the ability to empathize is an evaluative response, a much desired outcome of literature studies. Use of these books either individually or as a thematic unit of study allows for discussion or writing. The titles are grouped by theme, not by reading level.

Abuse
Blair, Maury and Doug Brendel. *Maury, Wednesday's Child*
Dizenzo, Patricia. *Why Me?*
Parrot, Andrea. *Coping with Date Rape and Acquaintance Rape*

Natural World Concerns
Caduto, M. and J. Bruchac. *Keepers of Earth*
Gay, Kathlyn. *Greenhouse Effect*
Johnson, Denis. *Fiskadaro*
Madison, Arnold. *It Can't Happen to Me*

Eating Disorders
Arnold, Caroline. *Too Fat, Too Thin, Do You Have a Choice?*
DeClements, Barthe. *Nothing's Fair in Fifth Grade*
Snyder, Anne. *Goodbye, Paper Doll*

Family
Cormier, Robert. *Tunes for Bears to Dance to*
Danzinger, Paula. *The Divorce Express*
Neufield, John. *Sunday Father*
Okimoto, Jean Davies. *Molly by any Other Name*
Peck, Richard. *Don't Look and It Won't Hurt*
Zindel, Paul. *I Never Loved Your Mind*

Stereotyping
Baklanov, Grigory. (Trans. by Antonina W. Bouis) *Forever Nineteen*
Greene, Betty. *Summer of My German Soldier*
Kerr, M.E. *Gentle Hands*
Reiss, Johanna. *The Upstairs Room*
Taylor, Mildred D. *Roll of Thunder, Hear Me Cry*
Wakatsuki-Houston, Jeanne and James D. Houston. *Farewell to Manzanarr*

Suicide and Death
Blume, Judy. *Tiger Eyes*
Bunting, Eve. *If I Asked You, Would You Stay?*
Gunther, John. *Death Be Not Proud*

Mazer, Harry. *When the Phone Rings*
Peck, Richard. *Remembering the Good Times*
Richter, Elizabeth. *Losing Someone You Love*
Strasser, Todd. *Friends Till the End*

Caution

Teachers should always use caution with reading materials that have a sensitive or controversial nature. They must be of the happenings in the school and outside community to spare students undue suffering. A child who has known a recent death in his family or circle of friends may need to distance himself from classroom discussion. Whenever open discussion of a topic brings pain or embarrassment, the child should not be further subjected. Older children and young adults will be able to discuss issues with greater objectivity and without making blurted, insensitive comments.

Teachers must be able to gauge the level of emotional development of the students when selecting subject matter and the strategies for studying it. Students or parents may consider some material objectionable. Should a student choose not to read an assigned material, the teacher can allow the student to select an alternate title. It is always advisable to notify parents if a particularly sensitive piece is to be studied.

In middle and secondary schools, the emphasis of reading instruction spans the range of comprehension skills: literal, inferential, and critical. Most instruction in grades five and six is based on the skills delineated in basal readers adopted for those grade levels. Reading instruction in grades seven through nine is usually part of the general language arts class instead of being a distinct subject in the curriculum, unless the instruction is remedial. Reading in tenth through twelfth grades is part of the literature curriculum—World, American, and British.

Teachers have many techniques to assure that students understand the text but these techniques vary with student age and ability.

READING EMPHASIS IN MIDDLE SCHOOL

Reading for comprehension of factual material—content area textbooks, reference books, and newspapers—is closely related to study strategies in the middle/junior high.

Organized study models teach students to locate main ideas and supporting details, to recognize sequential order, to distinguish fact from opinion, and to determine cause/effect relationships. One such model is the SQ3R method, a technique that enables students to learn the content of even large amounts of text (Survey, Question, Read, Recite, and Review Studying),

Strategies

Teacher-guided activities that require students to organize and to summarize information based on the author's explicit intent are pertinent strategies in middle grades. Evaluation techniques include oral and written responses to standardized or teacher-made worksheets.

Through reading fiction, students can develop skills for inferring meaning. Teachers can identify the skills to be studied, choose the appropriate reading resources, and develop activities to guide students' reading for meaning. To monitor the progress of acquiring these comprehension skills, teachers have at their disposal a variety of printed materials as well as individualized computer software programs.

Older middle school students should be given opportunities for more student-centered activities, such as the individual and collaborative selection of reading choices based on student interest, small group discussions of selected works, and greater written expression. Evaluation techniques include teacher monitoring and observation of discussions and written work samples.

Certain students may begin some fundamental critical interpretation, such as recognizing fallacious reasoning in news media, examining the accuracy of news reports and advertising, or explaining their reasons for preferring one author's writing to another's. Development of these skills may require a more learning-centered approach in which the teacher identifies a number of objectives and suggested resources from which the student may choose a course of study. Teachers can stress self-evaluation through a reading diary or they can encourage teacher and peer evaluation of creative projects resulting from such study.

> Learn more about
> **Monitoring Comprehension**
> http://www.indiana.edu/~l517/monitoring.html

Teachers should encourage one-on-one tutoring or peer-assisted reading instead of evaluating students as they read aloud before the entire class. However, occasional sharing of favored selections by both teachers and willing students is a good oral interpretation basic.

READING EMPHASIS IN HIGH SCHOOL

Students in high school literature classes should focus on interpretive and critical reading. Teachers should guide the study of the elements of inferential (interpretive) reading—drawing conclusions, predicting outcomes, and recognizing examples of specific genre characteristics, for example—and critical reading to judge the quality of the writer's work against recognized standards.

At this level students should understand the skills of language and reading that they are expected to master and be able to evaluate their own progress.

Strategies

Along with the requisites and prerequisites of most literature courses, teachers need to encourage students to pursue independent study and enrichment reading. Enabling students to be life-long learners is a fundamental goal of teaching.

The teacher becomes more facilitator than instructor. With the teacher's guidance, students should be able to diagnose their individual strengths and weaknesses, keep a record of progress, and interact with other students and the teacher in practicing skills.

Teachers should provide ample opportunities for oral interpretation of literature, special projects in creative dramatics, writing for publication in school literary magazines or newspapers, and speech/debate activities. A student portfolio provides for teacher and peer evaluation.

READING ASSESSMENT

Assessment is the practice of collecting information about children's progress, and evaluation is the process of judging the children's responses to determine how well they are achieving particular goals or demonstrating reading skills.

Assessment and evaluation are intricately connected in the literacy classroom. Assessment is necessary because teachers need ways to determine what students are learning and how they are progressing. In addition, assessment can be a tool which can also help students take ownership of their own learning and become partners in their ongoing development as readers and writers. In this day of public accountability, clear, definite and reliable assessment creates confidence in public education. There are two broad categories of assessment.

Formal assessment is composed of standardized tests and procedures carried out under circumscribed conditions. Formal assessments include state tests, standardized achievement tests, NAEP tests, and the like. **Informal assessment** uses observations and other non-standardized procedures to compile anecdotal and observation data/evidence of children's progress. It includes but is not limited to checklists, observations, and performance tasks.

SKILLS TO EVALUATE

- Ability to use syntactic cues when encountering an unknown word. Good readers will expect the word to fit the syntax they are familiar with. Poor readers may substitute a word that does not fit the syntax, and will not correct themselves.

- Ability to use semantic cues to determine the meaning of an unknown word. Good readers will consider the meanings of all the known words in the sentence. Poor readers may read one word at a time with no regard for the other words.

  - Ability to use schematic cues to connect words read with prior knowledge. Good readers will incorporate what they know with what the text says or implies. Poor readers may think only of the word they are reading without associating it with prior knowledge.

- Ability to use phonics cues to improve ease and efficiency in reading. Good readers will apply letter and sound associations almost subconsciously. Poor readers may have one of two kinds of problems.

  They may have underdeveloped phonics/skills, and use only an initial clue without analyzing vowel patterns before quickly guessing the word. Or they may use phonics skills in isolation, becoming so absorbed in the word "noises" that they ignore or forget the message of the text.

- Ability to process information from text. Readers should be able to get information from the text as well as store, retrieve, and integrate it for later use.

- Ability to use interpretive thinking to make logical predictions and inferences.

- Ability to use critical thinking to make decisions and insights about the text.

- Ability to use appreciative thinking to respond to the text, whether emotionally, mentally, or ideologically

Methods of Evaluation

- Assess students at the beginning of each year to determine grouping for instruction.

- Judge whether a student recognizes when a word does not make sense.

- Monitor whether the students corrects themselves if they know when to ignore and read on or when to reread a sentence.

- Looks for skill such as recognizing cause and effect, finding main ideas, and using comparison and contrast techniques.

- Keep dated records to follow individual progress. Focus on a few students each day. Grade them on a scale of 1-5 according to how well they perform certain reading abilities (e.g. Logically predicts coming events).

    Also include informal observations, such as "Ed was able to determine the meaning of the word 'immigrant' by examining the other words in the sentence."

- Remember that evaluation is important, but enjoyment of reading is the most important thing to emphasize. Keep reading as a pressure-free, fun activity so students do not become intimidated by reading. Even if the students are not meeting excellent standards, if they continue wanting to read each day that is a success!

COMPETENCY 2.0 LANGUAGE AND LINGUISTICS

Skill 2.1 Understanding the principles of language acquisition and development, including social, cultural, and historical influences and the role and nature of dialects.

LANGUAGE DEVELOPMENT

The way language skills are developed depends on many factors, some internal (the age of the child), some external (immigration). Teachers can use a variety of approaches to accommodate individual differences.

Learning Approach

Early theories of language development were formulated from learning theory research. The assumption was that language development evolved from learning the rules of language structures and applying them through imitation and reinforcement. This approach also assumed that language, cognitive and social developments were independent of each other.

Thus, children were expected to learn language from patterning after adults who spoke and wrote Standard English. No allowance was made for communication through child jargon, idiomatic expressions, or grammatical and mechanical errors resulting from too strict adherence to the rules of inflection ("child's" instead of "children") or conjugation ("runned" instead of "ran"). No association was made between physical and operational development and language mastery.

Linguistic Approach

Studies spearheaded by Noam Chomsky in the 1950s formulated the theory that language ability is innate and develops through natural human maturation as environmental stimuli trigger acquisition of syntactical structures appropriate to each exposure level. The assumption of a hierarchy of syntax downplayed the significance of semantics. Because of the complexity of syntax and the relative speed with which children acquire language, linguists attributed language development to biological rather than cognitive or social influences.

Cognitive Approach

Researchers in the 1970s proposed that language knowledge derives from both syntactic and semantic structures. Drawing on the studies of Piaget and other cognitive learning theorists, supporters of the cognitive approach maintained that children acquire knowledge of linguistic structures after they have acquired the cognitive structures necessary to process language. For example, joining words for specific meaning necessitates sensory motor intelligence.

Children must be able to coordinate movement and recognize objects before they can identify words to name the objects or word groups to describe the actions performed with those objects.

Adolescents must have developed the mental abilities for organizing concepts as well as concrete operations, predicting outcomes, and theorizing before they can assimilate and verbalize complex sentence structures, choose vocabulary for particular nuances of meaning, and examine semantic structures for tone and manipulative effect.

Sociocognitive Approach

Other theorists in the 1970s proposed that language development results from sociolinguistic competence. Language, cognitive, and social knowledge are interactive elements of total human development. Emphasis on verbal communication as the medium for language expression resulted in the inclusion of speech activities in most language arts curricula.

Unlike previous approaches, the sociocognitive approach allowed that determining the appropriateness of language in given situations for specific listeners is as important as understanding semantic and syntactic structures.

By engaging in conversation, children at all stages of development have opportunities to test their language skills, receive feedback, and make modifications. As a social activity, conversation is as structured by social order as grammar is structured by the rules of syntax. Conversation satisfies the learner's need to be heard and understood and to influence others. Thus, the choices of vocabulary, tone, and content are dictated by the learner's ability to assess the language knowledge of listeners. The speaker is constantly applying his cognitive skills to using language in a social interaction. If the capacity to acquire language is inborn, without an environment in which to practice language, children would not pass beyond grunts and gestures, as did primitive man.

Of course, the varying degrees of environmental stimuli to which children are exposed at all age levels create a slower or faster development of language. Some children are prepared to articulate concepts and recognize symbolism by the time they enter fifth grade because they have been exposed to challenging reading and conversations with well-spoken adults at home or in their social groups. Others are still trying to master the sight recognition skills and are not yet ready to combine words in complex patterns.

Benefits of the Sociocognitive Approach

This approach has tended to guide the whole language movement, currently in fashion. Most basal readers use an integrated, cross-curricular approach to successful grammar, language, and usage. Reinforcement becomes an intradepartmental responsibility.

Language incorporates diction and terminology across the curriculum. Standard usage is encouraged and supported by both the core classroom textbooks and current software for technology. Teachers need to acquaint themselves with the computer capabilities in their school district and at their individual school sites. Advances in new technologies require teachers to familiarize themselves with programs that would serve their students' needs. Students respond enthusiastically to technology.

Several highly effective programs are available in various formats to assist students with initial instruction or remediation. Grammar texts, such as the Warriner's series, employ various methods to reach individual learning styles. The school library media center should become a focal point for individual exploration.

Concerns for the Teacher

Because teachers must, by virtue of tradition and the dictates of the curriculum, teach grammar, usage, and writing as well as reading and later literature, the problem becomes when to teach what to whom.

The profusion of approaches to teaching grammar alone is mind-boggling. In the universities, we learn about transformational grammar, stratification grammar, sectoral grammar, and more. But in practice, most teachers, supported by presentations in textbooks and by the methods they learned themselves, keep coming back to the same traditional prescriptive approach—read and imitate—or structural approach—learn the parts of speech, the parts of sentence, punctuation rules, sentence patterns. After enough of the terminology and rules are stored in the brain, then we learn to write and speak. For some educators, the best solution is the worse—don't teach grammar at all.

The same problems occur in teaching usage. How much can we demand students communicate in only Standard English? Different schools of thought suggest that a study of dialect and idiom and recognition of various jargons is a vital part of language development. Social pressures, especially on students in middle and junior high schools, to be accepted within their peer groups and to speak the non-standard language spoken outside the school make adolescents resistant to the corrective, remedial approach.

In many communities where the immigrant populations are high, new words are entering English from other languages even as words and expressions that were common when we were children have become rare or obsolete.

Regardless of differences of opinion concerning language development, language arts teachers will be most effective using the styles and approaches with which they are is most comfortable. And, if they subscribe to a student-centered approach, they may find that the students have a lot to teach the teachers and each other. Moffett and Wagner in the Fourth Edition of *Student-centered Language Arts K-12* stress the three I's: individualization, interaction, and integration. Essentially, they are supporting the socio-cognitive approach to language development. By providing an opportunity for students to select their own activities and resources, their instruction is individualized. By centering on and teaching each other, students are interactive. Finally, by allowing students to synthesize a variety of knowledge structures, they integrate them. The teacher's role becomes that of a facilitator.

> Learn more about
> **Student Centered Learning**
> http://www.wcer.wisc.edu/step/ep301/Fall2000/Tochonites/stu_cen.html

Geographical Influences

Dialect differences are basically in pronunciation. Bostoners say "pahty" for "party" and Southerners blend words like "you all" into "y'all." Besides the dialect differences already mentioned, the biggest geographical factors in American English stem from minor word choice variances. Depending on the region where you live, when you order a carbonated, syrupy beverage most generically called a soft drink, you might ask for a "soda" in the South, or a "pop" in the Midwest. If you order a soda in New York, then you will get a scoop of ice cream in your soft drink, while in other areas you would have to ask for a "float."

Social Influences

Social influences are mostly those imposed by family, peer groups, and mass media. The economic and educational levels of families determine language use. Exposure to adults who encourage and assist children to speak well enhances readiness for other areas of learning and contributes to their ability to communicate their needs. Historically, children learned language, speech patterns, and grammar from members of the extended family just as they learned the rules of conduct within their family unit and community. In modern times, the mother in a nuclear family became the dominant force in influencing children's development. With increasing social changes, many children are not receiving the proper guidance in all areas of development, especially language.

Those who are fortunate to be in educational-day-care programs like Head Start or in certified preschools develop better language skills than those whose care is entrusted to untrained care providers. Once children enter elementary school, they are also greatly influenced by peer language. This peer influence becomes significant in adolescence as the use of teen jargon gives teenagers a sense of identity within their chosen group(s) and independence from the influence of adults. In some lower socio-economic groups, children use Standard English in school and street language outside the school. Some children of immigrant families become bilingual by necessity if no English is spoken in the home.

Research has shown a strong correlation between socio-economic characteristics and all areas of intellectual development. Traditional measurement instruments rely on verbal ability to establish intelligence. Research findings and test scores reflect that children reared in nuclear families providing cultural experiences and individual attention become more language proficient than those who are denied that security and stimulation.

Personal Influences

The rate of physical development and identifiable language disabilities also influence language development. Nutritional deficiencies, poor eyesight, and conditions such as stuttering or dyslexia can inhibit children's ability to master language. Unless diagnosed early, they can hamper communication into adulthood. These conditions also stymie the development of self-confidence and, therefore, the willingness to learn or to overcome the handicap. Children should receive proper diagnosis and positive corrective instruction.

In adolescence, children's choice of role models and decisions about their future determine the growth of identity. Rapid physical and emotional changes and the stress of coping with the pressure of sexual awareness make concentration on any educational pursuits difficult. The easier the transition from childhood to adulthood, the better the competence will be in all learning areas.

Middle school and junior high school teachers are confronted by a student body ranging from fifth graders who are still childish to eighth or ninth graders who, if not in fact, at least in their minds, are young adults. Teachers must approach language instruction as a social development tool with more emphasis on vocabulary acquisition, reading improvement, and speaking/writing skills. High school teachers can deal with the more formalized instruction of grammar, usage, and literature meant for older adolescents whose social development allows them to pay more attention to studies that will improve their chances for a better adult life.

As a tool, language must have relevance to students' real environment. Many high schools have developed practical English classes for business/ vocational students whose specific needs are determined by their desire to enter the workforce upon graduation. More emphasis is placed upon accuracy of mechanics and understanding verbal and written directions because these are skills desired by employers. Writing résumés, completing forms, reading policy and operations manuals, and generating reports are some of the desired skills. Emphasis is placed on higher-level thinking skills, including inferential thinking and literary interpretation, in literature classes for college-bound students.

Skill 2.2   Understanding elements of the history and development of the English language and American English, including linguistic change, etymology, and processes of word formation.

HISTORY AND DEVELOPMENT OF THE ENGLISH LANGUAGE

English is an Indo-European language that evolved through several periods. The origin of English dates to the settlement of the British Isles in the fifth and sixth centuries by Germanic tribes called the Angles, Saxons, and Jutes. The original Britons spoke a Celtic tongue while the Angles spoke a Germanic dialect.

Modern English derives from the speech of the Anglo-Saxons who imposed not only their language but also their social customs and laws on their new land. From the fifth to the tenth century, Britain's language was the tongue we now refer to as Old English. During the next four centuries, the many French attempts at English conquest introduced many French words to English. However, the grammar and syntax of the language remained Germanic.

> Learn more about the
> **History of the English Language**
> http://ebbs.english.vt.edu/hel/hel.html

Middle English, most evident in the writings of Geoffrey Chaucer, dates loosely from 1066 to 1509. William Caxton brought the printing press to England in 1474 and increased literacy. Old English words required numerous inflections to indicate noun cases and plurals as well as verb conjugations. Middle English continued the use of many inflections and pronunciations that treated these inflections as separately pronounced syllables. English in 1300 would have been written "Olde Anglishe" with the *e*'s at the ends of the words pronounced as our short *a* vowel. Even adjectives had plural inflections: "long dai" became "longe daies" pronounced "long-a day-as." Spelling was phonetic, thus every vowel had multiple pronunciations, a fact that continues to affect the language.

Modern English dates from the introduction of The Great Vowels Shift because it created guidelines for spelling and pronunciation. Before the printing press, books were copied laboriously by hand; the language was subject to the individual interpretation of the scribes. Printers and subsequently lexicographers like Samuel Johnson and America's Noah Webster influenced the guidelines. As reading matter was mass produced, the reading public was forced to adopt the speech and writing habits developed by those who wrote and printed books.

Despite many students' insistence to the contrary, Shakespeare's writings are in Modern English. Teachers should stress to students that language, like customs, morals, and other social factors, is constantly subject to change. Immigration, inventions, and cataclysmic events change language as much as any other facet of life is affected by these changes.

The domination of one race or nation over others can change a language significantly. Beginning with the colonization of the New World by England and Spain, English and Spanish became dominant languages in the Western hemisphere.

American English today is somewhat different in pronunciation and sometimes vocabulary from British English. The British call a truck a "lorry," baby carriages a "pram," short for "perambulator," and an elevator a "lift." The two languages have very few syntactical differences, and even the tonal qualities that were once so clearly different are converging.

Though Modern English is less complex than Middle English, having lost many unnecessary inflections, it is still considered difficult to learn because of its many exceptions to the rules. It has, however, become the world's dominant language by reason of the great political, military, and social power of England from the fifteenth to the nineteenth century and of America in the twentieth century.

Modern inventions—the telephone, phonograph, radio, television, and motion pictures—have especially affected English pronunciation. Regional dialects, once a hindrance to clear understanding, have fewer distinct characteristics. The speakers from different parts of the United States of America can be identified by their accents, but more and more as educators and media personalities stress uniform pronunciations and proper grammar, the differences are diminishing.

The English language has a more extensive vocabulary than any other language. Ours is a language of synonyms, words borrowed from other languages, and coined words—many of them introduced by the rapid expansion of technology.

Students should understand that language is in constant flux. They can demonstrate this when they use language for specific purposes and audiences. Negative criticism of a student's errors in word choice or sentence structures will inhibit creativity. Positive criticism that suggests ways to enhance communication skills will encourage exploration.

Language changes in all its manifestations: At the phonetic level, the sounds of a language will change as will its orthography (spelling). The vocabulary level will probably manifest the greatest changes. Changes in syntax are slower and less likely to occur. For example, English has changed in response to the influences of many other languages and cultures as well as internal cultural changes such as the development of the railroad and the computer; however, its syntax still relies on word order—it has not shifted to an inflected system even though many of the cultures that have impacted it do, in fact, have an inflected language, such as Spanish.

The most significance influence on a language is the blending of cultures. The Norman Conquest that brought the English speakers in the British Isles under the rule of French speakers changed the language, but the fact that English speakers did not adopt the language of the ruling class is significant—they did not become speakers of French. Even so, many vocabulary items entered the language in that period. The Great Vowel Shift that occurred between the 14th and 16th centuries is somewhat of a mystery although it's generally attributed to the migration to Southeast England following the plague of the Black Death. The Great Vowel Shift largely accounts for the discrepancy between orthography and speech—the difficult spelling system in modern English.

Colonization of other countries has also brought new vocabulary items into the language. Indian English has its own easily recognizable attributes as does Australian and North American English, and these cultural interactions have added to items in the usages of each other and in the language at large. The fact that English is the most widely spoken and understood language all over the world in the 21st century implies that it is constantly being changed by the globalized world.

Other influences, of course, impact language. The introduction of television and its domination by the United States has had great influence on the English that is spoken and understood all over the world. The same is true of the computerizing of the world (Tom Friedman called it "flattening" in his *The World is Flat: A Brief History of the Twenty-first Century*). New terms have been added ("blog"), old terms have changed meaning ("mouse"), and nouns have been verbalized ("prioritize").

Identification of Common Morphemes, Prefixes, and Suffixes

This aspect of language development is to help students look for structural elements within words that they can use independently to help them determine meaning. The terms listed below are generally recognized as the key structural analysis components.

Root Words: A root word is a word from which another word is developed. The second word can be said to have its "root" in the first. This structural component nicely lends itself to the illustration a tree with roots so that students can use a concrete image for an abstract concept.

An example of a root word is "bene" which means "good" or "well." English words from this Latin root include "benefit," "beneficial," "beneficent," and "beneficiary."

Students may also want to construct root words literally by using cardboard trees and/or actual roots from plants to create word family models. This is an effective way to help students own their root words.

Base Words: A base word is a stand-alone linguistic unit which cannot be deconstructed or broken down into smaller words. For example, in the word "re-tell," the base word is "tell."

Contractions: These are shortened forms of two words in which a letter or letters have been deleted. These deleted letters have been replaced by an apostrophe. For example, "hasn't" is the contraction for "has not."

Prefixes: These are beginning units of meaning which can be added (the vocabulary word for this type of structural adding is "affixed") to a base word or root word. They cannot stand-alone. They are also sometimes known as "bound morphemes," meaning that they cannot stand alone as a base word. Some examples of prefixes are "pre," "ex," "trans," and "sub."

Suffixes: These are ending units of meaning that can be "affixed" or added on to the ends of root or base words. Suffixes transform the original meanings of base and root words. Like prefixes, they are also known as "bound morphemes," because they cannot stand alone as words. Some examples of suffixes are "ing," "ful," "ness," and "er."

Inflectional endings: These are types of suffixes that impart a new meaning to the base or root word. These endings in particular change the gender, number, tense, or form of the base or root words. Just like other suffixes, these are also termed "bound morphemes." Some examples are "ette," "es," and "ed."

> Learn more about
> **Word Analysis**
> http://www.orangeusd.k12.ca.us/yorba/word_analysis.htm

Compound Words: These occur when two or more base words are connected to form a new word. The meaning of the new word is in some way connected with that of the base word. "Bookkeeper," besides being the only English word with three double letters in a row, is an example of a compound word.

The way language skills are developed depends on many factors, some internal (the age of the child), some external (immigration). Teachers can use a variety of approaches to accommodate individual differences.

Origins of English Words

Just as countries and families have histories, so do words. Knowing and understanding the origin of a word, where and how it has been used through the years, and the history of its meaning as it has changed are important components of the writing and language teacher's tool kit.

Never in the history of the English language, or any other language for that matter, have the forms and meanings of words changed so rapidly. When America was settled originally, immigration from many countries made it a "melting pot." Immigration accelerated rapidly within the first hundred years, resulting in pockets of language throughout the country.

When trains began to make transportation available and affordable, individuals from those various pockets came in contact with each other, shared vocabularies, and attempted to converse. From that time forward, every generation brought the introduction of a technology that made language interchange not only more possible but more important.

Radio began the trend to standardize dialects. A Bostonian might not be understood by a Houstonian, who might not be interested in turning the dial to hear the news or a drama or the advertisements of the vendors that had a vested interest in being heard and understood. Soap and soup producers knew a goldmine when they saw it and created a market for radio announcers and actors who spoke without a pronounced dialect. In return, listeners began to hear the English language in a dialect very different from the one they spoke, and as it settled into their thinking processes, it eventually made its way to their tongues; consequently, spoken English began to lose some of its local peculiarities.

This change has been a slow process, but most Americans can easily understand other Americans, no matter where they come from. They can even converse with a native of Great Britain with little difficulty. The introduction of television carried the evolution further as did the explosion of electronic communicating devices over the past fifty years.

An excellent example of the changes that have occurred in English is a comparison of Shakespeare's original works with modern translations. Without help, twenty-first-century Americans are unable to read the *Folio*.

On the other hand, teachers must constantly be mindful of the vocabularies and etymologies of their students, who are on the receiving end of the escalation brought about by technology and increased global influence and contact.

In the past, the Oxford English Dictionary has been the most reliable source for etymologies. Some of the collegiate dictionaries are also useful. *Merriam-Webster's 3rd Unabridged Dictionary* is useful in tracing the sources of words in American English. *Merriam-Webster's Unabridged Dictionary* may be out of date, so a teacher should also have a *Merriam-Webster's Collegiate Dictionary*, which is updated regularly.

> Check out the
> **Learning Resources of the OED**
> http://www.oed.com/learning/

In addition to etymologies, knowing how and when to label a usage "jargon" or "colloquial" is important. The teacher must be aware of the possibility that it's a word that is now accepted as standard. To be on top of this, the teacher must continually keep up with the etymological aids that are available, particularly online.

If you google "etymology," for instance, or even the word you're unsure of, you can find a multitude of sources. Don't trust a single one. The information should be validated by at least three sources. Wikipedia is very useful, but it can be changed by anyone who chooses, so any information on it should be backed up by other sources. If you go to http://www.etymonline.com/sources.php, you will find a long list of resources on etymology.

Spelling

Spelling in English is complicated because it is not phonetic—that is, it is not based on the one-sound/one letter formula used by many other languages. It is based on the Latin alphabet, which originally had twenty letters, consisting of the present English alphabet minus J, K, V, W, Y, and Z. The Romans added K to be used in abbreviations and Y and Z in words that came from the Greek. This 23-letter alphabet was adopted by the English, who developed W as a ligatured doubling of U and later J and V as consonantal variants of I and U. The result was our alphabet of 26 letters with upper case (capital) and lower case forms.

Spelling is based primarily on 15th century English. The problem is that pronunciation has changed drastically since then, especially long vowels and diphthongs. This Great Vowel Shift affected the seven long vowels.

For a long time, spelling was erratic—there were no standards. As long as the meaning was clear, spelling was not considered very important. Samuel Johnson tackled this problem, and his *Dictionary of the English Language* (1755) brought standards to spelling, so important once printing presses were invented. There have been some changes, of course, through the years, but spelling is still not strictly phonetic.

Despite many attempts to nudge the spelling into a more phonetic representation of the sounds, all have failed for the most part. A good example is Noah Webster's *Spelling Book* (1783), which was a precursor to the first edition (1828) of his *American Dictionary of the English Language*. While there are rules for spelling, and it's important that students learn the rules, there are also many exceptions; and memorizing exceptions and giving plenty of opportunities for practicing them seems the only solution for the teacher of English.

Skill 2.3 Understanding and applying the elements of traditional grammar, e.g., syntax, sentence types, sentence structure, parts of speech, modifiers, sentence combining, phrases and clauses, capitalization, and punctuation.

Understanding that syntax is the grammatical relationship of words in sentences, writers will craft sentences that convey their thoughts precisely. One of the first rules of grammar is to use complete sentences so a review of sentence structure is a first step.

SENTENCE COMPLETENESS

Recognize the sentence elements necessary to make a complete thought and use independent and dependent clauses properly. Proper punctuation will correct such errors.

Sentence Structure

You should recognize simple, compound, complex, and compound-complex sentences. Use dependent (subordinate) and independent clauses correctly to create these sentence structures.

Simple	Joyce wrote a letter.
Compound	Joyce wrote a letter, and Dot drew a picture.
Complex	While Joyce wrote a letter, Dot drew a picture.
Compound/Complex	When Mother asked the girls to demonstrate their new-found skills, Joyce wrote a letter, and Dot drew a picture.

Note: Do **not** confuse compound sentence elements with compound sentences.

Simple sentence with compound subject
   Joyce and Dot wrote letters.
   The girl in row three and the boy next to her were passing notes across the aisle.

Simple sentence with compound predicate
   Joyce wrote letters and drew pictures.
   The captain of the high school debate team graduated with honors and studied broadcast journalism in college.

Simple sentence with compound object of preposition
   Coleen graded the students' essays for style and mechanical accuracy.

Clauses and Phrases

Clauses are connected word groups that are composed of *at least* one subject and one verb. (A subject is the doer of an action or the element that is being joined. A verb conveys either the action or the link.)

   Students are waiting for the start of the assembly.
   Subject   Verb

   At the end of the play, students wait for the curtain to come down.
                           Subject   Verb

Clauses can be **independent** or **dependent**. Independent clauses can stand alone or can be joined to other clauses. Connect independent clauses with the coordinating conjunctions—*and, but, or, for,* or *nor*—when their content is of equal importance. Use subordinating conjunctions—*although, because, before, if, since, though, until, when, whenever, where*—and relative pronouns—*that, who, whom, which*—introduce clauses that express ideas that are subordinate to main ideas expressed in independent clauses.

Comma and coordinating conjunction
Independent clause	, for	Independent clause
	, and	Independent clause
	, nor	Independent clause
	, but	Independent clause
	, or	Independent clause
	, yet	Independent clause
	, so	Independent clause

Semicolon
Independent clause   ;   Independent clause

Subordinating conjunction, dependent clause, and comma
Dependent clause   ,   Independent clause

Independent clause followed by a subordinating conjunction that introduces a dependent clause
Independent clause   Dependent clause

Dependent clauses, by definition, contain at least one subject and one verb. However, they cannot stand alone as a complete sentence. They are structurally dependent on the main clause.

There are two types of dependent clauses: (1) those with a subordinating conjunction, and (2) those with a relative pronoun.

Sample subordinating conjunctions: *although, when, if, unless, because*

> <u>Unless a cure is discovered</u>, <u>many more people will die of the disease</u>.
>   Dependent clause   +   Independent clause

Sample relative pronouns: *who, whom, which, that*

> <u>The White House has an official website</u>, <u>which</u> <u>contains press releases, news updates, and biographies of the President and Vice-President</u>.
> (<u>Independent clause</u> + <u>relative pronoun</u> + <u>relative dependent clause</u>)

Be sure to place the conjunctions so that they express the proper relationship between ideas (cause/effect, condition, time, space).

> Incorrect: Because mother scolded me, I was late.
> Correct: *Mother scolded me because I was late.*
>
> Incorrect: The sun rose after the fog lifted.
> Correct: *The fog lifted after the sun rose.*

Notice that placement of the conjunction can completely change the meaning of the sentence. Main emphasis is shifted by the change.

> Although Jenny was pleased, the teacher was disappointed.
> Although the teacher was disappointed, Jenny was pleased.
>
> The boys who had written the essay won the contest.
> The boys who won the contest had written the essay.

While not syntactically incorrect, the second sentence makes it appear that the boys won the contest for something else before they wrote the essay.

Misplaced and Dangling Modifiers

Particular phrases that are not placed near the one word they modify often result in misplaced modifiers. Particular phrases that do not relate to the subject being modified result in dangling modifiers.

Error: Weighing the options carefully, a decision was made regarding the punishment of the convicted murderer.

Problem: Who is weighing the options? No one capable of weighing is named in the sentence; thus, the participle phrase weighing the options carefully dangles. This problem can be corrected by adding a subject of the sentence capable of doing the action.

Correction: *Weighing the options carefully, the judge made a decision regarding the punishment of the convicted murderer.*

Error: Returning to my favorite watering hole brought back many fond memories.

Problem: The person who returned is never indicated, and the participle phrase dangles. This problem can be corrected by creating a dependent clause from the modifying phrase.

Correction: *When I returned to my favorite watering hole, many fond memories came back to me.*

Error: One damaged house stood only to remind townspeople of the hurricane.

Problem: The placement of the misplaced modifier only suggests that the sole reason the house remained was to serve as a reminder. The faulty modifier creates ambiguity.

Correction: *Only one damaged house stood, reminding townspeople of the hurricane.*

Parallelism

You should recognize parallel structures using phrases (prepositional, gerund, participial, and infinitive) and omissions from sentences that create the lack of parallelism. Parallelism provides balance to the grammar and the ideas.

> Learn more about
> **Parallel Structure vs.**
> **Faulty Parallelism**
> http://jerz.setonhill.edu/writing/grammar/parallel.html

Prepositional phrase/single modifier
Incorrect: Coleen ate the ice cream with enthusiasm and hurriedly.
Correct: *Coleen ate the ice cream with enthusiasm and in a hurry.*
Correct: *Coleen ate the ice cream enthusiastically and hurriedly.*

Participial phrase/infinitive phrase
Incorrect: After hiking for hours and to sweat profusely, Joe sat down to rest and drinking water.
Correct: *After hiking for hours and sweating profusely, Joe sat down to rest and drink water.*

Recognition of Syntactical Redundancy or Omission

These errors occur when superfluous words have been added to a sentence or key words have been omitted from a sentence.

Redundancy
Incorrect: Joyce made sure that when her plane arrived that she retrieved all of her luggage.
Correct: Joyce made sure that when her plane arrived she retrieved all of her luggage.

Incorrect: He was a mere skeleton of his former self.

Correct: He was a skeleton of his former self.

Omission
Incorrect: Dot opened her book, recited her textbook, and answered the teacher's subsequent question.
Correct: *Dot opened her book, recited from the textbook, and answered the teacher's subsequent question.*

Avoidance of Double Negatives

This error occurs from positioning two negatives that, in fact, cancel each other in meaning.

Incorrect: Dot didn't have no double negatives in her paper.
Correct: *Dot didn't have any double negatives in her paper.*

PARTS OF SPEECH

The eight parts of speech form the syntactical framework on our language. While the study of grammar can be detailed, let's review some of the basics.

- Noun—names a person, place, or thing
- Pronoun—takes the place of one or more noun
- Verb—expresses action or state of being
- Adjective—describes, or modifies, a noun or a pronoun
- Adverb—modifies a verb, an adjective, or another adverb
- Conjunction—is a connecting word
- Preposition—relates a noun or a pronoun to another word in a sentence
- Interjection—expresses emotions

Nouns

A **noun** names a person, place, or thing/idea. A common noun names any person, place, or thing/idea; a proper noun names a particular person, place, thing/idea and will be capitalized.

	Person	Place	Thing/Idea	Idea
Common Noun	Actor	museum	ship	bravery
Proper Noun	Meryl Streep	The Smithsonian	*Titanic*	

Plural Nouns

The multiplicity and complexity of spelling rules based on phonics, letter doubling, and exceptions to rules—not mastered by adulthood—should be replaced by a good dictionary. As spelling mastery is also difficult for adolescents, our recommendation is the same. Learning the use of a dictionary and thesaurus will be a more rewarding use of time.

Most plurals of nouns that end in hard consonants or hard consonant sounds followed by a silent *e* are made by adding *s*. Some words ending in vowels only add *s*.

fingers, numerals, banks, bugs, riots, homes, gates, radios, bananas

Nouns that end in soft consonant sounds *s, j, x, z, ch,* and *sh,* add *es.* Some nouns ending in *o* add es.

>dresses, waxes, churches, brushes, tomatoes

Nouns ending in *y* preceded by a vowel just add *s.*

>boys, alleys

Nouns ending in *y* preceded by a consonant change the *y* to *i* and add *es.*

>babies, corollaries, frugalities, poppies

Some nouns' plurals are formed irregularly or remain the same.
>sheep, deer, children, leaves, oxen

Some nouns derived from foreign words, especially Latin, may make their plurals in two different ways - one of them Anglicized. Sometimes, the meanings are the same; other times, the two plurals are used in slightly different contexts. It is always wise to consult the dictionary.

>appendices, appendixes   criterion, criteria
>indexes, indices   crisis, crises

Make the plurals of closed (solid) compound words in the usual way except for words ending in *ful* which make their plurals on the root word.

>timelines, hairpins

Make the plurals of open or hyphenated compounds by adding the change in inflection to the word that change in number.

>fathers-in-law, courts-martial, masters of art, doctors of medicine

Make the plurals of letters, numbers, and abbreviations by adding *s.*

>fives and tens, IBMs, 1990s, *p*s and *q*s (Note that letters are italicized.)

Possessive Nouns

Make the possessives of singular nouns by adding an apostrophe followed by the letter *s ('s).*

>baby's bottle, father's job, elephant's eye, teacher's desk, sympathizer's protests, week's postponement

Make the possessive of singular nouns ending in *s* by adding either an apostrophe or an *('s)* depending upon common usage or sound. When making the possessive causes difficulty, use a prepositional phrase instead. Even with the sibilant ending, with a few exceptions, it is advisable to use the *('s)* construction.

> dress's color, species' characteristics or characteristics of the species, James' hat or James's hat, Delores's shirt. Make the possessive of plural nouns ending in *s* by adding the apostrophe after the *s;* horses' coats, jockeys' times, four days' time

Make possessives of plural nouns that do not end in *s* the same as singular nouns by adding *'s*.

> children's shoes, deer's antlers, cattle's horns

Make possessives of compound nouns by adding the inflection at the end of the word or phrase.

> the mayor of Los Angeles' campaign, the mailman's new truck, the mailmen's new trucks, my father-in-law's first wife, the keepsakes' values, several daughters-in-law's husbands

Note: Because a gerund functions as a noun, any noun preceding it and operating as a possessive adjective must reflect the necessary inflection. However, if the gerundive following the noun is a participle, no inflection is added.

> The general was perturbed by the private's sleeping on duty. (The word *sleeping* is a gerund, the object of the preposition *by.*)
> but
> The general was perturbed to see the private sleeping on duty. (The word *sleeping* is a participle modifying private.)

Pronoun

A pronoun takes the place of one or more noun and must agree with that noun in case and number. The noun to which the pronoun refers is called the "antecedent."

Proper Case Forms

Pronouns, unlike nouns, change case forms. Pronouns must be in the subjective, objective, or possessive form according to their function in the sentence.

	Subjective (Nominative)		Possessive		Objective	
	Singular	Plural	Singular	Plural	Singular	Plural
1st person	I	we	my	our	me	us
2nd person	You	you	your	your	you	you
3rd person	He she it	they	his her its	their	him her it	them

Relative Pronouns
> **Who**   Subjective/Nominative
> **Whom**   Objective
> **Whose**   Possessive

Rules for Clearly Identifying Pronoun Reference

Misuse of pronouns create agreement errors and cloud the meaning of the sentence. Here are a few tips to correct this common grammatical error.

Make sure that the antecedent reference is clear and cannot refer to something else. A "distant relative" is a relative pronoun or a relative clause that has been placed too far away from the antecedent to which it refers. It is a common error to place a verb between the relative pronoun and its antecedent.

Error: Return the books to the library that are overdue.

Problem: The relative clause "that are overdue" refers to the "books" and should be placed immediately after the antecedent.

Correction: *Return the books that are overdue to the library.*
                or
                Return the overdue books to the library.

A pronoun should not refer to adjectives or possessive nouns. Adjectives, nouns or possessive pronouns should not be used as antecedents. This will create ambiguity in sentences.

rror: In Todd's letter he told his mom he'd broken the priceless vase.

Problem: In this sentence the pronoun "he" seems to refer to the noun phrase "Todd's letter" though it was probably meant to refer to the possessive noun "Todd's."

Correction: *In his letter, Todd told his mom that he had broken the priceless vase.*

A pronoun should not refer to an implied idea. A pronoun must refer to a specific antecedent rather than an implied antecedent. When an antecedent is not stated specifically, the reader has to guess or assume the meaning of a sentence. Pronouns that do not have antecedents are called expletives. "It" and "there" are the most common expletives, though other pronouns can also become expletives as well. In informal conversation, expletives allow for casual presentation of ideas without supporting evidence. However, in more formal writing, it is best to be more precise.

Error: She said that it is important to floss every day.

Problem: The pronoun "it" refers to an implied idea.

Correction: *She said that flossing every day is important.*

Error: They returned the book because there were missing pages.

Problem: The pronouns "they" and "there" do not refer to the antecedent.

Correction: *The customer returned the book with missing pages.*

Using Who, That, and Which

Who, whom and **whose** refer to human beings and can either introduce essential or nonessential clauses. **That** refers to things other than humans and is used to introduce essential clauses. **Which** refers to things other than humans and is used to introduce nonessential clauses.

Error: The doctor that performed the surgery said the man would be fully recovered.

Problem: Since the relative pronoun is referring to a human, who should be used.

Correction: *The doctor who performed the surgery said the man would be fully recovered.*

ENG. LANGUAGE LIT. & COMP.

Error: That ice cream cone that you just ate looked really delicious.

Problem: That has already been used so you must use *which* to introduce the next clause, whether it is essential or nonessential.

Correction: *That ice cream cone, which you just ate, looked really delicious.*

Error: Tom and me have reserved seats for next week's baseball game.

Problem: The pronoun me is the subject of the verb have reserved and should be in the subjective form.

Correction: *Tom and I have reserved seats for next week's baseball game.*

Error: Who's coat is this?

Problem: The interrogative possessive pronoun is whose; who's is the contraction for who is.

Correction: *Whose coat is this?*

Error: The voters will choose the candidate whom has the best qualifications for the job.

Problem: The case of the relative pronoun *who* or *whom* is determined by the pronoun's function in the clause in which it appears. The word *who* is in the subjective case, and whom is in the objective. Analyze how the pronoun is being used within the sentence.

Correction: *The voters will choose the candidate who has the best qualifications for the job.*

Verbs

A verb expresses action or state of being. Most verbs show time (tense) by an inflectional ending to the word. Other irregular verbs take completely different forms.

Both regular and irregular verbs must appear in their standard forms for each tense. Note: the *ed* or *d* ending is added to regular verbs in the past tense and for past participles.

Infinitive	Past Tense	Past Participle
Bake	baked	baked

Irregular Verb Forms

Infinitive	Past Tense	Past Participle
Be	was, were	been
become	became	become
break	broke	broken
bring	brought	brought
choose	chose	chosen
come	came	come
do	did	done
draw	drew	drawn
eat	ate	eaten
fall	fell	fallen
forget	forgot	forgotten
freeze	froze	frozen
give	gave	given
go	went	gone
grow	grew	grown
have/has	had	had
hide	hid	hidden
know	knew	known
lay	laid	laid
lie	lay	lain
ride	rode	ridden
rise	rose	risen
run	ran	run
see	saw	seen
steal	stole	stolen
take	took	taken
tell	told	told
throw	threw	thrown
wear	wore	worn
write	wrote	written

Error: She should have went to her doctor's appointment at the scheduled time.

Problem: The past participle of the verb *to go* is *gone*. *Went* expresses the simple past tense.

Correction: *She should have gone to her doctor's appointment at the scheduled time.*

Error: My train is suppose to arrive before two o'clock.

Problem: The verb following *train* is a present tense passive construction which requires the present tense verb *to be* and the past participle.

Correction: *My train is supposed to arrive before two o'clock.*

Error: Linda should of known that the car wouldn't start after leaving it out in the cold all night.

Problem: *Should of* is a nonstandard expression. *Of* is not a verb.

Correction: *Linda should have known that the car wouldn't start after leaving it out in the cold all night.*

Subject-Verb Agreement

A verb agrees in number with its subject. Making them agree relies on the ability to identify the correct subject.

> One of the boys *was playing* too rough.
>
> No one in the class, not the teacher nor the students, was listening to the message from the intercom.
>
> The candidates, including a grandmother and a teenager, are debating some controversial issues.

If two singular subjects are connected by *and* the verb must be plural.

> A *man* and his *dog* were jogging on the beach.

If two singular subjects are connected by *or*, or *nor*, a singular verb is required.

> Neither Dot nor Joyce has missed a day of school this year.
> Either Fran or Paul is missing.

If one singular subject and one plural subject are connected by *or,* or *nor*, the verb agrees with the subject nearest to the verb.

> Neither the coach nor the players were able to sleep on the bus.

If the subject is a collective noun, its sense of number in the sentence determines the verb: singular if the noun represents a group or unit and plural if the noun represents individuals.

> The <u>House of Representatives has adjourned</u> for the holidays.
> The <u>House of Representatives have failed</u> to reach agreement on the subject of adjournment.

Use of Verbs (Tense)

Present tense is used to express that which is currently happening or is always true.

> Randy is playing the piano.

> Randy plays the piano like a pro.

Past tense is used to express action that occurred in a past time.

> Randy learned to play the piano when he was six years old.

Future tense is used to express action or a condition of future time.

> Randy will probably earn a music scholarship.

Present perfect tense is used to express action or a condition that started in the past and is continued to or completed in the present.

> Randy has practiced piano every day for the last ten years.

> Randy has never been bored with practice.

Past perfect tense expresses action or a condition that occurred as a precedent to some other past action or condition.

> Randy had considered playing clarinet before he discovered the piano.

Future perfect tense expresses action that started in the past or the present and will conclude at some time in the future.

> By the time he goes to college, Randy will have been an accomplished pianist for more than half of his life.

Use of Verbs: Mood

Indicative mood is used to make unconditional statements; subjunctive mood is used for conditional clauses or wish statements that pose conditions that are untrue. Verbs in subjunctive mood are plural with both singular and plural subjects.

>If I were a bird, I would fly.

>I wish I were as rich as Donald Trump.

Use of Verbs: Voice

A verb is in the **active voice** when its subject is the doer of the action. A verb is in the **passive voice** when its subject is the receiver of the action.

Active Voice	Passive Voice
The director adjourned the meeting. The subject, *director*, performs the action, *adjourned*.	**The meeting was adjourned by the director.** The subject, *meeting*, is not performing the action; instead, it is receiving the action, *was adjourned*.
The mechanic at the Shell station inspected Mrs. Johnson's automobile. The subject, *mechanic*, performed the action, *inspected*.	**Mrs. Johnson's automobile was inspected by the mechanic at the Shell station.** The subject, *automobile*, is not acting; it is receiving the action, *was inspected*.

How do you recognize passive voice? Look at the verb. A passive voice verb has at least two parts:
1. a form of the verb *to be (am, is, are, was, were, be, been)*
   The computer *was* installed by Datacorp.
2. a past participle form of the main verb (thrown, driven, planted, talked)
   The computer was *installed* by Datacorp.

- Sometimes the subject is in an object position in the sentence.
   The computer was installed by *Datacorp*. (object of preposition)

- Watch for a "by" statement between the verb phrase and the object.
   The computer was installed *by* Datacorp. (preposition)

- Sometimes the doer is not even present.
   The computer was installed. (By whom?)

Verb Conjugation

The conjugation of verbs follows the patterns used in the discussion of tense above. However, the most frequent problems in verb use stem from the improper formation of past and past participial forms.

>Regular verb: believe, believed, (have) believed

>Irregular verbs: run, ran, run; sit, sat, sat; teach, taught, taught

Other problems stem from the use of verbs that are the same in some tenses but have different forms and different meanings in other tenses.

>I lie on the ground. I lay on the ground yesterday. I have lain down. I lay the blanket on the bed. I laid the blanket there yesterday. I have laid the blanket down every night.

>The sun rises. The sun rose. The sun has risen.

>He raises the flag. He raised the flag. He had raised the flag.

>I sit on the porch. I sat on the porch. I have sat in the porch swing.

>I set the plate on the table. I set the plate there yesterday. I had set the table before dinner.

Adjectives and Adverbs

Adjectives are words that modify or describe nouns or pronouns. Adjectives usually precede the words they modify, but not always; for example, an adjective occurs after a linking verb. Adjectives answer what kind, how many, or which one.

Adverbs are words that modify verbs, adjectives, or other adverbs. They cannot modify nouns. Adverbs answer such questions as how, why, when, where, how much, or how often something is done. Many adverbs are formed by adding *ly*.

Error: The birthday cake tasted sweetly.

Problem: *Tasted* is a linking verb; the modifier that follows should be an adjective, not an adverb.

Correction: *The birthday cake tasted sweet.*

Error: You have done good with this project.

Problem: *Good* is an adjective and cannot be used to modify a verb phrase such as have done.

Correction: *You have done well with this project.*

Error: The coach was positive happy about the team's chance of winning.

Problem: The adjective *positive* cannot be used to modify another adjective, *happy*. An adverb is needed instead.

Correction: *The coach was positively happy about the team's chance of winning.*

Error: The fireman acted quick and brave to save the child from the burning building.

Problem: *Quick and brave* are adjectives and cannot be used to describe a verb. Adverbs are needed instead.

Correction: *The fireman acted quickly and bravely to save the child from the burning building.*

Conjunctions

A conjunction connects words, phrases, or clauses. It acts as a signal, indicating when a thought is added, contrasted, or altered.

Meet the FANBOYS! This mnemonic device will help students remember the seven coordinating conjunctions.

    For, And, Nor, But, Or, Yet, So

These are **coordinating conjunctions** that join similar elements.
    Strong and tall (adjectives)
    Easily and quickly (adverbs)
    Of the people, by the people, for the people (prepositional phrases)
    We disagreed, but we reached a compromise. (sentences)

Subordinating conjunctions connect clauses (subject-verb combinations) in a sentence. They signal that the clause is subordinate and cannot stand alone.

Subordinating Conjunctions			
after	because	though	whenever
although	before	till	where
as	if	unless	whereas
as if	since	until	wherever
as though	than	when	while

I will be grateful *if you will work on this project with me.*
Because I am running late, you will need to cover for me.

Prepositions

A preposition relates a noun or a pronoun to another word in a sentence. Think of prepositions as words that show relationships. Below is a partial list.

> Check out this
> **Guide to Grammar and Writing**
> http://grammar.ccc.commnet.edu/grammar/

about	above	according to	across	after	against
along	along with	among	apart from	around	as/as for
at	because of	before	behind	below	beneath
beside	between	beyond	by	by means of	concerning
despite	down	during	except	except for	excepting
for	from	in	in addition to	in back of	in case of
in front of	in place of	inside	in spite of	instead of	into
like	near	next	of	off	on
onto	on top of	out/out of	outside	over	past
regarding	round	since	through	throughout	till
to	toward	under	underneath	unlike	until
up/upon	up to	with	within	without	

Guidelines
- Include necessary prepositions.
    I graduated from high school. (not *I graduated high school.*)

- Omit unnecessary prepositions
    Both printers work well. (Not *Both of the printers* work well.)
    Where are the printers? (Not *Where are the printers at?*)

- Avoid the overuse of prepositions.
    We have received your application for credit at our branch in the Fresno area.
    We have received your Fresno credit application.

Interjections

An **interjection** is a word or group of words that express emotion, surprise, or disbelief. It has no grammatical connection to other words in a sentence.

Some Common Interjections			
aha	great	my	ouch
alas	ha	no	well
gee	hey	oh	wow
good grief	hooray	oops	yes

Guidelines
- When an interjection expresses strong emotion, it usually stands alone; it begins with a capital letter and ends with an exclamation point.
    Ouch! That paper cut really hurts.
    Good grief! My favorite store has closed.

- When an interjection expresses mild feeling, it is written as part of the sentence and is set off with commas.
    Yes, we will comply with your request.

CAPITALIZATION

Capitalize all proper names of persons (including specific organizations or agencies of government); places (countries, states, cities, parks, and specific geographical areas); and things (political parties, structures, historical and cultural terms, and calendar and time designations); and religious terms (any deity, revered person or group, sacred writings).

   Percy Bysshe Shelley, Argentina, Mount Rainier National Park, Grand Canyon, League of Nations, the Sears Tower, Birmingham, Lyric Theater, Americans, Midwesterners, Democrats, Renaissance, Boy Scouts of America, Easter, God, Bible, Dead Sea Scrolls, Koran

Capitalize proper adjectives and titles used with proper names.

   California gold rush, President John Adams, French fries, Homeric epic, Romanesque architecture, Senator John Glenn

Note: Some words that represent titles and offices are not capitalized unless used with a proper name.

Capitalized	Not Capitalized
Congressman McKay	the congressman from Florida
Commander Alger	commander of the Pacific Fleet
Queen Elizabeth	the queen of England

Capitalize all main words in titles of works of literature, art, and music.

PUNCTUATION

A basic way to show relationship of ideas in sentences is to use punctuation correctly and effectively. Competency exams will generally test the ability to apply the more advanced skills; thus, a limited number of more frustrating rules are presented here. Rules should be applied according to the American style of English, i.e. spelling *theater* instead of *theatre* and placing terminal marks of punctuation almost exclusively within other marks of punctuation.

Quotation Marks

The more troublesome punctuation marks involve the use of quotations.

Using Terminal Punctuation in Relation to Quotation Marks: In a quoted statement that is either declarative or imperative, place the period inside the closing quotation marks.

"The airplane crashed on the runway during takeoff."

If the quotation is followed by other words in the sentence, place a comma inside the closing quotations marks and a period at the end of the sentence.

"The airplane crashed on the runway during takeoff," said the announcer.

In most instances in which a quoted title or expression occurs at the end of a sentence, the period is placed before either the single or double quotation marks.

The educator worried, "The middle school readers were unprepared to understand Bryant's poem 'Thanatopsis.'"

Early book-length adventure stories like *Don Quixote* and *The Three Musketeers* are known as "picaresque novels."

There is an instance in which the final quotation mark would precede the period - if the content of the sentence were about a speech or quote so that the understanding of the meaning would be confused by the placement of the period.

> The first thing out of his mouth was "Hi, I'm home." *but*
> The first line of his speech began "I arrived home to an empty house".

In sentences that are interrogatory or exclamatory, the question mark or exclamation point should be positioned outside the closing quotation marks if the quote itself is a statement or command or cited title.

> Who decided to lead us in the recitation of the "Pledge of Allegiance"?

> Why was Tillie shaking as she began her recitation, "Once upon a midnight dreary..."?

> I was embarrassed when Mrs. White said, "Your slip is showing"!

In sentences that are declarative but the quotation is a question or an exclamation, place the question mark or exclamation point inside the quotation marks.

> The hall monitor yelled, "Fire! Fire!"

> "Fire! Fire!" yelled the hall monitor.

> Cory shrieked, "Is there a mouse in the room?" (In this instance, the question supersedes the exclamation.)

Using Double Quotation Marks with Other Punctuation: Quotations—whether words, phrases, or clauses—should be punctuated according to the rules of the grammatical function they serve in the sentence.

> The works of Shakespeare, "the bard of Avon," have been contested as originating with other authors.

> "You'll get my money," the old man warned, "when 'Hell freezes over'."

> Sheila cited the passage that began "Four score and seven years ago...." (Note the ellipsis followed by an enclosed period.)

> "Old Ironsides" inspired the preservation of the U.S.S. Constitution.

Use quotation marks to enclose the titles of shorter works: songs, short poems, short stories, essays, and chapters of books. (See "Using Italics" for punctuating longer titles.)

"The Tell-Tale Heart" - short story
"Casey at the Bat" - poem
"America the Beautiful" - song

Using Commas

Separate two or more coordinate adjectives modifying the same word and three or more nouns, phrases, or clauses in a list.

Maggie's hair was dull, dirty, and lice-ridden.

Dickens portrayed the Artful Dodger as skillful pickpocket, loyal follower of Fagin, and defendant of Oliver Twist.

Ellen daydreamed about getting out of the rain, taking a shower, and eating a hot dinner.

In Elizabethan England, Ben Jonson wrote comedy, Christopher Marlowe wrote tragedies, and William Shakespeare composed both.

Use commas to separate antithetical or complimentary expressions from the rest of the sentence.

The veterinarian, not his assistant, would perform the delicate surgery.

The more he knew about her, the less he wished he had known.

Randy hopes to, and probably will, get an appointment to the Naval Academy.

Using Semicolons

Use semicolons to separate independent clauses when the second clause is introduced by a transitional adverb. (These clauses may also be written as separate sentences, preferably by placing the adverb within the second sentence.)

The Elizabethans modified the rhyme scheme of the sonnet; thus, it was called the English sonnet.
or
The Elizabethans modified the rhyme scheme of the sonnet. It thus was called the English sonnet.

Use semicolons to separate items in a series that are long and complex or have internal punctuation.

> The Italian Renaissance produced masters in the fine arts: Dante Alighieri, author of the *Divine Comedy;* Leonardo da Vinci, painter of *The Last Supper;* and Donatello, sculptor of the *Quattro Coronati*, the four saints.

> The leading scorers in the WNBA were Haizhaw Zheng, averaging 23.9 points per game; Lisa Leslie, 22; and Cynthia Cooper, 19.5.

Using Colons

Place a colon at the beginning of a list of items. (Note its use in the sentence about Renaissance Italians previously.)

> The teacher directed us to compare Faulkner's three symbolic novels: *Absalom, Absalom; As I Lay Dying;* and *Light in August*.

Do **not** use a comma if the list is preceded by a verb.

> Three of Faulkner's symbolic novels are *Absalom, Absalom; As I Lay Dying,* and *Light in August*.

Using Dashes

Place dashes (called an "em" dash) to denote sudden breaks in thought.

> Some periods in literature—the Romantic Age, for example—spanned different time periods in different countries.

Use dashes instead of commas if commas are already used elsewhere in the sentence for amplification or explanation.

> The Fireside Poets included three Brahmans—James Russell Lowell, Henry David Wadsworth, Oliver Wendell Holmes—and John Greenleaf Whittier.

Using Italics

Use italics to punctuate the titles of long works of literature, names of periodical publications, musical scores, works of art and motion picture television, and radio programs. (When unable to write in italics, you can instruct students to underline in their own writing where italics would be appropriate.)

> *The Idylls of the King*　　*Hiawatha*　　*The Sound and the Fury*
> *Mary Poppins*　　*Newsweek*　　*The Nutcracker Suite*

TEACHER CERTIFICATION STUDY GUIDE

Skill 2.4 Understanding the elements of semantics, including ambiguity, euphemism, doublespeak, connotation, and jargon and how these elements affect meaning.

LEVELS OF LANGUAGE

Informal and formal language are distinctions made on the basis of the occasion as well as the audience. At a formal occasion, for example, a meeting of executives or of government officials, even conversational exchanges are likely to be more formal. Cocktail parties or golf games are examples where the language is likely to be informal. Formal language uses fewer or no contractions, less slang, longer sentences, and more organization in longer segments.

Speeches delivered to executives, college professors, government officials and other groups like this are likely to be formal. Speeches made to fellow employees are likely to be informal. Sermons tend to be formal; Bible lessons tend to be informal.

Slang comes about for many reasons: Amelioration is an important one that results often in euphemisms. Examples are "passed away" for dying or "senior citizens" for old people. Some usages have become so embedded in the language that their sources are long forgotten. For example, "fame" originally meant rumor. Some words originally intended as euphemisms, such as "mentally retarded" and "moron" to avoid using "idiot," have themselves become pejorative.

> Check out this link:
> **Do You Speak American?**
> http://www.pbs.org/speak/seatosea/standardamerican/hamlet/

Slang is lower in prestige than Standard English tends to first appear in the language of groups with low status is often taboo, and unlikely to be used by people of high status. It tends to displace conventional terms, either as shorthand or as a defense against perceptions associated with the conventional term.

Jargon is a specialized vocabulary. It may be the vocabulary peculiar to a particular industry such as computers ("firewall") or of a field such as religion ("vocation"). It may also be the vocabulary of a social group.

Black English is a good example. A Hardee's ad has two young men on the streets of Philadelphia discussing the merits of one of their sandwiches, and captions are required so others may understand what they're saying.

A whole vocabulary that has even developed its own dictionaries is the jargon of bloggers. The speaker must be knowledgeable about and sensitive to the jargon peculiar to the particular audience. That may require some research and some vocabulary development on the speaker's part.

ENG. LANGUAGE LIT. & COMP.

Technical language is a form of jargon. It is usually specific to an industry, profession, or field of study. Sensitivity to the language familiar to the particular audience is important.

Regionalisms are those usages that are peculiar to a particular part of the country. A good example is the second person plural pronoun: you. Because the plural is the same as the singular, various parts of the country have developed their own solutions to be sure that they are understood when they are speaking to more than one "you." In the South, "you-all" or "y'all" is common. In the Northeast, one often hears "youse." In some areas of the Middle West, "you'ns" can be heard.

Vocabulary also varies from region to region. A small stream is a "creek" in some regions but "crick" in some. In Boston, soft drinks are generically called "tonic," but it becomes "soda" in other parts of the northeast. It is "liqueur" in Canada, and "pop" when you get very far west of New York.

Euphemism and Doublespeak

Both euphemism and doublespeak substitute an agreeable or inoffensive term for one that might offend or suggest something unpleasant. It is the reason for the substitution that differentiates the terms.

Often euphemisms are used to maintain a more positive tone or to prevent offense. For example, *death* might be referred to as *passed away, crossed over*, or nowadays *passed*. The word *death* might be too hard for people to face. On the other hand, doublespeak connotes a deliberate obfuscation or confusion of the meaning. For example, the killing of innocent civilians in time of war is called *collateral damage*. Here *death* is so minimized that it disappears.

In fact, *euphemism* could be a euphemism for *doublespeak*.

SEMANTIC CONNOTATIONS

To teach language effectively, we need to understand that as human beings acquire language they realize that words have **denotative** and **connotative** meanings. Generally, denotative words point to things and connotative words deal with mental suggestions that the words convey.

The word *skunk* has a denotative meaning if the speaker can point to the actual animal as he speaks the word and intends the word to identify the animal. *Skunk* has connotative meaning depending upon the tone of delivery, the socially acceptable attitudes about the animal, and the speaker's personal feelings about the animal.

Informative Connotations

Informative connotations are definitions agreed upon by the society in which the learner operates. A *skunk* is "a black and white mammal of the weasel family with a pair of perineal glands which secrete a pungent odor." The *Merriam Webster Collegiate Dictionary* adds "...and offensive" odor. Identification of the color, species, and glandular characteristics are informative. The interpretation of the odor as *offensive* is affective.

Affective Connotations

Affective connotations are the personal feelings a word arouses. A child who has no personal experience with a skunk and its odor or has had a pet skunk will feel differently about the word *skunk* than a child who has smelled the spray or been conditioned vicariously to associate offensiveness with the animal denoted *skunk*.

> Learn more about **Connotation and Denotation in "Elements of Poetry"**
> http://bcs.bedfordstmartins.com/Virtualit/poetry/denotate_def.html

The very fact that our society views a skunk as an animal to be avoided will affect the child's interpretation of the word. In fact, you don't actually have to have seen a skunk (that is, have a denotative understanding) to use the word in either connotative expression. For example, one child might call another child a skunk, connoting an unpleasant reaction (affective use) or, seeing another small black and white animal, call it a skunk based on the definition (informative use).

Using Connotations

In everyday language, we attach affective meanings to words unconsciously; we exercise more conscious control of informative connotations. In the process of language development, the leaner must come not only to grasp the definitions of words but also to become more conscious of the affective connotations and how his listeners process these connotations. Gaining this conscious control over language makes it possible to use language appropriately in various situations and to evaluate its uses in literature and other forms of communication.

The manipulation of language for a variety of purposes is the goal of language instruction. Advertisers and satirists are especially conscious of the effect word choice has on their audiences. By evoking the proper responses from readers/listeners, we can prompt them to take action.

Choice of the medium through which the message is delivered to the receiver is a significant factor in controlling language. Spoken language relies as much on the gestures, facial expression, and tone of voice of the speaker as on the words that are spoken. Slapstick comics can evoke laughter without speaking a word. Young children use body language overtly and older children more subtly to convey messages. These refinements of body language are paralleled by an ability to recognize and apply the nuances of spoken language. To work strictly with the written work, the writer must use words to imply the body language.

AMBIGUITY

Ambiguity is any writing whose meaning cannot be determined by its context. Ambiguity may be introduced accidentally, confusing the readers and disrupting the flow of reading. If a sentence or paragraph jars upon reading, there is lurking ambiguity. It is particularly difficult to spot your own ambiguities, since authors tend to see what they mean rather than what they say.

For example, when Robert Frost writes "Good fences make good neighbors" in the poem "Mending Wall," students can spend much time discussing what that means in the context of the poem as well as in the context of their own lives.

> Read
> **"Mending Wall" by Robert Frost**
> http://www.writing.upenn.edu/~afilreis/88/frost-mending.html

Commonly Misused Words

Because of the richness of the English language and the immensity of the vocabulary, words with similar sounds are sometimes confused. Here is a partial list of commonly misused words. Use incorrectly, these words cause misunderstanding.

Accept is a verb meaning to receive or to tolerate. **Except** is usually a preposition meaning excluding. Except is also a verb meaning to exclude.

Advice is a noun meaning recommendation. **Advise** is a verb meaning to recommend.

Affect is usually a verb meaning to influence. **Effect** is usually a noun meaning result. Effect can also be a verb meaning to bring about.

An **allusion** is an indirect reference. An **illusion** is a misconception or false impression.

Add is a verb to mean to put together. **Ad** is a noun that is the abbreviation for the word advertisement.

Ain't is a common nonstandard contraction for the contraction aren't.

Allot is a verb meaning to distribute. **A lot** can be an adverb that means often, or to a great degree. It can also mean a large quantity.

Allowed is an adjective that means permitted. **Aloud** is an adverb that means audibly.

Bare is an adjective that means naked or exposed. It can also indicate a minimum. As a noun, **bear** is a large mammal. As a verb, bear means to carry a heavy burden.

Capitol refers to a city, capitol to a building where lawmakers meet. **Capital** also refers to wealth or resources.

A **chord** is a noun that refers to a group of musical notes. **Cord** is a noun meaning rope or a long electrical line.

Compliment is a noun meaning a praising or flattering remark. **Complement** is a noun that means something that completes or makes perfect.

Climactic is derived from climax, the point of greatest intensity in a series or progression of events. **Climatic** is derived from climate; it refers to meteorological conditions.

Discreet is an adjective that means tactful or diplomatic; **discrete** is an adjective that means separate or distinct.

Dye is a noun or verb used to indicate artificially coloring something. **Die** is a verb that means to pass away. Die is also a noun that means a cube-shaped game piece.

Elicit is a verb meaning to bring out or to evoke. **Illicit** is an adjective meaning unlawful

Emigrate means to leave one country or region to settle in another. **Immigrate** means to enter another country and reside there.

Fewer is used for countable items and **less** for amounts and quantities, such as fewer minutes but less time

Hoard is a verb that means to accumulate or store up. **Horde** is a large group.

Imply is to direct an interpretation toward other people; to **infer** is to deduce an interpretation from someone else's discourse.

Lead /lēd/ is a verb that means to guide or serve as the head of. It is also a noun /lĕd/ that is a type of metal.

Medal is a noun that means an award that is strung round the neck. **Meddle** is a verb that means to involve oneself in a matter without right or invitation. **Metal** is an element such as silver or gold. **Mettle** is a noun meaning toughness or guts.

Morning is a noun indicating the time between midnight and midday. **Mourning** is a verb or noun pertaining to the period of grieving after a death.

Past is a noun meaning a time before now (past, present and future). **Passed** is past tense of the verb "to pass."

Piece is a noun meaning a portion. **Peace** is a noun meaning the opposite of war.

Peak is a noun meaning the tip or height to reach the highest point. **Peek** is a verb that means to take a brief look. **Pique** is a verb meaning to incite or raise interest.

Principal is a noun meaning the head of a school or an organization or a sum of money. **Principle** is a noun meaning a basic truth or law.

Rite is a noun meaning a special ceremony. **Right** is an adjective meaning correct or direction. **Write** is a verb meaning to compose in writing.

Than is a conjunction used in comparisons; **then** is an adverb denoting time. That pizza is more than I can eat. Tom laughed, and then we recognized him.

Here's a mnemonic device to remember the difference. *Than* is used to *compare*; both words have the letter *a* in them. *Then* tells *when*; both are spelled the same, except for the first letter.

There is an adverb specifying place; it is also an expletive. Adverb: Sylvia is lying *there* unconscious. Expletive: *There* are two plums left. **Their** is a possessive pronoun. **They're** is a contraction of they are. Fred and Jane finally washed *their* car. *They're* later than usual today.

To is a preposition; **too** is an adverb; **two** is a number.

Your is a possessive pronoun; **you're** is a contraction of you are.

Other Confusing Words

Among is a preposition to be used with three or more items. **Between** is to be used with two items.

> Between you and me, I cannot tell the difference among those three Johnson sisters.

As is a subordinating conjunction used to introduce a subordinating clause; **like** is a preposition and is followed by a noun or a noun phrase.

> As I walked to the lab, I realized that the recent experiment findings were much like those we found last year.

Can is a verb that means to be able. **May** is a verb that means to have permission. They are only interchangeable in cases of possibility.

> I can lift 250 pounds.
> May I go to Alex's house?

Set is a transitive verb meaning to put or to place. Its principal parts are set, set, set. **Sit** is an intransitive verb meaning to be seated. Its principal parts are sit, sat, sat.

> I set my backpack down near the front door.
> They sat in the park until the sun went down.

Problem Phrases

Correct	Incorrect
Anyway	Anyways
Come to see me	Come and see me
Could have, would have, should have	Could of, would of, should of
Couldn't care less	Could care less
En route	In route
For all intents and purposes	For all intensive purposes
Regardless	Irregardless
Second, Third	Secondly, Thirdly
Supposed to	Suppose to
Toward	Towards
Try to	Try and
Used to	Use to

COMPETENCY 3.0   COMPOSITION AND RHETORIC

Skill 3.1 Understanding and applying elements of teaching writing, including:
- Individual and collaborative approaches to teaching writing, e.g., stages of the writing process (prewriting, drafting, revising, editing, publishing, evaluating) and how those stages work recursively.
- Tools and response strategies for assessing student writing, e.g., peer review, portfolios, holistic scoring, scoring rubrics, self-assessment, and conferencing.
- Common research and documentation techniques, e.g., gathering and evaluating data, using electronic and print media, and MLA and APA citations.

THE WRITING PROCESS

Writing is a recursive process. As students engage in the various stages of writing, they develop and improve not only their writing skills but their thinking skills as well. You will find varying approaches to teaching the writing process: some will combine stages; some will use different terminology. Their goal, however, are similar. Using a step-by-step process will help writers compose more efficiently and effectively.

Writing Process Approach 1

Prewriting Strategies

Students gather ideas before writing. Prewriting may include clustering, listing, brainstorming, mapping, free writing, and charting. If you provide many ways for students to develop ideas on a topic, you will increase their chances for success.

Listed below are the most common prewriting strategies students can use to explore, plan, and write on a topic. When teaching these strategies, remember that not all prewriting must eventually produce a finished piece of writing. In fact, in the initial lesson of teaching prewriting strategies, you might have students practice prewriting strategies without the pressure of having to write a finished product.

- Keep an idea book so that they can jot down ideas that come to mind.
- Write in a daily journal.
- Write down whatever comes to mind; this is called **free writing**. Students do not stop to make corrections or interrupt the flow of ideas. A variation of this technique is focused free writing—writing on a specific topic—to prepare for an essay.

- Make a list of all ideas connected with their topic; this is called **brainstorming**. Make sure students know that this technique works best when they let their mind work freely. After completing the list, students should analyze the list to see if a pattern or way to group the ideas.
- Ask the questions *who, what, when, where, why and how.* Help the writer approach a topic from several perspectives.
- Create a visual map on paper to gather ideas. Cluster circles and lines to show connections between ideas. Students should try to identify the relationship that exists between their ideas. If they cannot see the relationships, have them pair up, exchange papers and have their partners look for some related ideas.
- Observe details of sight, hearing, taste, touch, and taste.
- Visualize by making mental images of something and write down the details in a list.

After they have practiced with each of these prewriting strategies, ask them to pick out the ones they prefer and ask them to discuss how they might use the techniques to help them with future writing assignments. Remind them that they can use more than one prewriting strategy at a time. Also they may find that different writing situations may suggest certain techniques.

Writing

Students compose the first draft. Encourage them to write freely. If they get their ideas down first, then they can move to revising. If they have difficulty, have them write as they speak—perhaps have them dictate to another writer or recorder.

They might compose their first drafts on computer so they can quickly and easily type out their ideas. Encourage them to begin anywhere they want. Once they see their ideas on paper, they will be encouraged to continue.

Revising

Students examine their work and make changes in sentences, wording, details and ideas. Revise comes from the Latin word *revidere*, meaning "to see again." This step is often overlooked, unfortunately. Sometimes writers confuse it with proofreading. So students need to understand how important this process is. If they use a computer, they can move and delete without having to rewrite the entire paper. This eliminates some of the frustrations students face with this important but often overlooked step in the writing process.

Editing

Students proofread the draft for punctuation and mechanical errors. If they are using computers, they can run grammar and spell check; however, they should be taught not to rely on these devices. Sharing papers with their peers in this process can be worthwhile. A fresh look can reveal errors the writer has overlooked.

Publishing

Students may have their work displayed on a bulletin board, read aloud in class, or printed in a literary magazine or school anthology. A class blog of papers could stimulate interest in and out of the classroom. They may keep a portfolio of their work throughout the year.

These steps are recursive; as students engage in each aspect of the writing process, they may begin with prewriting, write, revise, write, revise, edit, and publish. They do not engage in this process in a lockstep manner; it is more circular.

Writing Process Approach 2

Here is another approach you might use with your students.

Prewriting Activities

1. As a class, discuss the topic.

2. Map out ideas, questions, and graphic organizers on the chalkboard.

3. Break into small groups to discuss different ways of approaching the topic and develop an organizational plan and create a thesis statement.

4. Research the topic if necessary.

Drafting/Revising

1. Students write first draft in class or at home.

2. Students engage in peer response and class discussion.

3. Using checklists or a rubric, students critique each other's writing and make suggestions for revising the writing.

4. Students revise the writing.

Editing and Proofreading

1. Students, working in pairs, analyze sentences for variety.

2. Students work in groups to read papers for punctuation and mechanics.

3. Students perform final edit.

Students need to be trained to become effective at proofreading, revising and editing strategies. Begin this process by using both desk-side and scheduled conferences. The following strategies are useful in guiding students through the final stages of the writing process.

- Provide some guide sheets or forms for students to use during peer responses.
- Allow students to work in pairs and limit the agenda.
- Model the use of the guide sheet or form for the entire class.
- Give students a time limit.
- Have the students read their partners' papers and ask at least three who, what, when, why, how questions. The students answer the questions and use them as a place to begin discussing the piece.
- Provide students with a series of questions that will assist them in revising their writing.
  - Do the details give a clear picture? Add details that appeal to more than just the sense of sight.
  - How effectively are the details organized? Reorder the details if it is needed.
  - Are the thoughts and feelings of the writer included? Add personal thoughts and feelings about the subject.

As you discuss revision, begin with discussing the definition of revise. Also, state that all writing must be revised in order to be improved. After students have revised their writing, it is time for the final edit and proofreading. Here are a few key points to remember when helping students learn to edit and proofread their work.

It is crucial that students are not taught grammar in isolation but in the context of the writing process. At this point in the writing process, a mini-lesson that focuses on some of the problems your students are having would be appropriate.

- Ask students to read their writing and check for specific errors like using a subordinate clause as a sentence.
- Provide students with a proofreading checklist to guide them as they edit their work.

You may think this exercise is simply catching errors in spelling or word use, but you should reframe your thinking about revising and editing. This is an extremely important step that often is ignored. Here are some questions you could ask:

- Is the reasoning coherent?
- Is the point established?
- Does the introduction make the reader want to read this discourse?
- What is the thesis? Is it proven?
- What is the purpose? Is it clear? Is it useful, valuable, and interesting?
- Is the style of writing so wordy that it exhausts the reader and interferes with engagement?
- Is the writing so spare that it is boring?
- Is the language appropriate? Is it too formal? Too informal? If jargon is used, is it appropriate?
- Are the sentences too uniform in structure?
- Are there too many simple sentences?
- Are too many of the complex sentences the same structure?
- Are the compounds truly compounds, or are they unbalanced?
- Are parallel structures truly parallel?
- If there are characters, are they believable?
- If there is dialogue, is it natural or stilted?
- Is the title appropriate?
- Does the writing show creativity, or is it boring?

Studies have clearly demonstrated that the most fertile area in teaching writing is this one. If students can learn to revise their own work effectively, they are well on their way to becoming effective, mature writers.

Word processing is an important tool for teaching this stage in the writing process. Requiring extensive revision in writing classrooms nowadays is not unreasonable and can be an important stage in the production of papers.

Microsoft Word has had a "tracking" capability in its last several upgrades, which carries revision a step further. Now the teacher and student can carry on a dialogue on the paper itself. The teacher's deletions and additions can be tracked, the student can respond, and the tracking will be facilitated by automatically putting the changes in a different color. The "comment" function makes it possible for both teacher and student to write notes at the exactly relevant point in the manuscript.

While a spelling checker is an appropriate first step, students should be reminded that they should not rely solely on spell checkers for proofreading. Noted for their failure to understand context, spell checkers will not help with incorrect homonyms or typos.

ASSESSING STUDENT WRITING

Creating a Supporting Environment

Viewing writing as a process allows teachers and students to see the writing classroom as a cooperative workshop where students and teachers encourage and support each other in each writing endeavor. Listed below are some techniques that help teachers facilitate and create a supportive classroom environment.

> Learn more about
> **Teaching and Managing Peer Review**
> http://www.utexas.edu/cola/progs/wac/highschool/hspeerreview/

1. Create peer response/support groups that are working on similar writing assignments. The members help each other in all stages of the writing process—from prewriting, writing, revising, editing, and publishing.

2. Provide several prompts to give students the freedom to write on a topic of their own. Writing should be generated out of personal experience and students should be introduced to in-class journals. One effective way to get into writing is to let them write often and freely about their own lives, without having to worry about grades or evaluation.

3. Respond in the form of a question whenever possible. Teacher/facilitator should respond non-critically and use positive, supportive language.

4. Respond to formal writing acknowledging the student's strengths and focusing on the composition skills demonstrated by the writing. A response should encourage the student by offering praise for what the student has done well. Give the student a focus for revision and demonstrate that the process of revision has applications in many other writing situations.

5. Provide students with readers' checklists so that students can write observational critiques of others' drafts. Then they can revise their own papers at home using the checklists as a guide.

6. Pair students so that they can give and receive responses. Pairing students keeps them aware of the role of an audience in the composing process and in evaluating stylistic effects.

7. Focus critical comments on aspects of the writing that can be observed in the writing. Comments like "I noticed you use the word 'is' frequently" will be more helpful than "Your introduction is dull" and will not demoralize the writer.

8. Provide the group with a series of questions to guide them through the group writing sessions.

When assessing and responding to student writing, you might consider these guidelines.

Responding to Non-graded Writing (Formative)

- Avoid using a red pen. Whenever possible use a #2 pencil.
- Explain the criteria that will be used for assessment in advance.
- Read the writing once while asking the question, "Is the student's response appropriate for the assignment?"
- Reread and make note at the end whether the student met the objective of the writing task.
- Responses should be non-critical and use supportive and encouraging language.
- Resist writing on or over the student's writing.
- Highlight the ideas you wish to emphasize, question, or verify.
- Encourage your students to take risks.

Responding to and Evaluating Graded Writing (Summative)

- Ask students to submit prewriting and rough-draft materials including all revisions with their final draft.
- For the first reading, use a holistic method, examining the work as a whole.
- When reading the draft for the second time, assess it using the standards previously established.
- Write your responses in the margin and use supportive language.
- Make sure you address the process as well as the product. It is important that students value the learning process as well as the final product.
- After scanning the piece a third time, write final comments at the end of the draft.

The last twenty years have seen great change in instruction in the English classroom. Gone are the days when literature is taught on Monday, grammar is taught on Wednesday, and writing is assigned on Friday. Integrating reading, writing, speaking, listening and viewing enables students to make connections between each aspect of language development during each class.

Suggestions for Integrating Language Arts

- Use prereading activities such as discussion, writing, research, and journals. Use writing to tap into prior knowledge before students read; engage students in class discussions about themes, issues, and ideas explored in journals, predicting the outcome and exploring related information.

- Use prewriting activities such as reading model essays, researching, interviewing others, combining sentences and other prewriting activities. Remember that developing language proficiency is a recursive process and involves practice in reading, writing, thinking, speaking, listening and viewing.

- Create writing activities that are relevant to students by having them write and share with real audiences.

- Connect correctness—including developing skills of conventional usage, spelling, grammar, and punctuation—to the revision and editing stage of writing. Review of mechanics and punctuation can be done with mini-lessons that use sentences from student papers, sentence combining strategies, and modeling passages of skilled writers.

- Connect reading, writing, listening, speaking, and viewing by using literature read as a springboard for a variety of activities.

RESEARCH AND DOCUMENTATION

Whether researching for your own purposes or teaching students to research, the best place to start research is usually at a library. Not only does it have numerous books, videos, and periodicals to use for references, the librarian is always a valuable resource for information and can help retrieve information. In spite of the abundance of online sources, researchers still need librarians.

> Those who declared librarians obsolete when the Internet rage first appeared are now red-faced. We need them more than ever. The Internet is full of "stuff" but its value and readability is often questionable. "Stuff" doesn't give you a competitive edge; high-quality related information does.
>
> -Patricia Schroeder,
> President of the Association of American Publishers

Gathering Data

Keep **content** and **context** in mind when researching. Don't be so wrapped up with how you are going to apply your resources to your project that you miss the author's entire purpose or message. Remember that there are multiple ways to get the information you need. Read an encyclopedia article about your topic to get a general overview, and then focus from there. Note important names of people associated with your subject, time periods, and geographic areas. Make a list of key words and their synonyms to use while searching for information. And finally, don't forget about articles in magazines and newspapers, or even personal interviews with experts related to your field of interest!

- Keep a record of any sources consulted during the research process.
- As you take notes, avoid unintentional plagiarism.
- Summarize and paraphrase in your own words without the source in front of you.

To be life-long learners, student should learn to conduct their own research. Thus, they need to know what resources are available to them and how to use them.

Dictionaries are useful for spelling, writing, and reading. Students looking up a word in the dictionary should be an expected behavior, not a punishment or busy work that has no reference to their current reading assignment.

Model the correct way to use the dictionary for some have never been taught proper dictionary skills. As the teacher, you need to demonstrate that as an adult reader and writer, you routinely and happily use the dictionary.

Encyclopedias in print or online are the beginning point for many research projects. While these entries may sometimes lack timeliness, they do provide students with general background.

Databases hold billions of records so students should be taught effective search techniques such as using key words and Boolean operators.

Learning that "and" and "or" will increase the number of hits while "not" or "and not" will decrease the number of hits can save researchers time and effort.

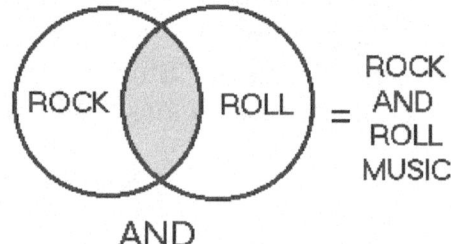

Learn more about **Boolean Operators** at http://www.bgsu.edu/colleges/library/info srv/lue/boolean.html

The **Internet** is a multi-faceted goldmine of information, but you must be careful to discriminate between reliable and unreliable sources. Use sites that are associated with an academic institution, such as a university or a scholarly organization. Typical domain names will end in "edu" or "org."

Students (and everyone) should evaluate any piece of information gleaned from the Internet. For example, if you google "etymology" you can find a multitude of sources. Don't trust a single one. The information should be validated by at least three sources. Wikipedia is very useful, but it can be changed by anyone who chooses, so any information on it should be backed up by other sources.

The resources used to support a piece of writing can be divided into two major groups: **primary** sources and **secondary** sources.

Primary sources are works, records, and the like that were created during the period being studied or immediately after it. Secondary sources are works written significantly after the period being studied and based upon primary sources. Primary sources are the basic materials that provide raw data and information. Secondary sources are the works that contain the explications of, and judgments on, this primary material.

Primary sources include the following kinds of materials:
- Documents that reflect the immediate, everyday concerns of people: memoranda, bills, deeds, charters, newspaper reports, pamphlets, graffiti, popular writings, journals or diaries, records of decision-making bodies, letters, receipts, snapshots, and others.
- Theoretical writings which reflect care and consideration in composition and an attempt to convince or persuade. The topic will generally be deeper and more pervasive values than is the case with "immediate" documents. These may include newspaper or magazine editorials, sermons, political speeches, or philosophical writings.
- Narrative accounts of events, ideas, and trends written with intentionality by someone contemporary with the events described.
- Statistical data, although statistics may be misleading.
- Literature and nonverbal materials, novels, stories, poetry and essays from the period, as well as coins, archaeological artifacts, and art produced during the period.

Secondary sources include the following kinds of materials:
- Books written on the basis of primary materials about the period of time.
- Books written on the basis of primary materials about persons who played a major role in the events under consideration.
- Books and articles written on the basis of primary materials about the culture, the social norms, the language, and the values of the period.
- Quotations from primary sources.
- Statistical data on the period.

- The conclusions and inferences of other historians.
- Multiple interpretations of the ethos of the time.

Questions for Analyzing Sources

To determine the authenticity or credibility of your sources, consider these questions:

> Learn more about **Assessing the Credibility of Online Sources**
> http://www.webcredible.co.uk/user-friendly-resources/web-credibility/assessing-credibility-online-sources.shtml

1. Who created the source and why? Was it created through a spur-of-the-moment act, a routine transaction, or a thoughtful, deliberate process?
2. Did the recorder have firsthand knowledge of the event? Or, did the recorder report what others saw and heard?
3. Was the recorder a neutral party, or did the recorder have opinions or interests that might have influenced what was recorded?
   Did the recorder produce the source for personal use, for one or more individuals, or for a large audience?
4. Was the source meant to be public or private?
5. Did the recorder wish to inform or persuade others? (Check the words in the source. The words may tell you whether the recorder was trying to be objective or persuasive.) Did the recorder have reasons to be honest or dishonest?
6. Was the information recorded during the event, immediately after the event, or after some lapse of time? How large a lapse of time?

Paraphrasing

Paraphrasing is the art of rewording text. The goal is to maintain the original purpose of the statement while translating it into your own words. Your newly generated sentence can be longer or shorter than the original. Concentrate on the meaning, not on the words. Do not change concept words, special terms, or proper names. There are numerous ways to paraphrase effectively:

- Change the key words' form or part of speech. Example: "American news **coverage** is frequently **biased** in favor of Western views," becomes "When American journalists **cover** events, they often display a Western **bias**."

- Use synonyms of "relationship words." Look for a relationship word, such as **contrast, cause,** or **effect,** and replace it with a word that conveys a similar meaning, thus creating a different structure for your sentence. Example: "**Unlike** many cats, Purrdy can sit on command," becomes "Most cats are not able to be trained, **but** Purrdy can sit on command."

- Use synonyms of phrases and words. Example: "The Beatnik writers were relatively unknown at **the start of the decade**," becomes "**Around the early 1950s**, the Beatnik writers were still relatively unknown."

- Change passive voice to active voice or move phrases and modifiers. Example: "Not to be outdone by the third graders, the fourth grade class added a musical medley to their Christmas performance," becomes "The fourth grade class added a musical medley to their Christmas performance to avoid being showed up by the third graders."

- Use reversals or negatives that do not change the meaning of the sentence. Example: "That burger chain is only found in California," becomes "That burger chain is not found on the east coast."

- Cite anything that is not common knowledge. This includes direct quotes as well as ideas or statistics.

Documentation

Documentation is an important skill in incorporating outside information into a piece of writing. Students must learn that research is more than cut and paste from the Internet and that plagiarism is a serious academic offense.

This skill pertains to recognizing that stealing intellectual property is an academic and, in some cases, a legal crime; because it is so, students need to learn how to give credit where credit is due.

Students need to be aware of the rules that apply to borrowing ideas from various sources. Increasingly, consequences for violations of these rules (plagiarism) are becoming more severe, and students are expected to be aware of how to avoid such problems. Pleading ignorance is less and less of a defense. Such consequences include failing a particular assignment, losing credit for an entire course, expulsion from a learning environment, and civil penalties. Software exists that enables teachers and other interested individuals to determine quickly whether a given paper includes plagiarized material. As members of society in the information age, students are expected to recognize the basic justice of intellectual honesty and to conform to the systems meant to ensure it.

There are several style guides for documenting sources. Each guide has its own particular ways of signaling that information has been directly borrowed or paraphrased, and familiarity with at least where to find the relevant details of the major style guides is an essential for students. Many libraries publish overviews of the major style guides for students to consult, most bookstores will carry full guides for the major systems, and relevant information is readily available on the web as well.

Documentation of sources takes two main forms. The first form applies to citing sources in the text of the document or as footnotes or endnotes. In-text documentation is sometimes called parenthetical documentation and requires specific information within parentheses placed immediately after borrowed material. Footnotes or endnotes are placed either at the bottom of relevant pages or at the end of the document.

Beyond citing sources in the text, style guides also require a bibliography, a references section, or a works cited section at the end of the document. Sources for any borrowed material are to be listed according to the rules of the particular guide. In some cases, it may be required to include a works consulted listing even though no material is directly cited or paraphrased to the extent that an in-text citation would be required.

The major style guides to be familiar with include the *Modern Language Association Handbook* (MLA), the *Manual of the American Psychological Association* (APA), the *Chicago Manuel of Style*, *Turabian*, and *Scientific Style and Format: the CBE Manual*.

> Learn more about
> **MLA Works Cited Documentation**
> http://www.studyguide.org/MLAdocumentation.htm

Documentation of sources from the Internet is particularly involved and continues to evolve at a pace often requiring visiting the latest online update available for a particular style guide.

Tips for Documentation

Keep a record of all sources consulted during the research process.
As you take notes, avoid unintentional plagiarism. Summarize and paraphrase in your own words without the source in front of you. If you use a direct quote, copy it exactly as written and enclose in quotation marks.

Cite anything that is not common knowledge. This includes direct quotes as well as ideas or statistics.

Within the body of your document follow this blueprint for standard attribution following MLA style.

1. Begin the sentence with, "According to _____,"

2. Proceed with the material being cited, followed by the page number in parentheses.

In-Text Citation Example

According to Steve Mandel, "our average conversational rate of speech is about 125 words per minute" (78).

Once students have mastered this basic approach, they can learn more sophisticated methods such as embedding information.

Each source used within the document will have a complete citation in a bibliography or works cited page.

Works Cited Entry

Mandel, Steve. *Effective Presentation Skills*. Menlo Park, California: Crisp Publications, 1993.

Skill 3.2 **Understanding and evaluating rhetorical features in writing, including:**

- Purposes for writing and speaking and the role of the audience within varying contexts.
- Organization in a piece of writing and the creation and preservation of coherence.
- Strategies for the organization, development, and presentation of print, electronic, and visual media.
- Discourse aims, e.g., creative, expository, persuasive.
- Methods of argument and types of appeals, e.g., argumentative strategies, analogy, extended metaphor, allusion.
- Style, tone, voice, and point of view as part of rhetorical strategy.
- Recognition of bias, distinguishing between fact and opinion, and identifying stereotypes, inferences, and assumptions.

PURPOSES FOR WRITING AND SPEAKING AND THE ROLE OF THE AUDIENCE WITHIN VARYING CONTEXTS

Tailoring language for a particular **audience** is an important skill. Writing to be read by a business associate will surely sound different from writing to be read by a younger sibling. Not only are the vocabularies different, but the formality or informality of the discourse will need to be adjusted.

Two characteristics that determine language style are **degree of formality** and **word choice**. The most formal language does not use contractions or slang while the most informal language will probably feature a more casual use of common sayings and anecdotes. Formal language will use longer sentences and will not sound like a conversation. The most informal language will use shorter sentences (not necessarily simple sentences—but shorter constructions) and may sound like a conversation.

In both formal and informal writing, there exists a **tone**, the writer's attitude toward the material and/or readers. Tone may be playful, formal, intimate, angry, serious, ironic, outraged, baffled, tender, serene, depressed, and so on. The overall tone of a piece of writing is dictated by both the subject matter and the audience. Tone is also related to the actual word choice which make up the document, as we attach affective meanings to words, called their **connotations**. Gaining this conscious control over language makes it possible to use language appropriately in various situations and to evaluate its uses in literature and other forms of communication. By evoking the proper responses from readers or listeners, we can prompt them to take action.

Using the following questions is an excellent way to assess the audience and tone of a given piece of writing.

1. Who is your audience (friend, teacher, business person, someone else)?

2. How much does this person know about you and/or your topic?

3. What is your purpose (to prove an argument, to persuade, to amuse, to register a complaint, to ask for a raise, etc)?

4. What emotions do you have about the topic (nervous, happy, confident, angry, sad, no feelings at all)?

5. What emotions do you want to register with your audience (anger, nervousness, happiness, boredom, interest)?

6. What persona do you need to create in order to achieve your purpose?

7. What choice of language is best suited to achieving your purpose with your particular subject (slang, friendly but respectful, formal)?

8. What emotional quality do you want to transmit to achieve your purpose (matter of fact, informative, authoritative, inquisitive, sympathetic, angry), and to what degree do you want to express this tone?

In the past, teachers have assigned reports, paragraphs, and essays that focused on the teacher as the audience with the purpose of explaining information. However, for students to be meaningfully engaged in their writing, they must write for a variety of reasons. Writing for different audiences and aims enables students to be more involved in their writing. If they write for the same audience and purpose, they will continue to see writing as just another assignment. Listed below are suggestions that give students an opportunity to write in more creative and critical ways.

- Write letters to the editor, to a college, to a friend, to another student that would be sent to the intended audience.
- Write stories that would be read aloud to a group (the class, another group of students, to a group of elementary school students) or published in a literary magazine or class anthology.
- Write plays that would be performed.
- Have students discuss the parallels between the different speech styles we use and writing styles for different readers or audiences.
- Allow students to write a particular piece for different audiences.

As part of the prewriting exercises, have students identify the audience. Expose students to writing that is on the same topic but with a different audience and have them identify the variations in sentence structure and style. Remind your students that it is not necessary to identify all the specifics of the audience in the initial stage of the writing process but that at some point they must make some determinations about audience.

Guidelines for Assessing your Audience

Now that you know your purpose and have the information, you need to assess your audience. What does your audience know and what does it need to know? Here are some questions to consider.

Values: What is important to this group of people? What is their background and how will that affect their perception of your speech?

Needs: Find out in advance what the audience's needs are. Why are they listening to you? Find a way to satisfy their needs.

Constraints: What might hold the audience back from being fully engaged in what you are saying, or agreeing with your point of view, or processing what you are trying to say? These could be political reasons, which make them wary of your presentation's ideology from the start, or knowledge reasons, in which the audience lacks the appropriate background information to grasp your ideas. Avoid this last constraint by staying away from technical terminology, slang, or abbreviations that may be unclear to your audience.

Demographic Information: Take the audience's size into account as well as the location of the presentation. Demographics could include age, gender, education, religion, income level and other such countable characteristics.

ORGANIZATION IN A PIECE OF WRITING AND THE CREATION AND PRESERVATION OF COHERENCE

In writing or speaking, you can be convincing if you follow the three basic principles of unity, coherence, and emphasis.

Unity: All ideas must relate to the controlling thesis. At the simplest level, this means that all sentences must develop the topic sentence of a paragraph. By extension, then, all paragraphs must develop the thesis statement of the essay; all chapters must develop the main idea of the book. All ideas must develop the argument.

Coherence: One way to achieve unity is to show the relationship of ideas by using transitional words, phrases, sentences, and paragraphs. Using coordinating conjunctions (for, and, nor, but, or, yet, so), subordinating conjunctions (because, since, whenever), or transitional adverbs (however, therefore) is an effective way to show logical order and thus create coherence. Another way to show the relationship of ideas is to use an appropriate strategy (spatial, chronological, cause and effect, classification, comparison/contrast) to arrange details.

Emphasis: By placing your stronger arguments in areas of importance, you emphasize the significance of the ideas. In direct order, the main ideas are stated first and then supported by reasons or details. In indirect order, the support is provided first (in either increasing or decreasing order of importance) so that the end is a well-defended argument.

Using Transition

A mark of maturity in writing is the effective use of transitional devices at all levels. For example, a topic sentence can be used to establish continuity, especially if it is positioned at the beginning of a paragraph. The most common use would be to refer to what has preceded, repeat it, or summarize it and then go on to introduce a new topic. An essay by W. H. Hudson uses this device: "Although the potato was very much to me in those early years, it grew to be more when I heard its history." It summarizes what has preceded, makes a comment on the author's interest, and introduces a new topic: the history of the potato.

Another example of a transitional sentence could be, "Not all matters end so happily." This refers to the previous information and prepares for the next paragraph, which will be about matters that do not end happily. This transitional sentence is a little more forthright: "The increase in drug use in our community leads us to another general question."

Another fairly simple and straightforward transitional device is the use of numbers or their approximation: "First, I want to talk about the dangers of immigration; second, I will discuss the enormity of the problem; third, I will propose a reasonable solution."

An entire paragraph may be transitional in purpose and form. In "Darwiniana," Thomas Huxley used a transitional paragraph:

> So much, then, by way of proof that the method of establishing laws in science is exactly the same as that pursued in common life. Let us now turn to another matter (though really it is but another phase of the same question), and that is, the method by which, from the relations of certain phenomena, we prove that some stand in the position of causes toward the others.

The most common transitional device is a single word. Some examples: *and, furthermore, next, moreover, in addition, again, also, likewise, similarly, finally, second.* There are many, but they should be used correctly and judiciously. See chart "Common Transitions" below.

In marking student papers, a teacher can encourage a student to think in terms of moving coherently from one idea to the next by making transitions between the two. If the shift from one thought to another is too abrupt, the student can be asked to provide a transitional paragraph. Provide lists of possible transitions and encourage students to have the list at hand when composing essays. These are good tools for nudging students to more mature writing styles.

STRATEGIES FOR THE ORGANIZATION, DEVELOPMENT, AND PRESENTATION OF PRINT, ELECTRONIC, AND VISUAL MEDIA

Media's impact on today's society is immense and ever increasing. As children, we watch programs on television that are amazingly fast-paced and visually rich. Parents' roles as verbal and moral teachers are diminishing in response to the much more stimulating guidance of the television set. Adolescence, which used to be the time for going out and exploring the world first hand, is now consumed by the allure of MTV, popular music, and video games. Young adults are exposed to uncensored sex and violence.

> Learn more about
> **Integrating Technology in the Classroom**
> http://www.glencoe.com/sec/teachingtoday/tiparchive.phtml/3

ENG. LANGUAGE LIT. & COMP.

But media's effect on society is beneficial and progressive at the same time. Its effect on education in particular provides special challenges and opportunities for teachers and students.

Thanks to satellite technology, urban classrooms and rural villages can receive instructional radio and television programs. CD-ROMs enable students to learn information through a virtual reality experience. The Internet allows instant access to unlimited data and connects people across all cultures through shared interests. Educational media, when used in a productive way, enriches instruction and makes it more individualized, accessible, and economical.

Common Transitions

Logical Relationship	Transitional Expression
Similarity	also, in the same way, just as ... so too, likewise, similarly
Exception/Contrast	but, however, in spite of, on the one hand ... on the other hand, nevertheless, nonetheless, notwithstanding, in contrast, on the contrary, still, yet, although
Sequence/Order	first, second, third, next, then, finally, until
Time	after, afterward, at last, before, currently, during, earlier, immediately, later, meanwhile, now, presently, recently, simultaneously, since, subsequently, then
Example	for example, for instance, namely, specifically, to illustrate
Emphasis	even, indeed, in fact, of course, truly
Place/Position	above, adjacent, below, beyond, here, in front, in back, nearby, there
Cause and Effect	accordingly, consequently, hence, so, therefore, thus, as a result, because, consequently, hence, if...then, in short
Additional Support or Evidence	additionally, again, also, and, as well, besides, equally important, further, furthermore, in addition, moreover, then
Conclusion/Summary	finally, in a word, in brief, in conclusion, in the end, in the final analysis, on the whole, thus, to conclude, to summarize, in sum, in summary
Statement support	most important, more significant, primarily, most essential
Addition	again, also, and, besides, equally important, finally, furthermore, in addition, last, likewise, moreover, too
Clarification	actually, clearly, evidently, in fact, in other words, obviously, of course, indeed

A common classroom assignment that applies to this skill is to view the movie version of a book studied by a particular class, to compare and contrast the two media, and to argue which did the better job of conveying the intended message(s).

It is difficult to convey the same message across different media because of the dynamics specific to those media. The degree of difficulty increases as the complexity of the message does. Nonetheless, certain general observations inform the discussion.

A **print message** has two kinds of unique features. Some seem to be positive. For instance, print messages have longevity; they are also easily portable. Print messages appeal almost exclusively to the mind, and allow students to recursively read sections that warrant more thought. Other features of print seem potentially negative. For instance, a print message requires an active reader; without such a reader, print messages are not very effective. Print messages are not accessible to non-readers.

A **graphic message** in the hands of an artistic genius can produce images that seem to be Jungian archetypes. More commonly, a graphic message gives a quick overview of some quantifiable situation. Some learners find that graphic information works for them better than print, and many struggling readers find graphic messages more helpful, too. However, compared to print, graphic messages convey a much shorter range of information. If the particular graphic is inspiring, the inspirations it conveys are subject to the descriptions of the various readers who view it. With print, the inspired scripts are already there for the reader, provided the reader is applying active reading skills.

Tips for using print media and visual aids
- Use pictures over words whenever possible.
- Present one key point per visual.
- Use no more than 3-4 colors per visual to avoid clutter and confusion.
- Use contrasting colors such as dark blue and bright yellow.
- Use a maximum of 25-35 numbers per visual aid.
- Use bullets instead of paragraphs when possible.
- Make sure it is student-centered, not media-centered. Delivery is just as important as the media presented.
- Keep the content simple and concise (avoid too many lines, words, or pictures)
- Balance substance and visual appeal
- Make sure the text is large enough for the class to read
- Match the information to the format that will fit it best

Tips for using film and television
- Study programs in advance.
- Obtain supplementary materials such as printed transcripts of the narrative or study guides.
- Provide your students with background information, explain unfamiliar concepts, and anticipate outcomes.
- Assign outside readings based on student viewing.
- Ask cuing questions.
- Watch along with students.
- Observe students' reactions.
- Follow up viewing with discussions and related activities.

An **audio message** allows for messages delivered with attention to prosody. Students who can't read can access the material. Audio messages invite the listener to form mental images consistent with the topic of the audio. Audio messages allow the learners to close their eyes for better mental focus. Listening to an audio message is a more passive modality than reading a print message. As a rule, people read faster than normal speech patterns, so print conveys more information in a given time span.

An **audiovisual** message offers the easiest accessibility for learners. It has the advantages of each, the graphic and the audio, medium. Learners' eyes and ears are engaged. Non-readers get significant access to content. On the other hand, viewing an audiovisual presentation is an even more passive activity than listening to an audio message because information is coming to learners effortlessly through two senses. Activities to foster a critical perspective on an audiovisual presentation serve as valuable safeguards against any overall and unwelcome passivity.

The use of technology has broadened and enriched the entire communication process. Teachers and students who learn to use these resources effectively will expand their capabilities inside and outside the classroom.

Multimedia refers to a technology for presenting material in both visual and verbal forms. This format is especially conducive to the classroom, since it reaches both visual and auditory learners.

> Check out the
> **Language of Media Literacy:
> A Glossary of Terms**
> http://www.medialit.org/reading_room/article565.html

Knowing how to select effective teaching software is the first step in efficient multi-media education. First, decide what you need the software for (creating spreadsheets, making diagrams, or creating slideshows). Consult magazines such as *Popular Computing, PC World, MacWorld,* and *Multimedia World* to learn about the newest programs available.

Go to a local computer store and ask a customer service representative to help you find the exact equipment you need. If possible, test the programs you are interested in. Check reviews in magazines such as *Consumer Reports, PCWorld, Electronic Learning* or *Multimedia Schools* to ensure the software's quality.

Software Programs for Producing Teaching Material
- Adobe
- CorelDRAW!
- Claris Works
- Harvard Graphics
- Microsoft Word
- Aldus Freehand
- DrawPerfect
- PC Paintbrush
- Visio
- Microsoft Power Point

Multimedia Teaching Model

Teaching students how to follow a process will help them simplify their research. Here's one model to follow:

Step 1. Diagnose
- Figure out what students need to know.
- Assess what students already know.

Step 2. Design
- Design tests of learning achievement.
- Identify effective instructional strategies.
- Select suitable media.
- Sequence learning activities within program.
- Plan introductory activities.
- Plan follow-up activities.

Step 3. Procure
- Secure materials at hand.
- Obtain new materials.

Step 4. Produce
- Modify existing materials.
- Craft new materials.

Step 5. Refine
- Conduct small-scale test of program.
- Evaluate procedures and achievements.
- Revise program accordingly.
- Conduct classroom test of program.
- Evaluate procedures and achievements.
- Revise in anticipation of next school term.

DISCOURSE AIMS

Basic expository writing simply gives information not previously known about a topic or is used to explain or define one. Facts, examples, statistics, cause and effect, direct tone, objective rather than subjective delivery, and non-emotional information are presented in a formal manner.

Descriptive writing centers on person, place, or object, using concrete and sensory words to create a mood or impression and arranging details in a chronological or spatial sequence.

Narrative writing is developed using an incident or anecdote or related series of events. Chronology, the 5 W's, topic sentence, and conclusion are essential ingredients.

Persuasive writing implies the writer's ability to select vocabulary and arrange facts and opinions in such a way as to direct the actions of the listener/reader. Persuasive writing may incorporate exposition and narration as they illustrate the main idea.

Journalistic writing is theoretically free of author bias. It is essential when relaying information about an event, person, or thing that it be factual and objective. Provide students with an opportunity to examine newspapers and create their own. Many newspapers have educational programs that are offered free to schools.

Different Methods of Oral Communication

Different from the basic writing forms of discourse is the art of **debating, discussion, and conversation**. The ability to use language and logic to convince the audience to accept your reasoning and to side with you is an art. This form of writing/speaking is extremely confined or structured, and logically sequenced with supporting reasons and evidence. At its best, it is the highest form of propaganda. A position statement, evidence, reason, evaluation and refutation are integral parts of this writing schema.

> Learn more about
> **Oral Communication Skills**
> http://www.glencoe.com/sec/teachingtoday/weeklytips.phtml/88

Interviewing provides opportunities for students to apply expository and informative communication. It teaches them how to structure questions to evoke fact-filled responses. Compiling the information from an interview into a biographical essay or speech helps students list, sort, and arrange details in an orderly fashion.

Speeches that encourage them to describe persons, places, or events in their own lives or oral interpretations of literature help them sense the creativity and effort used by professional writers.

The memorization and **recitation** of poetry allow students a level of familiarity and a deeper comprehension of a poem than is available upon simply reading or studying the words. The act of recitation involves projecting yourself into the poet's position, fully personifying the emotions and ideas of the poem as conveyed through language. To fully convey the meaning of a poem in recitation, students learn to make important decisions regarding style, tone of voice, projection, speed or slowness, emotional tenor, and character.

Public speaking skills are enhanced through recitation as students who memorize and recite poetry become cognizant of the power of words, which has relevance in many different walks of life. Students also become aware of the connections between traditional poetic forms and contemporary ones, such as hip hop, slam, song lyrics, and performance poetry, making palpable a connection between historical periods and the current moment. Memorization of "classics" of poetry is an excellent way for students to study elements of prosody (rhyme, meter, conventions of open & closed form) in an activated context, rather than just in a book, supplying them a wide range of techniques and tools for their own future writing and reading.

Delivery Techniques

As a teacher, you recognize the importance of delivering your message. While written communications is discussed in later sections, let's consider oral communications now. Instruct your students on the ways that verbal and non-verbal communication can affect the way a presentation is understood. You can model these techniques.

Posture: Maintain a straight, but not stiff posture. Instead of shifting weight from hip to hip, point your feet directly at the audience and distribute your weight evenly. Keep shoulders towards the audience. If you have to turn your body to use a visual aid, turn 45 degrees and continue speaking towards the audience.

Movement: Instead of staying glued to one spot or pacing back and forth, stay within four to eight feet of the front row of your audience. Take a step or half-step to the side every once in a while. If you are using a lectern, feel free to move to the front or side of it to engage your audience more. Avoid distancing yourself from the audience; you want them to feel involved and connected.

Gestures: Gestures can maintain a natural atmosphere when speaking publicly. Use them just as you would when speaking to a friend. They shouldn't be exaggerated, but they should be used for added emphasis. Avoid keeping your hands in your pockets or locked behind your back, wringing your hands and fidgeting nervously, or keeping your arms crossed.

Eye Contact: Many people are intimidated by using eye contact when speaking to large groups. Interestingly, eye contact usually *helps* the speaker overcome speech anxiety by connecting with the attentive audience and easing feelings of isolation. Instead of looking at a spot on the back wall or at your notes, scan the room and make eye contact for one to three seconds per person.

In addition to the content of your presentation, you want to use a strong delivery. As with most skills, the key is practice, practice, practice. Record and play back your presentation to hear how you sound.

Voice: Many people fall into one of two traps when speaking: using a monotone or talking too fast. These are both caused by anxiety. A monotone restricts your natural inflection but can be remedied by releasing tension in upper and lower body muscles. Subtle movement will keep you loose and natural.

> Learn more about
> **Using Your Voice**
> http://www.longview.k12.wa.us/mmhs/wyatt/pathway/voice.html

Talking too fast, on the other hand, is not necessarily bad if you are exceptionally articulate. If you are not a strong speaker or if you are talking about very technical items, the audience will easily become lost.

When you talk too fast and begin tripping over your words, consciously pause after every sentence you say. Don't be afraid of brief silences. The audience needs time to absorb what you are saying.

Volume: Problems with volume, whether too soft or too loud, can usually be overcome with practice. If you tend to speak too softly, have someone stand in the back of the room and signal you when your volume is strong enough. If possible, have someone in the front of the room as well to make sure you're not overcompensating with excessive volume.

Conversely, if you have a problem with speaking too loud, have the person in the front of the room signal you when your voice is soft enough and check with the person in the back to make sure it is still loud enough to be heard. In both cases, note your volume level for future reference. Don't be shy about asking your audience, "Can you hear me in the back?" Suitable volume is beneficial for both you and the audience.

Pitch: Pitch refers to the length, tension, and thickness of your person's vocal bands. As your voice gets higher, the pitch gets higher. In oral performance, pitch reflects the emotional arousal level. More variation in pitch typically corresponds to more emotional arousal but can also be used to convey sarcasm or highlight specific words.

While these skills are essential for you to be an effective teacher, you want your students to develop these techniques as well. By encouraging the development of proper techniques for oral presentations, you are enabling your students to develop self-confidence for higher levels of communication.

METHODS OF ARGUMENT AND TYPES OF APPEALS

The art of rhetoric was first developed in Ancient Greece. Its pioneer was Socrates, who recognized the crucial role that rhetoric played in education, politics, and story telling. Socrates argued that, presented effectively, speech could evoke any desired emotion or opinion. His method of dialectic syllogism, known today as the Socratic Method, pursued truth through a series of questions. Socrates established three types of appeals used in persuasive speech:

Types of Appeal

Ethos: Refers to the credibility of the speaker. It establishes the speaker as a reliable and trustworthy authority by focusing on the speaker's credentials.

Pathos: Refers to the emotional appeal made by the speaker to the listeners. It emphasizes the fact that the audience responds to ideas with emotion. For example, when the government is trying to persuade citizens to go to war for the sake of "the fatherland," it is using the appeal to *pathos* to target their love of their country.

Logos: Refers to the logic of the speaker's argument. It uses the idea that facts, statistics, and other forms of evidence can convince an audience to accept a speaker's argument. Remember that information can be just as, if not more, persuasive than appeal tactics.

Today, rhetoric's evolution can be traced back to ancient Athens in many facets of our society. The structure of many governments and judicial systems reflect rhetorical tactics established by the Greeks so long ago. The media has taken rhetoric to a whole new level and has refined it to a very skilled art. Every word as well as the method of presentation is carefully planned. The audience is taken into account and speech tailored to their needs and motivations. Though the content has changed, this concept has been around since Socrates contemplated it thousands of years ago.

Advertising Techniques

Because students are very interested in the types of approaches advertisers use, you can develop high-interest assignments requiring them to analyze commercial messages. What is powerful about Nike's "Just Do It" campaign? What is the appeal of Jessica Simpson's eponymous perfume?

Beauty Appeal: Beauty attracts us; we are drawn to beautiful people, places, and things.

Celebrity Endorsement: This technique associates product use with a well-known person. By purchasing this product we are led to believe that we will attain characteristics similar to the celebrity.

Compliment the Consumer: Advertisers flatter the consumer who is willing to purchase their product. By purchasing the product the consumer is recognized by the advertisers for making a good decision with the selection.

Escape: Getting away from it all is very appealing; you can imagine adventures you cannot have; the idea of escape is pleasurable.

Independence/Individuality: This technique associates product with people who can think and act for themselves. Products are linked to individual decision making.

Intelligence: This technique associates product with smart people who can't be fooled.

Lifestyle: This technique associates product with a particular style of living/way of doing things.

Nurture: Every time you see an animal or a child, the appeal is to your paternal or maternal instincts, so this technique associates products with taking care of someone.

Peer Approval: This technique associates product use with friendship/acceptance. Advertisers can also use this negatively to make you worry that you'll lose friends if you don't use a certain product.

Rebel: This technique associates products with behaviors or lifestyles that oppose society's norms.

Rhetorical Question: This technique poses a question to the consumer that demands a response. A question is asked and the consumer is supposed to answer in such a way that affirms the product's goodness.

Scientific/Statistical Claim: This provides some sort of scientific proof or experiment, very specific numbers, or an impressive sounding mystery ingredient.

Unfinished Comparison/Claim: This technique uses phrases such as "Works better in poor driving conditions!" Works better than what?

Deductive and Inductive Reasoning

The two forms of reasoning to support an argument are *inductive* or *deductive*. Inductive reason goes from the particular to the general. In other words, I observe that all the green apples I have ever tasted are sour. 1) I have tasted some from my grandfather's orchard, 2) I have tasted the Granny Smiths that my mother buys in the grocery store and makes pies from, 3) I taste the green apples in my friend's kitchen. (All particular instances or bits of evidence.) All are sour (conclusion). Then I can *generalize* that all green apples are sour. This is inductive reasoning, a very prevalent aspect of the way we think and deal with each other and essential to persuasive discourse.

Deductive reasoning, on the other hand, reverses the order by going from general to particular. The generalization drawn in the previous illustration, "All green apples are sour" can be used to make a statement about a particular apple. A new variety of green apples has appeared in the grocery store. Arguing from the generalization that all green apples are sour, I may reject this new variety because I am sure that they are going to be sour. Deductive reasoning is based on the syllogism:

> Learn more about
> **Deductive and Inductive Argument**
> http://www.iep.utm.edu/d/ded-ind.htm

    All green apples are sour.
    This apple is green.
    Therefore, this apple is sour.

When a prosecutor presents a trial in a courtroom, he typically puts forth the statement of fact: On November 2 in an alley between Smith and Jones Street at the 400 block, Stacy Highsmith was brutally raped and murdered. The coroner has concluded that she was bludgeoned with a blunt instrument at or around midnight and her body was found by a shopkeeper the next morning. (There may be other "knowns" presented in the statement of fact.)

Following the laying out of the facts of the case, the prosecutor will use inductive reasoning (a series of particulars) to accuse the person on trial for the crime. For example, Terry Large, the accused, 1) was seen in the neighborhood at 11:30 p.m. on November 2. 2) He was carrying a carpenter's tool kit, which was later recovered, and 3) a hammer with evidence of blood on it was found in that tool kit. 4) The blood was tested and it matched the victim's DNA. (All particulars leading to a conclusion.) Ultimately, the prosecutor will reach the generalization: Terry Large murdered Stacy Highsmith in the alley in the middle of the night on November 2.

Throughout history, theories of rhetoric have been developed, adopted, modified, and discarded. Here are three variations of persuasive speech.

Fact: Similar to an informative speech, a persuasive speech on a question of fact seeks to find an answer where there isn't a clear one. The speaker evaluates evidence and attempts to convince the audience that their conclusion is correct. The challenge is to accept a certain carefully crafted view of the facts presented.

Value: This kind of persuasion tries to convince the audience that a certain thing is good or bad, moral or immoral, valuable or worthless. It focuses less on knowledge and more on beliefs and values.

Policy: This speech is a call to action, arguing that something should be done, improved, or changed. Its goal is action from the audience, but it also seeks passive agreement with the proposition proposed. It appeals to both reason and emotion, and tells listeners what they can do and how to do it.

Logical Fallacies

A fallacy is, essentially, an error in reasoning. In persuasive speech, logical fallacies are instances of reasoning flaws that make an argument invalid. For example, a premature generalization occurs when you form a general rule based on only one or a few specific cases, which do not represent all possible cases. An illustration of this is the statement, "Bob Marley was a Rastafarian singer. Therefore, all Rastafarians sing."

A common fallacy in reasoning is the *post hoc ergo propter hoc* ("after this, therefore because of this") or the false-cause fallacy. These occur in cause/effect reasoning, which may either go from cause to effect or effect to cause.

They happen when an inadequate cause is offered for a particular effect; when the possibility of more than one cause is ignored; and when a connection between a particular cause and a particular effect is not made.

> Learn more about
> **Post Hoc Fallacy**
> http://www.sjsu.edu/depts/itl/graphics/adhom/posthoc.html

> An example of a *post hoc*: Our sales shot up thirty-five percent after we ran that television campaign; therefore the campaign caused the increase in sales.

It might have been a cause, of course, but more evidence is needed to prove it.

> An example of an **inadequate cause for a particular effect**: An Iraqi truck driver reported that Saddam Hussein had nuclear weapons; therefore, Saddam Hussein is a threat to world security.

More causes are needed to prove the conclusion.

> An example of **ignoring the possibility of more than one possible cause**: John Brown was caught out in a thunderstorm and his clothes were wet before he was rescued; therefore, he developed influenza the next day was because he got wet.

Being chilled may have played a role in the illness, but Brown would have had to contract the influenza virus before he would come down with it whether or not he had gotten wet.

> An example of **failing to make a connection between a particular cause and an effect** assigned to it. Anna fell into a putrid pond on Saturday; on Monday she came down with polio; therefore, the pond caused the polio.

This, of course, is not acceptable unless the poliovirus is found in a sample of water from the pond. A connection must be proven.

Argumentation

A logical argument consists of three stages. First, **state the premises** of the argument. These are the propositions which are necessary for the argument to continue. They are the evidence or reasons for accepting the argument and its conclusions.

Premises (or assertions) are often indicated by phrases such as "because," "since," "obviously," and so on. (The phrase "obviously" is often viewed with suspicion, as it can be used to intimidate others into accepting suspicious premises. If something doesn't seem obvious to you, don't be afraid to question it. You can always say, "Oh, yes, you're right, it is obvious" when you've heard the explanation.)

Next, **use the premises** to derive further propositions by a process known as inference. In inference, one proposition is arrived at on the basis of one or more other propositions already accepted. There are various forms of valid inference. The propositions arrived at by inference may then be used in further inference. Inference is often denoted by phrases such as "implies that" or "therefore."

Finally, **conclude the argument** with the proposition that is affirmed on the basis of the premises and inference. Conclusions are often indicated by phrases such as "therefore," "it follows that" "we conclude" and so on. The conclusion is often stated as the final stage of inference.

Classical Argument

The classical argument structure below uses unity, coherence, and emphasis effectively. In its simplest form, the classical argument has five main parts:

The **introduction**, which warms up the audience, establishes goodwill and rapport with the readers, and announces the general theme or thesis of the argument.

The **narration**, which summarizes relevant background material, provides any information the audience needs to know about the environment and circumstances that produce the argument, and set up the stakes—what's at risk in this question.

The **confirmation**, which lays out in a logical order (usually strongest to weakest or most obvious to most subtle) the claims that support the thesis, providing evidence for each claim.

The **refutation** and concession, which looks at opposing viewpoints to the writer's claims, anticipating objections from the audience, and allowing as much of the opposing viewpoints as possible without weakening the thesis.

The **summation**, which provides a strong conclusion, amplifies the force of the argument and shows the readers that this solution is the best at meeting the circumstances.

STYLE, TONE, VOICE, AND POINT OF VIEW AS PART OF RHETORICAL STRATEGY

Style and Tone

Often writers have an emotional stake in the subject; and their purpose, either explicitly or implicitly, is to convey those feelings to the reader. In such cases, the writing is generally subjective: that is, it stems from opinions, judgments, values, ideas, and feelings.

In literature, style means a distinctive manner of expression and applies to all levels of language, beginning at the phonemic level with word choices, alliteration, assonance, and others, moving to the syntactic level, characterized by length of sentences, choice of structure and phraseology (diction), and patterns, and even extending beyond the sentence to paragraphs and chapters. Critical readers determine what is distinctive about the writer's use of these elements. All of these are instrumental in creating tone.

The tone of a written passage is the author's attitude toward the subject matter. The tone (mood, feeling) is revealed through the qualities of the writing itself and is a direct product of such stylistic elements as language and sentence structure. The tone of the written passage is much like a speaker's voice; instead of being spoken, however, it is the product of words on a page.

Tone may be thought of generally as positive, negative, or neutral. Below is a statement about snakes that demonstrates this.

> Many species of snakes live in Florida. Some of those species, both poisonous and non-poisonous, have habitats that coincide with those of human residents of the state.

The voice of the writer in this statement is neutral. The sentences are declarative (not exclamations or fragments or questions). The adjectives are few and nondescript—*many, some, poisonous* (balanced with *non-poisonous*). Nothing much in this brief paragraph would alert the reader to the feelings of the writer about snakes. The paragraph has a neutral, objective, detached, impartial tone.

Then again, if the writer's attitude toward snakes involves admiration, or even affection, the tone would generally be positive:

> Florida's snakes are a tenacious bunch. When they find their habitats invaded by humans, they cling to their home territories as long as they can, as if vainly attempting to fight off the onslaught of the human hordes.

An additional message emerges in this paragraph: the writer quite clearly favors snakes over people. The writer uses adjectives like *tenacious* to describe feelings about snakes. The writer also humanizes the reptiles, making them brave, beleaguered creatures. Obviously, the writer is more sympathetic to snakes than to people in this paragraph.

If the writer's attitude toward snakes involves active dislike and fear, then the tone would also reflect that attitude by being negative:

> Countless species of snakes, some more dangerous than others, still lurk on the urban fringes of Florida's towns and cities. They will often invade domestic spaces, terrorizing people and their pets.

Here, obviously, the snakes are the villains. They *lurk,* they *invade,* and they *terrorize.* The tone of this paragraph might be said to be distressed about snakes.

In the same manner, a writer can use language to portray characters as good or bad. A writer uses positive and negative adjectives, as seen above, to convey the manner of a character.

Voice and Point of View

There are at least thirteen possible choices for point of view (voice) in literature as demonstrated and explained by Wallace Hildick in his *13 Types of Narrative*. However, for purposes of helping students write essays about literature, three, or possibly four, are adequate.

The importance of teaching students to use this aspect of a piece of literature to write about it is not just as an analytic exercise but also should help them think about how a writer's choices impact the overall effect of the work.

Point of view or voice is essentially through whose eyes the reader sees the action. The most common is the **third-person objective**. If the story is seen from this point of view, the reader watches the action, hears the dialogue, reads descriptions and from all of those must deduce characterization—what sort of person a character is. In this point of view, an unseen narrator tells the reader what is happening, using the third person, he, she, it, they. The effect of this point of view is usually a feeling of distance from the plot. More responsibility is on the reader to make judgments than in other points of view. However, the author may intrude and evaluate or comment on the characters or the action.

> Learn more about
> **Writing Fiction**
> http://crofsblogs.typepad.com/fiction/2003/07/narrative_voice.html

The voice of the **first-person** narrator is often used also. The reader sees the action through the eyes of an actor in the story who is also telling the story. In writing about a story that uses this voice, the narrator must be analyzed as a character. What sort of person is this? What is this character's position in the story—observer, commentator, and actor? Can the narrator be believed, or is he/she biased? The value of this voice is that, while the reader is able to follow the narrator around and see what is happening through that character's eyes, the reader is also able to feel what the narrator feels. For this reason, the writer can involve the reader more intensely in the story itself and move the reader by invoking feelings—pity, sorrow, anger, hate, confusion, disgust. Many of the most memorable novels, such as Jane Austen's *Jane Eyre*, are written in this point of view.

Another voice often used may best be titled **omniscient** because the reader is able to get into the mind of more than one character or sometimes all the characters. This point of view can also bring greater involvement of the reader in the story. By knowing what a character is thinking and feeling, the reader is able to empathize when a character feels great pain and sorrow, which tends to make a work memorable, such as Leo Tolstoy's *War and Peace*. On the other hand, knowing what a character is thinking makes it possible to get into the mind of a pathological murderer and may elicit horror or disgust.

Omniscient can be broken down into **third-person omniscient** or **first-person omniscient**. In third-person omniscient, the narrator is not seen or known or acting in the story but is able to watch and record not only what is happening or being said but also what characters are thinking. In first-person omniscient on the other hand, the narrator plays a role in the story but can also record what other characters are thinking.

It is possible, of course, that the narrator is the pathological murderer, which creates an effect quite different than a story where the thoughts of the murderer are known but the narrator is standing back and reporting his behavior, thoughts, and intents.

Point of view or voice is a powerful tool in the hands of a skillful writer. The questions to be answered in writing an essay about a literary work are: What point of view has this author used? What effect does it have on the story? If it had been written in a different voice, how would the story be different?

Most credible literary works are consistent in point of view but not always, so consistency is another aspect that should be analyzed. Does the point of view change? Where does it vary? Does it help or hurt the effect of the story?

RECOGNITION OF BIAS, DISTINGUISHING BETWEEN FACT AND OPINION, AND IDENTIFYING STEREOTYPES, INFERENCES, AND ASSUMPTIONS

Your students will enjoy sharing their opinions. Some of them may be voicing what they have heard from others, while some are discovering their own voices. All are trying to make sense of their worlds. Helping them distinguish between fact and opinion, realize conclusions, and make inferences develops critical reasoning.

Bias in Interpretation

Everyone is biased in some way because everyone has a perspective—a way of perceiving or preferring. While objectivity is a goal, we often fall short with our subjective perceptions and attitudes. What we want to avoid, however, is to be so slanted that we are unfairly biased. This weakens are credibility and undercuts the force of our argument.

What we need to do then is to avoid conscious bias and be sensitive to unconscious bias because preconceptions can compromise integrity of research. Conscious (deliberate) bias is unethical. Unconscious bias can be difficult to detect and/or control. It reflects the mentality of the analyst. You should be mentally alert to detect bias. Avoid racial, sexist, ageist, ethnic, and religious bias whenever possible. Sometimes the bias is more subtle and thus harder to detect.

Personal bias—For example, a researcher with an on-the-job injury may be partial in job safety studies.

Cultural bias—For example, a person with a strong work ethic may be partial in a study of the chronically unemployed.

Professional bias—For example, a teacher with a set work pattern may not be receptive to an alternative method.

Evaluating Sources

When evaluating sources, first go through this checklist to make sure the source is even worth reading:
- Title (How relevant is it to your topic?)
- Date (How current is the source?)
- Organization (What institution is this source coming from?)
- Length (How in depth does it go?)

Check for signs of bias:
- Does the author or publisher have political ties or religious views that could affect their objectivity?
- Is the author or publisher associated with any special-interest groups that might only see one side of an issue, such as Greenpeace or the National Rifle Association?
- How fairly does the author treat opposing views?
- Does the language of the piece show signs of bias?

Keep an open mind while reading, and don't let opposing viewpoints prevent you from absorbing the text. Remember that you are not judging the author's work, you are examining its assumptions, assessing its evidence and weighing its conclusions.

Facts and Opinions

Facts are statements that are verifiable. **Opinions** are statements that must be supported in order to be accepted. Facts are used to support opinions. For example, "Jane is a bad girl" is an opinion. However, "Jane hit her sister with a baseball bat" is a *fact* upon which the opinion is based. Judgments are opinions—decisions or declarations based on observation or reasoning that express approval or disapproval. Facts report what has happened or exists and come from observation, measurement, or calculation. Facts can be tested and verified whereas opinions and judgments cannot. They can only be supported with facts.

Most statements cannot be so clearly distinguished. "I believe that Jane is a bad girl" is a fact. The speaker knows what he/she believes. However, it obviously includes a judgment that could be disputed by another person who might believe otherwise. Judgments are not usually so firm. They are, rather, plausible opinions that provoke thought or lead to factual development.

See chart on Fact and Opinion below.

Conclusions

Conclusions are drawn as a result of a line of reasoning. Whether inductive or deductive, a conclusion is an analysis of what the data means. Given all the facts, all the opinions, all the details, the reader can draw a conclusion.

> Joe DiMaggio, a Yankees' center-fielder, was replaced by Mickey Mantle in 1952.

This is a fact. If necessary, evidence can be produced to support this.

> First-year players are more ambitious than seasoned players.

This is an opinion. There is no proof to support that every first-year player feels this way.

Fact vs. Opinion

Use the chart below to identify both facts and opinions in a text and be sure to explain how you know the details you write down are either facts or opinions.

	Text Details & Direct Quotes From the Text	Explain How You Know the Details are Facts or Opinions
Facts		
Opinions		

http://www.greece.k12.ny.us/instruction/ela/6-12/Tools/factvsopinion.pdf

COMPETENCY 4.0 INTERPRETING LITERATURE: POETRY

Skill 4.1 Interpret a poetry selection from English, American, or world literature

COMPETENCY 5.0 INTERPRETING LITERATURE: PROSE

Skill 5.1 Interpret a prose selection from English, American, or world literature of any period.

These two essays will have the same format and will be approached in the same way. The only distinction is the form of literature being discussed. See this book's preface for scoring rubric.

Each is one of four essays that you will write in a two-hour period, so you will want to budget thirty minutes per essay. Plan to spend five or ten minutes reading the prompt and selection carefully. Spend another five minutes prewriting. Use whatever method works well for you: outline, free write, make brief notes. Spend ten to fifteen minutes writing your essay and use the remaining time to edit.

Read the prompt very closely. It will typically ask you to focus on a particular theme. Make sure to focus on what the prompt is suggesting instead of discussing irrelevant aspects of the text.

Poetry: Read the poem carefully. If you cannot understand it, read it again as if you were saying it aloud. Look at the punctuation within the poem. This often helps you understand the grouping of ideas. In this discussion, we'll focus on "Do not go gentle into that good night," by Dylan Thomas.

Prose: While prose is not usually as dense as poetry and possibly more easily understood, you should still do a careful read of the selection. In this discussion, we'll focus on "The Story of an Hour," a very short but extremely powerful short story.

OVERVIEW FOR WRITING THE ESSAY

In their training to be scorers for these essays, readers are told to think of these essays as somewhat polished first drafts. However, that does not mean you can be hasty or careless. Your essay should reflect the same standards you would expect of your students. Use the standard five paragraph essay if you are comfortable with it but you are free to use whatever development strategy in which you feel confident and capable.

Provide an introduction. In your opening paragraph, establish the purpose of your essay. Avoid direct statements, such as "In this essay, I will analyze the literary elements in Dylan Thomas' poem 'Do not go gentle into that good night.'" Avoid the obvious, such as "Kate Chopin uses diction and style in her short story 'The Story of an Hour.'" All writers have a style and use diction.

Instead, write an interesting paragraph that will hook the reader's attention and still explain your main thesis and purpose.

Develop your thesis clearly. Your essay should have unity, coherence, and balance. This is not the time to throw in everything you know about poetry or prose. You must have control of your ideas and your writing style.

Analyze; Avoid Paraphrase or Summary

In these essays, you should analyze how the various literary elements or devices (Skill 1.2) develop the theme and/or enhance the effect of the poem or prose selection. Yes, Dylan Thomas writes about his father's death in "Do not go gentle into that good night"—that is obvious. What's needed, however, is an analysis of how Thomas uses metaphor, repetition, and rhyme to develop the beseeching tone. Why does he use the villanelle, a light verse form, for such a serious subject?

Summarizing the plot of "The Story of an Hour" is a low-level skill, and your goal here is to convince your reader that you have the critical thinking skills of an English teacher. Relate the events only as a way of illustrating the thesis, which leads to the next point.

Show, Don't Tell

Provide specific examples from the work to support the points you make. Do not write "Dylan Thomas uses many metaphors for death in his poem." Instead, incorporate lines from the poem to prove your point.

> Comparing death to darkness, Thomas pleads with his father to fight against "the good night" and to "rage against the dying of the light."

Do not make claims you are unsure about. An inaccurate claim is worse than a brief response. For example, in "The Story of an Hour," Chopin is deliberately ambiguous in her closing lines. But to write that "Chopin's closing line indicates that the main character dies from the joy of seeing her husband" is not supported by the details the story.

While you may be hurrying to meet the time requirements, be sure to close your essay effectively. Restate your thesis but don't merely repeat it. You have made your case and your closing should be a sound recapitulation of the main ideas.

Irritations for English Teachers

Most scorers for teacher certification essays are experienced English instructors who have developed personal biases against common problems in essays. They will overlook some of them but would hope that prospective English teachers would not make these mistakes. However, when the writer has little or no control over spelling, grammar, and punctuation, the score on the essay is naturally affected. Here's an incomplete list of thorny irritations. You should also review information in **Skill 2.2**.

Using *its* and *it's* incorrectly. *Its* is the possessive pronoun; *it's* is the contraction for it is.

Using the apostrophe incorrectly. Review the use of apostrophes in making nouns possessive. Review plural possessives.

Using the existential *it*. Begin sentences with strong subjects. Be sure the pronoun *it* has a clear antecedent. For example, "It is important to note" is a weak sentence beginning. Instead, you could write "Repetition is an important element in Dylan Thomas' poem. "It was a dark and stormy night" is unnecessarily repetitive. Instead, write "The night was dark and stormy."

Misspelling literary terms and incorrect word choice. For example, don't write *smile* for *simile* or confuse *affect* and *effect*.

Writing illegibly. Although scorers are trained to look past poor handwriting, this is sometimes hard and the psychological impact on your score cannot be measured. Scorers should be able to read your essay once. If your handwriting is weak, then print your response. If your handwriting is flowery and decorative, simplify it. Don't dot your *i's* with hearts or end words with fancy curlicues.

General Strategies for Writing an Essay

The strategies below which apply to your own experience in writing essays for the certification exam can also be adapted for your students.

The essay that you are to write must demonstrate the ability to write on a literary topic. As you practice the steps provided to prepare for this test, please keep in mind that this review will not teach you how to analyze literature. It is expected that analyzing literature has been a focus of your course of study. The following steps in writing an essay in a timed situation will aid you in preparing to write the essay in the most time efficient manner possible. Keep in mind that a good essay has focus, organization, support, and correct usage.

Understanding the Question

When you receive your question, the first task is to decide what the question is asking you to do. Look for key words that will establish the purpose of your essay. Examine the following chart and review the key words and purpose each word establishes. Please note that for each key word the purpose and an example are illustrated.

KEY WORD	PURPOSE	EXAMPLE
Analyze	To examine the parts of a literary selection	Read a passage and analyze how the author achieves tone using diction and imagery
Compare	To identify the similarities	Read "I Hear America Singing" by Walt Whitman and "Chicago" by Carl Sandburg and compare each poet's attitude about America.
Contrast	To identify the differences	Read "Thanatopsis" by Bryant and "Do not go gentle into that good night" by Dylan Thomas and contrast how each poet uses imagery to express his distinct views of death.
Discuss	Examine in detail	Read a poem and discuss how the poet establishes the mood using imagery and word choice.
Explain	Provide reasons, examples or clarify the meaning	Read the opening passage of *The Great Gatsby* and explain how the author establishes the tone of the novel.

When writing an essay on literature, consider the following before you begin to prewrite.

Identify the elements for analysis. If you are asked to examine the tone of poem, you might need to look at imagery and word choice. If you are asked to examine prose and explain how a writer creates mood, you should examine the diction, style, imagery, syntax, structure, and selection of detail.

Decide on your main idea. Use the question as a guideline. However, do not merely restate the question. Make sure that in restating the topic you have taken a position on how you will answer the prompt. For example, you might be asked to read Whitman's poem "I Hear America Singing" and discuss not only the tone of the poem but also how Whitman creates the tone. If you wish to receive a high score on the essay, state your main idea clearly.

A well-crafted thesis statement can help both writers and readers. Writers can stay on topic and develop their thesis statement with appropriate and relevant details. Readers can better understand the main idea and the supporting ideas.

By following these steps, writers can develop the skill to formulate clear and strong thesis statements.

Write the Thesis Statement

First, you should identify the topic.
> I am going to write about the tone and how it is created in the poem "I Hear America Singing" by Walt Whitman.

Second, state your point of view about the topic.
> The upbeat and optimistic tone of Whitman's poem is created by his word choice, structure and imagery.

Third, summarize the main points you will make in your essay.
> Whitman creates an optimistic tone through his choice of words, parallel structure, and images.

State the Main Point of Each Body Paragraph and Organize Support

Using a five-paragraph essay format is one of many ways to respond to literature. It is a basic structure that encourages development and coherence. As writers become more sophisticated, they will progress beyond this formula.

PARAGRAPH	PURPOSE	SUPPORT
1st Intro	Main idea statement	
2nd 1st body paragraph	Main point 1	Quotes or specifics from the text with analysis or explanation of how each detail supports your main point.
3rd 2nd body Paragraph	Main point 2	Quotes or specifics from the text with analysis or explanation of how each detail supports your main point.
4th 3rd Body Paragraph	Main point 3	Quotes or specifics from the text with analysis or explanation of how each detail supports Your main point.
5th Closing	Summarize ideas	

Consider Audience, Purpose, and Tone

Keep in mind as you write this essay that your purpose is to demonstrate literary skill by reading an unfamiliar passage or poem and examining its elements. It is crucial to avoid giving a summary of the piece or writing your personal reaction to the work. Your audience is familiar with the piece and thus does not need to have the work summarized. In fact, the readers of your essay have been trained to look for focus, organization, support, and correct usage. Finally, the tone is formal.

Techniques to Maintain Focus

- **Focus on a main point.** The point should be clear to readers, and all sentences in the paragraph should relate to it.

- **Start the paragraph with a topic sentence.** This should be a general, one-sentence summary of the paragraph's main point, relating back to the thesis and forward to the content of the paragraph. (A topic sentence is sometimes unnecessary if the paragraph continues a developing idea clearly introduced in a preceding paragraph, or if the paragraph appears in a narrative of events where generalizations might interrupt the flow of the story.)

- **Stick to the point.** Eliminate sentences that do not support the topic sentence.

- **Be flexible.** If you do not have enough evidence to support the claim of your topic sentence, do not fall into the trap of wandering or introducing new ideas within the paragraph. Either find more evidence, or adjust the topic sentence to corroborate with the evidence that is available.

CRITICAL APPROACHES

To analyze a work of literature, no matter the genre, you can use the critical approaches discussed below. Some are more appropriate than others for particular texts. Not all works can be viewed through the lens of feminism or Marxism, for example.

The New Criticism

New Criticism treats literary texts as independent entities requiring little or no consideration of external factors such as the identity of the author or the society in which he or she lives. Proponents of the New Criticism believe that the literary text itself is the paramount concern.

Works are analyzed, evaluated, and interpreted through what is called "close reading." Close reading emphasizes genre and literary form; a work's theme and a writer's rendition of it; plot and character development; poetic meter, rhythm, and, if applicable, rhyme; metaphor, simile, and other figurative or literal imagery; evaluation of literary quality; analysis and interpretation of a work's meaning.

The goal of close reading is to arrive, without biographical or sociological distractions, at an objective understanding and appreciation of a literary work

Resources for Literary Theory
http://vos.ucsb.edu/browse.asp?id=2718

The New Criticism's approach is summed up in two key literary anthologies: *Understanding Poetry* (4th ed.) and *Understanding Fiction*, both edited by Cleanth Brooks and Robert Penn Warren..

Structuralism and Deconstructionism

The structural approach is to examine the structure of a literary work without regard for external influences. This is an attempt to quantify objectively certain criteria that a work must follow. Emphasis is placed on the work as a whole and its place within its genre.

In deconstruction theory, only the text itself is examined. This is done through a very close reading. Formulated by Jacques Derrida in the 1960s, it has been unjustly called "destruction criticism" because of its detailed analytical approach.

Both of these theories are much more complex that explained here and require further study.

Marxist Criticism

Based on the ideas of Karl Marx, some of the key components of this critical theory follow:

- Class conflict drives the history of human civilization.

- The capitalists or bourgeoisie (those who possess and control economic capital) exploit and oppress the proletariat (the working classes) for their own economic and political benefit.

- The workers must therefore unite to overthrow the capitalists and their socio-economic system. This will result in a "dictatorship of the proletariat" that will create a classless society in which most, if not all, private property is abolished in favor of collective ownership. The result will be a "workers' paradise"; eventually the nation-states themselves will dissolve and be replaced by a unitary, worldwide communist society free of class conflict.

- Marxist orthodoxy holds that the triumph of communism is inevitable, and that Marxist doctrine is validated by its scientific and materialist approach to history.

- Therefore the Marxist critic uses these ideas to scrutinize literary works, which are analyzed and interpreted to determine their "revolutionary" or "proletarian," "bourgeois" or "reactionary," character.

- Works focused primarily on social injustice and abuses of power have drawn sustained attention from Marxist critics. These include: *The Jungle* by Upton Sinclair; Stephen Crane's *Maggie, a Girl of the Streets*; Theodore Dreiser's *Sister Carrie* and *An American Tragedy*; John Steinbeck's *Grapes of Wrath*; Virginia Woolf's *A Room of One's Own*; and Dostoevsky's *Crime and Punishment* and *The Brothers Karamazov*.

Feminist Criticism

Feminist critics emphasize the ways that literary works are informed and inspired by an author's gender, by an author's ideas about gender and gender roles, and by social norms regarding gender. Of prime concern to the feminist critical enterprise is the advocacy of women as intellectual, social, and artistic equals to men. Feminist criticism is not limited to works by women, nor is it hostile or opposed to male writers or males in general.

"Feminism" could just as easily be referred to as "feminisms." There are a variety of schools of thought that make the plural form more accurate than the singular. Some feminists emphasize class, others race, still others sexual orientation, when critiquing texts or social norms and conditions affecting women's lives.

When introducing feminist writing and criticism to high school students, teachers should consider giving a comprehensive summary of what feminism is, and when, where, and why it arose. Some students will likely have the impression that feminism originated in the 1960s, despite the fact that it has existed for over 200 years. To counter any such misconceptions, teachers can assign excerpts or entire works by these 18th or 19th century authors:

- Mary Wollstonecraft
- Margaret Fuller
- Sojourner Truth
- Susan B. Anthony
- Elizabeth Cady Stanton
- Frederick Douglass

Some popular 20th century works relevant to feminist thought and suitable for high school students are listed below.

- *A Room of One's Own* by Virginia Woolf (nonfiction)
- *The Yellow Wallpaper* by Charlotte Perkins Gilman (novella)
- *The Color Purple* by Alice Walker (novel)
- *Beloved* by Toni Morrison (novel)
- *Good Woman* by Lucille Clifton (poems)
- *She Had Some Horses* by Joy Harjo (poems)
- *The Joy Luck Club* by Amy Tan (novel)
- *The Secret Life of Bees* by Sue Monk Kidd (novel)

There are numerous up-to-date anthologies of women's literature and feminist criticism available through major publishers. The groundbreaking anthology, *The New Feminist Criticism*, edited by Elaine Showalter, offers an excellent variety of feminist essays on Western literature. Some of these essays are rather dated but the collection does give a solid overview of key concerns that animated "second wave" feminism in the 1960s and 70s.

Psychoanalytic, or Freudian, Criticism

Based initially on the works of Sigmund Freud, this theory has been expanded to include the ideas of other psychoanalysts.

Freudian psychoanalysis holds that the human mind is a tripartite structure composed of the id, which generates and seeks to satisfy all of a person's urges and desires; the superego, which "polices" and counters the id; and the ego, which is the psychic result of the id/superego conflict. The ego is characterized by a person's thoughts and behaviors.

The formation of human character—including sexual behavior—begins at birth. The infant is said to pass through various stages—the oral stage, the anal stage, and so on—as its needs and urges arise and are either satisfied or frustrated; and as it learns (or doesn't learn) to master human relationships and bodily functions.

All humans are said to have inexorable conflicts between drives such as Eros and Thanatos (the sex drive and the death wish), which are also played out in the contests between id and superego.

Neurotic behavior results from fixations on one of the above physical factors, or from an imbalance in the powers of the id and superego, or from deeply embedded (unconscious) memories of pleasant or unpleasant experiences, or from a combination of these. Neurosis is usually rooted in infancy or early childhood.

To discover the nature of a person's mind, the psychoanalyst looks for recurrent thoughts, images, speech patterns, and behaviors evident in the person being analyzed. By carefully observing (especially listening to) a patient, the psychoanalyst uncovers previously unknown truths about the hows and whys of the patient's predicament.

The psychoanalytic literary critic applies Freudian theories to writings and authors in order to better understand the psychological underpinnings of literary works, writers, and, sometimes, society itself.

Writers that have garnered much attention from Freudian critics include Edgar Allen Poe, the Marquis de Sade, Moses, Madame de Stahl, and William S. Burroughs. Not surprisingly, sex and violence feature prominently in these writers' works. Representative examples of psychoanalytic criticism include "Moses and Monotheism" by Sigmund Freud, and *Edgar Allen Poe* by Marie Bonaparte.

Reader-Response

In this critical theory, the readers create meaning through their individual understandings and responses. Some critics focus solely on the readers' experiences; other critics experiment on defined groups to determine reader response.

COMPETENCY 6.0 ISSUES IN ENGLISH: UNDERSTANDING LITERARY ISSUES

Skill 6.1 Evaluate the argument and rhetorical features of a passage that addresses an issue in the study of English.

In this essay, you will be reading a passage that addresses an issue in the study of English. The text may deal with topics such as the nature of literary interpretation, the value of studying literature, the qualities that define the discipline of literary study, or the kind of literary works we choose to read and teach and why we make those choices.

To prepare for this essay, review the information for **Competency 4.0 and 5.0** and apply the same process and skills. See this book's preface for scoring rubric.

Also, review **Skill 3.2** to help you evaluate both the argument and rhetorical features of the passage.

Sample Essay

The following is an example of an essay promoting reading for enjoyment within the classroom. As you read it, note the way the author develops the idea.

> Reading for enjoyment enables us to go to places in the world we will never be able to visit; we can learn about the enchantments of a particular place, so we will set a goal of going there someday. When *Under the Tuscan Sun* by Frances Mayes was published, it became a best seller. It also increased tourism to Italy. Many of the readers of that book visited Italy for the first time in their lives.
>
> In fiction, we can live through experiences that we will never encounter. We delve into feelings that are similar to our own or are so far removed from our own that we are filled with wonder and curiosity. In fact, we read because we're curious—curious to visit, experience, and know new and different things. The reader lives with a crowd of people and a vast landscape. The reading is constantly enriching life, and the mind is constantly expanding. To read is to grow. Sometimes the experience of reading a particular book or story is so delicious that we go back and read it again and again, such as the works of Jane Austen. We keep track of what is truly happening in the world when we read current best-sellers because they not only reflect what everyone else is interested in right now, they can influence trends. We can know in-depth what television news cannot cram in by reading publications like *Time* and *Newsweek*.

How do we model this wonderful gift for our students? We can bring those interesting stories into our classrooms and share the excitement we feel when we discover them. We can relate things that make us laugh so students may see the humor and laugh with us. We can vary the established curriculum to include something we are reading that we want to share. The tendency of students nowadays is to receive all of their information from television or the Internet. It's important for the teacher to help students understand that television and the Internet are not substitutes for reading. They should be an accessory, an extension, and a springboard for reading.

Another way teachers can inspire students to become readers is to assign a book that you have never read before and read along with them, chapter by chapter. Run a contest and the winner gets to pick a book that you and they will read chapter by chapter. If you are excited about it and are experiencing satisfaction from the reading, that excitement will be contagious. Be sure that the discussion sessions allow for students to relate what they are thinking and feeling about what they are reading. Lively discussions and the opportunity to express their own feelings will lead to more spontaneous reading.

You can also hand out a reading list of your favorite books and spend some time telling the students what you liked about each. Make sure the list is diverse so include nonfiction along with fiction. Don't forget that a good biography or autobiography may encourage students to read beyond thrillers and detective stories.

When the class is discussing the latest movie, whether formally as a part of the curriculum or informally and incidentally, if the movie is based on a book, this is a good opportunity to demonstrate how much more can be derived from the reading than from the watching. Or how the two combined make the experience more satisfying and worthwhile. What incidents or characters are missing from the Harry Potter movies? How does Anne Hathaway in *Pride and Prejudice* match Austen's description of Elizabeth Bentley?

Share with your students the excitement you have for reading. Successful writers are usually good readers. The two go hand-in-hand.

Prewriting Analysis

After reading the above selection, a writer, using the information in **Skill 3.2**, might make these notes before writing the essay.

1. *Uses logical appeal (logos) to argue that reading for enjoyment is worthwhile.* Provides facts and examples to persuade the audience.

2. *Uses fact, value, and policy as a rhetorical strategy.*
   - Facts: evaluates evidence to convince the reader; carefully crafts view of the facts.
   - Value: persuades reader that reading for enjoyment if valuable; the focus here is less on knowledge and more on belief and values.
   - Policy: calls audience to action by providing strategies to model reading for enjoyment.

3. *Uses some elements of the classical argument*
   - The **introduction**, which warms up the audience, establishes goodwill and rapport with the readers, and announces the general theme or thesis of the argument.

     ➢ Writer assert that "Reading for enjoyment enables us to go to places in the world we never be able to visit," draws the audience in by using "we" ("we can learn about the enchantments of a particular place" and then establishes rapport ("we will set a goal of going there someday"). The writer engages the audience by referring to popular movie.

   - The **narration**, which summarizes relevant background material, provides any information the audience needs to know about the environment and circumstances that produce the argument, and set up the stakes—what's at risk in this question.

     Writer provides additional support and illustrates what is at stake.
     ➢ We can live through experiences that we will never encounter
     ➢ We delve into feelings that are similar to our own or are so far removed from our own that we are filled with wonder and curiosity.
     ➢ We keep track of what is truly happening in the world when we read current best-sellers because they not only reflect what everyone else is interested in right now, they can influence trends. We can know in-depth what television news cannot cram in.

   - The **confirmation**, lays out in a logical order (usually strongest to weakest or most obvious to most subtle) the claims that support the thesis, providing evidence for each claim.

     ➢ We read because we're curious

- The reading is constantly enriching life, and the mind is constantly expanding.
- To read is to grow.

- We keep track of what is truly happening in the world when we read current best-sellers because they not only reflect what everyone else is interested in right now, they can influence trends. We can know in-depth what television news cannot cram in.

- The **refutation and concession**, which looks at opposing viewpoints to the writer's claims, anticipating objections from the audience, and allowing as much of the opposing viewpoints as possible without weakening the thesis.

  - The tendency of students nowadays is to receive all of their information from television or the Internet. It's important for the teacher to help students understand that television and the Internet are not substitutes for reading. They should be an accessory, an extension, and a springboard for reading.

- The **summation**, which provides a strong conclusion, amplifies the force of the argument and shows the readers that this solution is the best at meeting the circumstances.

  - Share with your students the excitement you have for reading. Successful writers are usually good readers. The two go hand-in-hand.

COMPETENCY 7.0 ISSUES IN ENGLISH: LITERARY ISSUES AND LITERARY TEXTS

Skill 7.1 Take and defend a position on an issue in the study of English, using references to works of literature to support that position.

This essay deals with similar topics as the one preceding it, but instead of evaluating someone else's argument, you will create and defend your own.

To write your essay, follow the General Strategies for Writing an Essay as discussed in **Competency 4.0**. See this book's preface for scoring rubric.

Choose a stance to take on the statement provided. Then develop a thesis statement that incorporates two literary works from the list provided as support for your argument.

Although the literary works provided will change, they may include some of the works below:

Chinua Achebe, *Things Fall Apart*
Isabel Allende, *The House of the Spirits*
Jane Austen, *Pride and Prejudice*
Pearl S. Buck, *The Good Earth*
Sandra Cisneros, *The House on Mango Street*
Joseph Conrad, *Heart of Darkness*
Charles Dickens, *Great Expectations*
Ralph Ellison, *Invisible Man*
F. Scott Fitzgerald, *The Great Gatsby*
William Golding, *Lord of the Flies*
Lorraine Hansberry, *A Raisin in the Sun*
Ernest Hemingway, *A Farewell to Arms*
Homer, *The Odyssey*
Zora Neale Hurston, *Their Eyes Were Watching God*

Franz Kafka, *The Metamorphosis*
Maxine Hong Kingston, *The Woman Warrior*
Jamaica Kincaid, *Annie John*
Arthur Miller, *Death of a Salesman*
N. Scott Momaday, *House Made of Dawn*
J. D. Salinger, *The Catcher in the Rye*
William Shakespeare, *Romeo and Juliet*
Leslie Marman Silko, *Ceremony*
Mark Twain, *The Adventures of Huckleberry Finn*
Alice Walker, *The Color Purple*
Edith Wharton, *Ethan Frome*
Elie Wiesel, *Night*
Tennessee Williams, *The Glass Menagerie*

TEACHER CERTIFICATION STUDY GUIDE

COMPETENCY 8.0 TEACHING LITERATURE

Skill 8.1 Choose a work from a list of literary works provided. This will be used as the basis for your response.

PEDAGOGY

In this section of the test, you will respond to two constructed questions on teaching literature and responding to student writing in a one-hour time period. See **Competency 9.0** for responding to student writing.

For the response on teaching literature, select a work that you know well. Given the time constraints, you will not be able to develop a plan for a work with which you have limited knowledge.

Identify two literary features of the work that are central to teaching it. These are two concepts that you would want students to come away with after reading the particular text. Topics to focus on might include characterization techniques, literary devices, and narration choices. Cite specific examples from the work to support these concepts.

Identify two obstacles to understanding that students might experience when encountering the work. They should be specific to the work selected, not just a general discussion of problems students could face with any piece of literature.

Describe two instructional activities that would help students understand the literary features and/or overcome obstacles to understanding. Explain exactly how the activities would lead to greater understanding and conquering of obstacles in the text. See **Skill 3.1** for literature teaching techniques.

Demonstrate understanding of the varied kinds of knowledge, abilities, and skills that students bring to the English classroom. Consider a multimedia approach and discuss the most appropriate choices. Consider an integrated curriculum plan that would incorporate concepts from other subjects, such as history or science.

Identify the assessment methods you would use to determine how well your objectives were met.

To write your essay, follow the General Strategies for Writing an Essay discussed in **Competency 4.0**

TEACHER CERTIFICATION STUDY GUIDE

Comparison/Contrast Essay

Because you will be comparing (similarities) and contrasting (differences) two literary works, you should review the appropriate organizational strategies.

One particularly useful plan is the whole-by-whole strategy where you organize your essay by the main topics, such as the literary features. The subtopics would be the areas of analysis. A sample outline might look like this.

I. Open with strong introductory paragraph and thesis statement
II. Introduce literary feature 1 and give examples
    A. Obstacle 1
        1. Explain obstacle
        2. Describe two instructional activities
        3. Identify assessment methods
    B. Obstacle 2
        1. Explain obstacle
        2. Describe two instructional activities
        3. Identify assessment methods
III. Introduce literary feature 2 and give examples
    A. Obstacle 1
        1. Explain obstacle
        2. Describe two instructional activities
        3. Identify assessment methods
    B. Obstacle 2
        1. Explain obstacle
        2. Describe two instructional activities
        3. Identify assessment methods
IV. Close with recapitulation

To **compare**, use these conjunctions and expressions:

Short Conjunctions	Longer Expressions
Similarly, Likewise, ...the same... ...the same as... ...also... ..., too. both	In the same way, X is similar to Y in that (they)... X and Y are similar in that (they)... Like X, Y [verb]... In like manner, One way in which X is similar to Y is (that)... Another way in which X is similar to Y is (that)...

http://lrs.ed.uiuc.edu/students/fwalters/compcont.html

To **contrast**, use these conjunctions and expressions:

Short Conjunctions	Subordinating Conjunctions
However, In contrast, By contrast, ..., but ..., yet	On the other hand, even though + [sentence] although + [sentence] whereas + [sentence] unlike + [sentence] while + [sentence] nevertheless,

http://lrs.ed.uiuc.edu/students/fwalters/compcont.html

The literary works you will have to choose from are subject to change; the following list includes popular choices:

Chinua Achebe, *Things Fall Apart*
Henry James, *The Turn of the Screw*
Maya Angelou, *I Know Why the Caged Bird Sings*
Franz Kafka, *The Metamorphosis*
James Baldwin, *Go Tell It on the Mountain*
Jamaica Kincaid, *Annie John*
Beowulf
Harper Lee, *To Kill a Mockingbird*
Pearl S. Buck, *The Good Earth*
Lois Lowry, *The Giver*
Sandra Cisneros, *The House on Mango Street*
Arthur Miller, *The Crucible*
Stephen Crane, *The Red Badge of Courage*
George Orwell, *Animal Farm*
Charles Dickens, *Great Expectations*
William Shakespeare, *Romeo and Juliet*
Frederick Douglass, *Narrative of the Life of Frederick Douglass*
Leslie Marmon Silko, *Ceremony*
F. Scott Fitzgerald, *The Great Gatsby*
John Steinbeck, *The Grapes of Wrath*
Anne Frank, *The Diary of Anne Frank*
Amy Tan, *The Joy Luck Club*
William Gibson, *The Miracle Worker*
Mildred Taylor, *Roll of Thunder, Hear My Cry*
Lorraine Hansberry, *A Raisin in the Sun*
J. R. R. Tolkien, *The Hobbit*
Nathaniel Hawthorne, *The Scarlet Letter*
Thornton Wilder, *Our Town*
Homer, *The Odyssey*

Teachers should be familiar with professional resources that aid them in recognizing reader responses and teaching students the process of assessing their responses. One exceptional tool is Laurence Perrine's *Sound and Sense*, cited in the bibliography. Both the text itself and the teacher manual that accompanies it provide excellent activities that contribute to the student's ability to make interpretive and evaluative responses.

In addition, a variety of good student resources are available in most school and public libraries that provide models of critical analyses. The Twayne publications are book-length critiques of individual titles or of the body of work of a given author. *The Modern Critical Interpretations* series, edited by Harold Bloom, offers a collection of critical essays on individual titles in each book.

Gale Research Company also provides several series: *Nineteenth Century Literature Criticism, Twentieth Century Literature Criticism*, and *Contemporary Literary Criticism*, to name a few. These encyclopedic sets contain reprints of literary magazine articles that date from the author's own lifetime to the present. Students doing independent research will find these are invaluable tools.

PEDAGOGY SCORING FOR COMPETENCY 8.0 TEACHING LITERATURE

The question consists of three parts. The score range is 0 to 6. Points are distributed as follows:

Part A—2 points
> 1 point for each appropriate literary feature central to the work of literature. Each literary feature must be specific to the work chosen and appropriate for the grade level.

Part B—2 points
> 1 point for each appropriate obstacle to understanding, including the explanation for why the obstacle is likely. Each obstacle must be specific to the work chosen and appropriate for the grade level.

Part C—2 points
> 1 point for the discussion of each appropriate instructional activity designed to help students understand the literary features and/or overcome obstacles to understanding. Each instructional activity must be specific to the work chosen and appropriate for the grade level.

If the response contains a significant number of errors in the conventions of standard written English, one point will be subtracted from the total points earned for the question. Responses on a literary work other than one chosen from the list provided in the question will receive a score of 0.

The criteria for evaluating whether a literary feature, obstacle, or instructional activity is "appropriate" are established through a "model answers" methodology. This methodology is described as follows.

The "Model Answers" Methodology

For each question, experienced English teachers are asked to write representative responses that, in their estimation, are consistent with the knowledge that prospective beginning English teachers should have. These teachers are carefully chosen to represent the diverse perspectives and situations relevant to the testing population.

The question writer uses these "model answers" to develop a question-specific scoring guide for the question, creating a list of specific examples that would receive full credit. This list is considered to contain *examples* of correct answers, not all the possible correct answers.

The question-specific scoring guides based on model answers provide the basis for choosing the papers that will serve as benchmark and sample papers for the purpose of training the scorers at the scoring session for the question.

During the scoring session while reading student papers, scorers can add new answers to the scoring guide as they see fit.

Training at the scoring session is aimed to ensure that scorers do not score papers on the basis of their opinions or their own preferences but rather make judgments based on the carefully established criteria in the scoring guide.

COMPETENCY 9.0 RESPONDING TO STUDENT WRITING

Skill 9.1 Read an authentic piece of student writing and then assess the strengths and weaknesses of the writing. Identify errors in the conventions of standard written English and create a follow-up assignment that addresses the strengths or weaknesses of the student's writing.

PEDAGOGY

In the second of the two constructed response, you will read and assess a student paper. To prepare for this, begin by reviewing Skill 3.1 for tips on assessing student writing. Here are some additional guidelines.

Always **identify the positive aspects first**. What did the student writer do correctly? What are the strengths of the paper? Address the student by name and provide substantive feedback. To say "nice job" or "good try" will not help the student become a better writer. Be specific, such as "You explained irony very clearly."

Identify the weaknesses. This includes the content as well as the mechanics. Students are easily discouraged, especially when they think they have written a good paper and have it returned with red marks all over it. This feedback is very important so you want to be tactful and instructive, not demeaning. Sometimes you can use questions to make your point: "Did you review this last paragraph carefully for sentence errors?"

Be specific with your recommendations for revision. State not only what needs to be changed but also how to change it. Indicate where students can receive help. Suggest resources (visit the Writing Center, have another student peer review, visit an online grammar site). Even though students would prefer that you guide them through every step, you want them to develop independent learning skills that will benefit them throughout their lives.

Try to target major problems before pointing out minor ones. Marking spelling, capitalization, and punctuation errors is quickly done so spend more time discussing content, organization, and coherence.

Personalize the lesson plan as much as possible to reflect a clear understanding of the student's needs.

Create a follow-up assignment that focuses on the student's weaknesses. A typical assignment would have the student correct and rewrite this particular essay. Establish your criteria for achieving success and set a deadline.

TEACHER CERTIFICATION STUDY GUIDE

To write your essay, follow the General Strategies for Writing an Essay discussed in **Competency 4.0**

Pedagogy Scoring For Competency 9.0 Responding To Student Writing

The question consists of four parts. The score range is 0 to 6. Points are distributed as follows.

Part A—1 point for the identification of one significant strength and explanation of how it contributes to the paper's effectiveness.

Part B—1 point for the identification of one significant weakness and explanation of how it interferes with the paper's effectiveness.

Part C—2 points: 1 point for the correct identification of each of the two specific errors.

Part D—2 points for the discussion of the follow-up assignment that is connected to the strengths or weaknesses of the student's paper and that contributes to the development of the student as a writer.

If the response contains a significant number of errors in the conventions of standard written English, one point will be subtracted from the total points earned for the question. Responses on a literary work other than one chosen from the list provided in the question will receive a score of 0.

The criteria for evaluating whether a strength, weakness, error, or follow-up assignment is awarded the point or points are established through the "Model Answers" methodology. See the above description.

Resources

Abrams, M. H. ed. *The Norton Anthology of English Literature*. 6th ed. 2 vols. New York: Norton, 1979.

A comprehensive reference for English literature, containing selected works from *Beowulf* through the twentieth century and information about literary criticism.

Beach, Richard. "Strategic Teaching in Literature." *Strategic Teaching and Learning: Cognitive Instruction in the Content Areas*. Edited by Beau Fly Jones and others. ASCD Publications, 1987: 135-159.

A chapter dealing with a definition of and strategic teaching strategies for literature studies.

Brown, A. C. and others. *Grammar and Composition* 3rd Course. Boston: Houghton Mifflin, 1984.

A standard ninth-grade grammar text covering spelling, vocabulary, reading, listening, and writing skills.

Burmeister, L. E. *Reading Strategies for Middle and Secondary School Teachers*. Reading, MA: Addison-Wesley, 1978.

A resource for developing classroom strategies for reading and content area classes, using library references, and adapting reading materials to all levels of students.

Carrier, W. and B. Neumann, eds. *Literature from the World*. New York: Scribner, 1981.

A comprehensive world literature text for high school students, with a section on mythology and folklore.

Cline, R. K. J. and W. G. McBride. *A Guide to Literature for Young Adults: Background, Selection, and Use*. Glenview, IL: Scott Foresman, 1983.

A literature reference containing sample readings and an overview of adolescent literature and the developmental changes that affect reading.

Coater, R.B., Jr., ed. "Reading Research and Instruction." *Journal of the College Research Association*. Pittsburgh, PA: 1995.

A reference tool for reading and language arts teachers, covering the latest research and instructional techniques.

Corcoran, B. and E. Evans, eds. *Readers, Texts, Teachers.* Upper Montclair, NJ: Boynton/Cook, 1987.

A collection of essays concerning reader response theory, including activities that help students interpret literature and help the teacher integrate literature into the course study.

Cutting, Brian. *Moving on in Whole Language: The Complete Guide for Every Teacher.* Bothell, WA: Wright Group, 1992.

A resource of practical knowledge in whole language instruction.

Damrosch, L. and others. *Adventures in English Literature.* Orlando, FL: Harcourt, Brace, Jovanovich, 1985.

One of many standard high school English literature textbooks with a solid section on the development of the English language.

Davidson, A. *Literacy 2000 Teacher's Resource. Emergent Stages 1 & 2.* 1990.

Devine, T. G. *Teaching Study Skills: A Guide for Teachers.* Boston: Allyn and Bacon, 1981.

Duffy, G. G. and others. *Comprehension Instruction: Perspectives and Suggestions.* New York: Longman, 1984.

Written by researchers at the Institute of Research on Teaching and the Center for the Study of Reading, this reference includes a variety of instructional techniques for different levels.

Fleming, M. ed. *Teaching the Epic.* Urbana, IL: NCTE, 1974.

Methods, materials, and projects for the teaching of epics with examples of Greek, religious, national, and American epics.

Flood, J. Ed. *Understanding Reading Comprehension: Cognition, Language, and the Structure of Prose.* Newark, DE: IRA, 1984.

Essays by preeminent scholars dealing with comprehension for learners of all levels and abilities.

Fry, E. B. and others. *The Reading Teacher's Book of Lists.* Edgewood Cliffs, NJ: Prentice-Hall, 1984.

A comprehensive list of book lists for students of various reading levels.

Garnica, Olga K. and Martha L. King. *Language, Children, and Society*. New York: Pergamon Press, 1981.

Gere, A. R. and E. Smith. *Attitude, Language and Change*. Urbana, IL: NCTE, 1979.

A discussion of the relationship between standard English and grammar and the vernacular usage, including various approaches to language instruction.

Hayakawa, S. I. *Language in Thought and Action*. 4th ed. Orlando, Fl: Harcourt, Brace, Jovanovich, 1979.

Hook, J. N. and others. *What Every English Teacher Should Know*. Champaign, IL: NCTE, 1970.

Research-based text that summarizes methodologies and specific application for use with students.

Johnson, D. D. and P. D. Pearson. *Teaching Reading Vocabulary*. 2nd ed. New York: Holt, Rinehart, and Winston, 1984.

A student text that stresses using vocabulary study in improving reading comprehension, with chapters on instructional components in the reading and content areas.

Kaywell, I. F. Ed. *Adolescent Literature as a Complement to the Classics*. Norwood, MA: Christopher-Gordon Pub., 1993.

A correlation of modern adolescent literature to classics of similar themes.

Mack, M. Ed. *World Masterpieces*. 3rd ed. 2 vols. New York: Norton, 1973.

A standard world literature survey, with useful introductory material on a critical approach to literature study.

McLuhan, M. *Understanding Media: The Extensions of Man*. New York: Signet, 1964.

The most classic work on the effect media has on the public and the power of the media to influence thinking.

McMichael, G. ed. *Concise Anthology of American Literature*. New York: Macmillan, 1974.

A standard survey of American literature text.

Moffett, J. *Teaching the Universe of Discourse*. Boston: Houghton Mifflin, 1983.

A significant reference text that proposes the outline for a total language arts program, emphasizing the reinforcement of each element of the language arts curriculum to the other elements.

Moffett, James and Betty Jane Wagner. *Student-Centered Language Arts K-12*. 4th ed. Boston: Houghton Mifflin, 1992.

Nelms, B. F., ed. *Literature in the Classroom: Readers, Texts, and Contexts*. Urbana, IL: NCTE, 1988.

Essays on adolescent and multicultural literature, social aspects of literature, and approaches to literature interpretation.

Nilsen, A. P. and K. L. Donelson. *Literature for Today's Young Adults*. 2nd ed. Glenview, IL: Scott, Foresman, and Co., 1985.

An excellent overview of young adult literature - its history, terminologies, bibliographies, and book reviews.

Perrine, L. *Literature: Structure, Sound, and Sense*. 5th ed. Orlando, FL: Harcourt, Brace, Jovanovich, 1988.

A much revised text for teaching literature elements, genres, and interpretation.

Piercey, Dorothy. *Reading Activities in Content Areas: An Ideabook for Middle and Secondary Schools*. 2nd ed. Boston: Allyn and Bacon, 1982.

Pooley, R. C. *The Teaching of English Usage*. Urbana, IL: NCTE, 1974.

A revision of the important 1946 text, which discusses the attitudes toward English usage through history and recommends specific techniques for usage instruction.

Probst, R. E. *Response and Analysis: Teaching Literature in Junior and Senior High School*. Upper Montclair, NJ: Boynton/Cook, 1988.

A resource that explores reader response theory and discusses student-centered methods for interpreting literature. Contains a section on the progress of adolescent literature.

Pyles, T. and J. Alges. *The Origin and Development of the English Language*. 3rd ed. Orlando, FL: Harcourt, Brace, Jovanovich, 1982.

A history of the English language; sections on social, personal, historical, and geographical influences on language usage.

Readence, J. E. and others. *Content Area Reading: An Integrated Approach*. 2nd ed. Dubuque, IA: Kendall/Hunt, 1985.

A practical instruction guide for teaching reading in the content areas.

Robinson, H. Alan. *Teaching Reading and Study Strategies: The Content Areas*. Boston: Allyn and Bacon, 1978.

Roe, B. D. and others. *Secondary School Reading Instruction: The Content Areas*. 3rd ed. Boston: Houghton Mifflin, 1987.

A resource of strategies for the teaching of reading for language arts teachers with little reading instruction background.

Rosenberg, D. *World Mythology: An Anthology of the Great Myths and Epics*. Lincolnwood, IL: National Textbook, 1986.

Presents selections of main myths from which literary allusions are drawn. Thorough literary analysis of each selection.

Rosenblatt, L. M. *The Reader, the Text, the Poem. The Transactional Theory of the Literary Work*. Southern Illinois University Press, 1978.

A discussion of reader-response theory and reader-centered methods for analyzing literature.

Santeusanio, Richard P. *A Practical Approach to Content Area Reading*. Reading, MA.: Addison-Wesley Publishing Co., 1983.

Strickland, D. S. and others. *Using Computers in the Teaching of Reading*. New York: Teachers College Press, 1987.

Resource for strategies for teaching and learning language and reading with computers and recommendations for software for all grades.

Sutherland, Zena and others. *Children and Books*. 6th ed. Glenview, IL: Scott, Foresman, and Co., 1981.

Thorough study of children's literature, with sections on language development theory and chapters on specific genres with synopses of specific classic works for child/adolescent readers.

Tchudi, S. and D. Mitchell. *Explorations in the Teaching of English*. 3rd ed. New York: Harper Row, 1989.

A thorough source of strategies for creating a more student-centered involvement in learning.

Tompkins, Gail E. *Teaching Writing: Balancing Process and Product*. 2nd ed. New York: Macmillan, 1994.

A tool to aid teachers in integrating recent research and theory about the writing process, writing reading connections, collaborative learning, and across the curriculum writing with practices in the fourth through eighth grade classrooms.

Warriners, J. E. *English Composition and Grammar*. Benchmark ed. Orlando, FL: Harcourt, Brace, Jovanovich, 1988.

Standard grammar and composition textbook, with a six-book series for seventh through twelfth grades; includes vocabulary study, language history, and diverse approaches to writing process.

Sample Test

Section I: Essay Test

Given are several prompts, reflecting the need to exhibit a variety of writing skills. In most testing situations, 30 minutes would be allowed to respond to each of the prompts. Some tests may allow 60 minutes for the essay to incorporate more than one question or allow for greater preparation and editing time. Read the directions carefully and organize your time wisely.

Section II: Multiple-choice Test

This section contains 125 questions. In most testing situations, you would be expected to answer from 35-40 questions within 30 minutes. If you time yourself on the entire battery, take no more than 90 minutes.

Section III: Answer Key

Section I: Essay Prompts

Prompt A

Write an expository essay discussing effective teaching strategies for developing literature appreciation with a heterogeneous class of ninth graders. Select any appropriate piece(s) of world literature to use as examples in the discussion.

Prompt B

After reading the following passage from Aldous Huxley's *Brave New World,* discuss the types of reader responses possible with a group of eight graders.

> He hated them all—all the men who came to visit Linda. One afternoon, when he had been playing with the other children - it was cold, he remembered, and there was snow on the mountains - he came back to the house and heard angry voices in the bedroom. They were women's voices, and they were words he didn't understand; but he knew they were dreadful words. Then suddenly, crash! something was upset; he heard people moving about quickly, and there was another crash and then a noise like hitting a mule, only not so bony; then Linda screamed. 'Oh, don't, don't, don't!' she said. He ran in. There were three women in dark blankets. Linda was on the bed. One of the women was holding her wrists. Another was lying across her legs, so she couldn't kick. The third was hitting her with a whip. Once, twice, three times; and each time Linda screamed.

Prompt C

Write a persuasive letter to the editor on any contemporary topic of special interest. Employ whatever forms of discourse, style devices, and audience appeal techniques that seem appropriate to the topic.

TEACHER CERTIFICATION STUDY GUIDE

Section II: Multiple-choice Test

Explanation of Rigor

Easy: The majority of test takers would get this question correct. It is a simple understanding of the facts and/or the subject matter is part of the basics of an education for teaching English.

Average Rigor: This question represents a test item that most people would pass. It requires a level of analysis or reasoning and/or the subject matter exceeds the basics of an education for teaching English.

Rigorous: The majority of test takers would have difficulty answering this question. It involves critical thinking skills such as a very high level of abstract thought, analysis or reasoning, and it would require a very deep and broad education for teaching English.

Part A

Each underlined portion of sentences 1-10 contains one or more errors in grammar, usage, mechanics, or sentence structure. Circle the choice which best corrects the error without changing the meaning of the original sentence.

1. Joe <u>didn't hardly know his cousin Fred</u> who'd had a rhinoplasty. (Skill 2.3, Easy)

   A. hardly did know his cousin Fred

   B. didn't know his cousin Fred hardly

   C. hardly knew his cousin Fred

   D. didn't know his cousin Fred

   E. didn't hardly know his cousin Fred

<u>Mixing the batter for cookies</u>, the cat licked the Crisco from the cookie sheet. (Skill 2.3, Average Rigor)

   A. While mixing the batter for cookies

   B. While the batter for cookies was mixing

   C. While I mixed the batter for cookies

   D. While I mixed the cookies

   E. Mixing the batter for cookies

2.

ENG. LANGUAGE LIT. & COMP.   170

3. Mr. Smith <u>respectfully submitted his resignation and had</u> a new job. (Skill 2.3, Average Rigor)

   A. respectfully submitted his resignation and has

   B. respectfully submitted his resignation before accepting

   C. respectfully submitted his resignation because of

   D. respectfully submitted his resignation and had

4. Wally <u>groaned</u>, "Why do I have to do an oral interpretation <u>of "The Raven."</u> (Skill 2.3, Average Rigor)

   A. groaned "Why… of 'The Raven'?"

   B. groaned "Why… of "The Raven"?

   C. groaned ", Why… of "The Raven?"

   D. groaned, "Why… of "The Raven."

5.

<u>The coach offered her assistance but</u> the athletes wanted to practice on their own. (Skill 2.3, Rigorous)

   A. The coach offered her assistance, however, the athletes wanted to practice on their own.

   B. The coach offered her assistance: furthermore, the athletes wanted to practice on their own.

   C. Having offered her assistance, the athletes wanted to practice on their own.

   D. The coach offered her assistance; however, the athletes wanted to practice on their own.

   E. The coach offered her assistance, and the athletes wanted to practice on their own.

6. The Taj Mahal has been designated one of the Seven Wonders of the World, and people know it for its unique architecture. (Skill 2.3, Rigorous)

   A. The Taj Mahal has been designated one of the Seven Wonders of the World, and it is known for its unique architecture.

   B. People know the Taj Mahal for its unique architecture, and it has been designated one of the Seven Wonders of the World.

   C. People have known the Taj Mahal for its unique architecture, and it has been designated of the Seven Wonders of the World.

   D. The Taj Mahal has designated itself one of the Seven Wonders of the World.

7. Walt Whitman was famous for his composition, *Leaves of Grass*, serving as a nurse during the Civil War, and a devoted son (Skill 2.3, Rigorous)

   A. *Leaves of Grass*, his service as a nurse during the Civil War, and a devoted son

   B. composing *Leaves of Grass*, serving as a nurse during the Civil War, and being a devoted son

   C. his composition, *Leaves of Grass*, his nursing during the Civil War, and his devotion as a son

   D. his composition *Leaves of Grass*, serving as a nurse during the Civil War and a devoted son

   E. his composition *Leaves of Grass*, serving as a nurse during the Civil War. and a devoted son

8. **A teacher must know not only her subject matter but also the strategies of content teaching. (Skill 2.3, Rigorous)**

   A. must not only know her subject matter but also the strategies of content teaching

   B. not only must know her subject matter but also the strategies of content teaching

   C. must not know only her subject matter but also the strategies of content teaching

   D. must know not only her subject matter but also the strategies of content teaching

9. **There were fewer pieces of evidence presented during the second trial. (Skill 2.4, Easy)**

   A. fewer peaces

   B. less peaces

   C. less pieces

   D. fewer pieces

10. **The teacher implied from our angry words that there was conflict between you and me. (Skill 2.4, Average Rigor)**

    A. Implied... between you and I

    B. Inferred... between you and I

    C. Inferred... between you and me

    D. Implied... between you and me

Part B

Directions: Select the best answer in each group of multiple choices.

11. Sometimes readers can be asked to demonstrate their understanding of a text. This might include all of the following except   (Skill 1.1, Average Rigor)

    A. role playing.

    B. paraphrasing.

    C. storyboarding a part of the story with dialogue bubbles.

    D. reading the story aloud

12. Which of the following reading strategies calls for higher order cognitive skills? (Skill 1.1, Average Rigor)

    A. Making predictions

    B. Summarizing

    C. Monitoring

    D. Making inferences

13. Which definition is the best for defining diction? (Skill 1.2, Easy)

    A. The specific word choices of an author to create a particular mood or feeling in the reader.

    B. Writing which explains something thoroughly.

    C. The background, or exposition, for a short story or drama.

    D. Word choices that help teach a truth or moral.

14. In the following quotation, addressing the dead body of Caesar as though he were still a living being is to employ an (Skill 1.2, Average Rigor)

    > O, pardon me, though
    > Bleeding piece of earth
    > That I am meek and gentle with
    > These butchers.
    >   -Marc Antony from
    > *Julius Caesar*

    A. apostrophe

    B. allusion

    C. antithesis

    D. anachronism

15. The literary device of personification is used in which example below? (Skill 1.2, Average Rigor)

    A. "Beg me no beggary by soul or parents, whining dog!"

    B. "Happiness sped through the halls cajoling as it went."

    C. "O wind thy horn, thou proud fellow."

    D. "And that one talent which is death to hide."

16. An extended metaphor comparing two very dissimilar things (one lofty one lowly) is a definition of a/an (Skill 1.2, Average Rigor)

    A. antithesis.

    B. aphorism.

    C. apostrophe.

    D. conceit.

17. Which of the following is a characteristic of blank verse? (Skill 1.2, Average Rigor)

    A. Meter in iambic pentameter

    B. Clearly specified rhyme scheme

    C. Lack of figurative language

    D. Unspecified rhythm

18. Which is the best definition of free verse, or *vers libre*? (Skill 1.2, Average Rigor)

    A. Poetry, which consists of an unaccented syllable followed by an unaccented sound.

    B. Short lyrical poetry written to entertain but with an instructive purpose.

    C. Poetry, which does not have a uniform pattern of rhythm.

    D. A poem which tells the story and has a plot

19. Which term best describes the form of the following poetic excerpt? (Skill 1.2, Rigorous)

> And more to lulle him in his slumber soft,
> A trickling streake from high rock
> tumbling downe,
> And ever-drizzling raine upon the loft.
> Mixt with a murmuring winde, much like a swowne
> No other noyse, nor peoples troubles cryes.
> As still we wont t'annoy the walle'd towne,
> Might there be heard: but careless Quiet lyes,
> Wrapt in eternall silence farre from enemyes.

A. Ballad

B. Elegy

C. Spenserian stanza

D. *Octava rima*

20. In the phrase "The Cabinet conferred with the President," Cabinet is an example of a/an (Skill 1.2, Rigorous)

A. metonym

B. synecdoche

C. metaphor

D. allusion

21. What syntactic device is most evident from Abraham Lincoln's "Gettysburg Address"? (Skill 1.2, Rigorous)

> It is rather for us to be here dedicated to the great task remaining before us -- that from these honored dead we take increased devotion to that cause for which they gave the last full measure of devotion—that we here highly resolve that these dead shall not have died in vain -- that this nation, under God, shall have a new birth of freedom—and that government of the people, by the people, for the people, shall not perish from the earth.

A. Affective connotation

B. Informative denotations

C. Allusion

D. Parallelism

22. A traditional, anonymous story, ostensibly having a historical basis, usually explaining some phenomenon of nature or aspect of creation, defines a/an (Skill 1.3, Easy)

A. proverb.

B. idyll.

C. myth.

D. epic.

23. Which of the following is not a characteristic of a fable? (Skill 1.3, Easy)

    A. Animals that feel and talk like humans.

    B. Happy solutions to human dilemmas.

    C. Teaches a moral or standard for behavior.

    D. Illustrates specific people or groups without directly naming them.

24. Which poem is typified as a villanelle? (Skill 1.3, Rigorous)

    A. "Do not go gentle into that good night"

    B. "Dover Beach"

    C. *Sir Gawain and the Green Knight*

    D. *Pilgrim's Progress*

25. In classic tragedy, a protagonist's defeat is brought about by a tragic flaw which is called (Skill 1.3, Rigorous)

    A. hubris

    B. hamartia

    C. catharsis

    D. the skene

26. Which sonnet form describes the following? (Skill 1.3, Rigorous)

    My galley charg'd with forgetfulness,
    Through sharp seas, in winter night doth pass
    'Tween rock and rock; and eke mine enemy, alas,
    That is my lord steereth with, cruelness.
    And every oar a thought with readiness,
    As though that death were light in such a case.
    An endless wind doth tear the sail apace
    Or forc'ed sighs and trusty fearfulness.
    A rain of tears, a cloud of dark
        disdain,
    Hath done the wearied cords great hinderance,
    Wreathed with error and eke
        with ignorance.
    The stars be hid that led me to this pain
    Drowned is reason that should me consort,
    And I remain despairing of the poet

    A. Petrarchan or Italian sonnet

    B. Shakespearian or Elizabethan sonnet

    C. Romantic sonnet

    D. Spenserian sonnet

27. What is the salient literary feature of this excerpt from an epic? (Skill 1.3, Rigorous)

> Hither the heroes and the nymphs resorts,
> To taste awhile the pleasures of a court;
> In various talk th'instructive hours they passed,
> Who gave the ball, or paid the visit last;
> One speaks the glory of the English Queen,
> And another describes a charming Indian screen;
> A third interprets motion, looks, and eyes;
> At every word a reputation dies.

A. Sprung rhythm

B. Onomatopoeia

C. Heroic couplets

D. Motif

28. The tendency to emphasize and value the qualities and peculiarities of life in a particular geographic area exemplifies (Skill 1.4, Easy)

A. pragmatism.

B. regionalism.

C. pantheism.

D. abstractionism.

29. Charles Dickens, Robert Browning, and Robert Louis Stevenson were (Skill 1.4, Easy)

A. Victorians.

B. Medievalists.

C. Elizabethans.

D. Absurdists.

30. Among junior-high school students of low-to-average readability levels, which work would most likely stir reading interest? (Skill 1.4, Easy)

A. *Elmer Gantry*, Sinclair Lewis

B. *Smiley's People*, John Le Carre

C. *The Outsiders*, S.E. Hinton

D. *And Then There Were None*, Agatha Christie.

31. What is considered the first work of English literature because it was written in the vernacular of the day? (Skill 1.4, Easy)

A. *Beowulf*

B. *Le Morte d'Arthur*

C. *The Faerie Queene*

D. *Canterbury Tales*

32. Considered one of the first feminist plays, this Ibsen drama ends with a door slamming symbolizing the lead character's emancipation from traditional societal norms. (Skill 1.4, Average Rigor)

    A. *The Wild Duck*

    B. *Hedda Gabler*

    C. *Ghosts*

    D. *The Doll's House*

33. Which of the following titles is known for its scathingly condemning tone? (Skill 1.4, Average Rigor)

    A. Boris Pasternak's *Dr Zhivago*

    B. Albert Camus' *The Stranger*

    C. Henry David Thoreau's "On the Duty of Civil Disobedience"

    D. Benjamin Franklin's "Rules by Which a Great Empire May Be Reduced to a Small One"

34. American colonial writers were primarily (Skill 1.4, Average Rigor)

    A. Romanticists.

    B. Naturalists.

    C. Realists.

    D. Neo-classicists.

35. Arthur Miller wrote *The Crucible* as a parallel to what twentieth century event? (Skill 1.4, Average Rigor)

    A. Sen. McCarthy's House un-American Activities Committee Hearing

    B. The Cold War

    C. The fall of the Berlin wall

    D. The Persian Gulf War

36. Which of the writers below is a renowned Black poet? (Skill 1.4, Average Rigor)

    A. Maya Angelou

    B. Sandra Cisneros

    C. Richard Wilbur

    D. Richard Wright

37. Which of the following is not a theme of Native American writing? (Skill 1.4, Average Rigor)

    A. Emphasis on the hardiness of the human body and soul

    B. The strength of multi-cultural assimilation

    C. Contrition for the genocide of native peoples

    D. Remorse for the love of the Indian way of life

38. The writing of Russian naturalists is (Skill 1.4, Average Rigor)

    A. optimistic.

    B. pessimistic.

    C. satirical.

    D. whimsical.

39. Most children's literature prior to the development of popular literature was intended to be didactic. Which of the following would not be considered didactic? (Skill 1.4, Average Rigor)

    A. "A Visit from St. Nicholas" by Clement Moore

    B. *McGuffy's Reader*

    C. Any version of Cinderella

    D. Parables from the Bible

40. Written on the sixth grade reading level, most of S. E. Hinton's novels (for instance, *The Outsiders*) have the greatest reader appeal with (Skill 1.4, Average Rigor)

    A. sixth graders.

    B. ninth graders.

    C. twelfth graders.

    D. adults.

41. Children's literature became established in the (Skill 1.4, Average Rigor)

    A. seventeenth century

    B. eighteenth century

    C. nineteenth century

    D. twentieth century

42. After watching a movie of a train derailment, a child exclaims, "Wow, look how many cars fell off the tracks. There's junk everywhere. The engineer must have really been asleep." Using the facts that the child is impressed by the wreckage and assigns blame to the engineer, a follower of Piaget's theories would estimate the child to be about (Skill 1.4, Rigorous)

    A. ten years old.

    B. twelve years old.

    C. fourteen years old.

    D. sixteen years old.

43. The most significant drawback to applying learning theory research to classroom practice is that (Skill 1.4, Rigorous)

   A. today's students do not acquire reading skills with the same alacrity as when greater emphasis was placed on reading classical literature.

   B. development rates are complicated by geographical and cultural In analyzing literature and in looking for ways to bring a work to life for an audience, the use of comparable themes and ideas from other pieces of literature and from one's own life experiences, including from reading the daily newspaper, is very important and useful.

   C. homogeneous grouping has contributed to faster development of some age groups.

   D. social and environmental conditions have contributed to an escalated maturity level than research done twenty of more years ago would seem to indicate.

44. Which of the following is the best definition of existentialism? (Skill 1.4, Rigorous)

   A. The philosophical doctrine that matter is the only reality and that everything in the world, including thought, will and feeling, can be explained only in terms of matter.

   B. Philosophy that views things as they should be or as one would wish them to be.

   C. A philosophical and literary movement, variously religious and atheistic, stemming from Kierkegaard and represented by Sartre.

   D. The belief that all events are determined by fate and are hence inevitable.

45. The following lines from Robert Browning's poem "My Last Duchess" come from an example of what form of dramatic literature? (Skill 1.4, Rigorous)

> That's my last Duchess painted on the wall,
> Looking as if she were alive. I call
> That piece a wonder now: Fràa Pandolf's hands
> Worked busily a day and there she stands.
> Will 't please you sit and look at her?

A. Tragedy

B. Comic opera

C. Dramatis personae

D. Dramatic monologue

46. "Every one must pass through Vanity Fair to get to the celestial city" is an allusion from a (Skill 1.4, Rigorous)

A. Chinese folk tale.

B. Norse saga.

C. British allegory.

D. German fairy tale.

47. Which author did not write satire? (Skill 1.4, Rigorous)

A. Joseph Addison

B. Richard Steele

C. Alexander Pope

D. John Bunyan

48. What were two major characteristics of the first American literature? (Skill 1.4, Rigorous)

A. Vengefulness and arrogance

B. Bellicosity and derision

C. Oral delivery and reverence for the land

D. Maudlin and self-pitying egocentricism

49. **Hoping to take advantage of the popularity of the Harry Potter series, a teacher develops a unit on mythology comparing the story and characters of Greek and Roman myths with the story and characters of the Harry Potter books. Which of these is a commonality that would link classical literature to popular fiction? (Skill 1.4, Rigorous)**

   A. The characters are gods in human form with human-like characteristics.

   B. The settings are realistic places in the world where the characters interact as humans would.

   C. The themes center on the universal truths of love and hate and fear.

   D. The heroes in the stories are young males and only they can overcome the opposing forces.

50. **In the following poem, what literary movement is reflected? (Skill 1.4, Rigorous)**

   "My Heart Leaps Up" by William Wordsworth

   My heart leaps up when I behold
      A rainbow in the sky:
   So was it when my life began;
   So is it now I am a man;
   So be it when I shall grow old,
      Or let me die!
   The Child is father of the Man;
   And I could wish my days to be
   Bound each to each by natural piety

   A. Neo-classicism

   B. Victorian literature

   C. Romanticism

   D. Naturalism

51. In preparing a unit on 20th century immigration you prepare a list of books for students to read. Which book would not be appropriate for this topic? (Skill 1.5, Average Rigor)

   A. *The Things They Carried* by Tim O'Brien

   B. *Exodus* by Leon Uris

   C. *The Joy Luck Club* by Amy Tan

   D. *Tortilla Flats* by John Steinbeck

52. To explore the relationship of literature to modern life, which of these activities would not enable students to explore comparable themes? (Skill 1.5, Average Rigor)

   A. After studying various world events, such as the Palestinian-Israeli conflict, students write an updated version of *Romeo and Juliet* using modern characters and settings.

   B. Before studying *Romeo and Juliet,* students watch *West Side Story.*

   C. Students research the major themes of *Romeo and Juliet* by studying news stories and finding modern counterparts for the story.

   D. Students would explore compare the romantic themes of *Romeo and Juliet* and *The Taming of the Shrew.*

53. Mr. Phillips is creating a unit to study *To Kill a Mockingbird* and wants to familiarize his high school freshmen with the attitudes and issues of the historical period. Which activity would familiarize students with the attitudes and issues of the Depression-era South? (Skill 1.5, Rigorous)

   A. Create a detailed timeline of 15-20 social, cultural, and political events that focus on race relations in the 1930s.

   B. Research and report on the life of its author Harper Lee. Compare her background with the events in the book.

   C. Watch the movie version and note language and dress.

   D. Write a research report on the stock market crash of 1929 and its effects.

54. Which choice below best defines naturalism? (Skill 1.5, Rigorous)

   A. A belief that the writer or artist should apply scientific objectivity in his/her observation and treatment of life without imposing value judgments.

   B. The doctrine that teaches that the existing world is the best to be hoped for.

   C. The doctrine that teaches that God is not a personality, but that all laws, forces and manifestations of the universe are God-related.

   D. A philosophical doctrine that professes that the truth of all knowledge must always be in question.

55. The students in Mrs. Cline's seventh grade language arts class were invited to attend a performance of *Romeo and Juliet* presented by the drama class at the high school. To best prepare, they should (Skill 1.6, Average Rigor)

    A. read the play as a homework exercise.

    B. read a synopsis of the plot and a biographical sketch of the author.

    C. examine a few main selections from the play to become familiar with the language and style of the author.

    D. read a condensed version of the story and practice attentive listening skills.

56. What is the best course of action when a child refuses to complete a reading/ literature assignment on the grounds that it is morally objectionable? (Skill 1.6, Average Rigor)

    A. Speak with the parents and explain the necessity of studying this work

    B. Encourage the child to sample some of the text before making a judgment

    C. Place the child in another teacher's class where they are studying an acceptable work

    D. Provide the student with alternative selections that cover the same performance standards that the rest of the class is learning.

57. The English department is developing strategies to encourage all students to become a community of readers. From the list of suggestions below, which would be the least effective way for teachers to foster independent reading? (Skill 1.6, Average Rigor)

   A. Each teacher will set aside a weekly 30-minute in-class reading session during which the teacher and students read a magazine or book for enjoyment.

   B. Teacher and students develop a list of favorite books to share with each other.

   C. The teacher assigns at least one book report each grading period to ensure that students are reading from the established class list.

   D. The students gather books for a classroom library so that books may be shared with each other.

58. Which of the following responses to literature typically give middle school students the most problems? (Skill 1.6, Average Rigor)

   A. Interpretive

   B. Evaluative

   C. Critical

   D. Emotional

59. Which of the following is a formal reading-level assessment? (Skill 1.6, Average Rigor)

   A. A standardized reading test

   B. A teacher-made reading test

   C. An interview

   D. A reading diary

60. Which of the following would be the most significant factor in teaching Homer's *Iliad* and *Odyssey* to any particular group of students? (Skill 1.6, Average Rigor)

    A. Identifying a translation on the appropriate reading level

    B. Determining the students' interest level

    C. Selecting an appropriate evaluative technique

    D. Determining the scope and delivery methods of background study

61. Which of the following definitions best describes a parable? (Skill 1.6, Average Rigor)

    A. A short entertaining account of some happening, usually using talking animals as characters.

    B. A slow, sad song or poem, or prose work expressing lamentation.

    C. An extensive narrative work expressing universal truths concerning domestic life.

    D. A short, simple story of an occurrence of a familiar kind, from which a moral or religious lesson may be drawn.

62. Which teaching method would best engage underachievers in the required senior English class? (Skill 1.6, Average Rigor)

    A. Assign use of glossary work and extensively footnoted excerpts of great works.

    B. Have students take turns reading aloud the anthology selection

    C. Let students choose which readings they'll study and write about.

    D. Use a chronologically arranged, traditional text, but assigning group work, panel presentations, and portfolio management

63. How will literature help students in a science class understand the following passage? (Skill 1.6, Rigorous)

> Just as was the case more than three decades ago, we are still sailing between the Scylla of deferring surgery for too long and risking irreversible left ventricular damage and sudden death, and the Charibdas of operating too early and subjecting the patient to the early risks of operation and the later risks resulting from prosthetic valves.
> --E. Braunwald, *European Heart Journal,* July 2000

A. They will recognize the allusion to Scylla and Charibdas from Greek mythology and understand that the medical community has to select one of two unfavorable choices.

B. They will recognize the allusion to sailing and understand its analogy to doctors as sailors navigating unknown waters.

C. They will recognize that the allusion to Scylla and Charibdas refers to the two islands in Norse mythology where sailors would find themselves shipwrecked and understand how the doctors feel isolated by their choices.

D. They will recognize the metaphor of the heart and relate it to Eros, the character in Greek mythology who represents love. Eros was the love child of Scylla and Charibdas.

64. Which is not a Biblical allusion? (Skill 1.6, Rigorous)

A. The patience of Job

B. Thirty pieces of silver

C. "Man proposes; God disposes"

D. "Suffer not yourself to be betrayed by a kiss"

65. Before reading a passage, a teacher gives her students an anticipation guide with a list of statements related to the topic they are about to cover in the reading material. She asks the students to indicate their agreement or disagreement with each statement on the guide. This activity is intended to (Skill 1.6, Rigorous)

   A. elicit students' prior knowledge of the topic and set a purpose for reading.

   B. help students to identify the main ideas and supporting details in the text.

   C. help students to synthesize information from the text.

   D. help students to visualize the concepts and terms in the text.

66.
66. Recognizing empathy in literature is mostly a/an (Skill 1.6, Rigorous)

   A. emotional response.

   B. interpretive response.

   C. critical response.

   D. evaluative response.

67. If a student has a poor vocabulary, the teacher should recommend first that (Skill 2.1, Average Rigor)

   A. the student read newspapers, magazines and books on a regular basis.

   B. the student enroll in a Latin class.

   C. the student write the words repetitively after looking them up in the dictionary.

   D. the student use a thesaurus to locate synonyms and incorporate them into his/her vocabulary

68. Which of the following sentences contains a subject-verb agreement error? (Skill 2.1, Average Rigor)

   A. Both mother and her two sisters were married in a triple ceremony.

   B. Neither the hen nor the rooster is likely to be served for dinner.

   C. My boss, as well as the company's two personnel directors, have been to Spain.

   D. Amanda and the twins are late again.

69. The synonyms *gyro, hero,* and *submarine* reflect which influence on language usage? (Skill 2.1, Average Rigor)

   A. Social

   B. Geographical

   C. Historical

   D. Personal

70.

70. Which aspect of language is innate? (Skill 2.1, Rigorous)

   A. Biological capability to articulate sounds understood by other humans

   B. Cognitive ability to create syntactical structures

   C. Capacity for using semantics to convey meaning in a social environment

   D. Ability to vary inflections and accents

71. To understand the origins of a word, one must study the (Skill 2.2, Easy)

   A. synonyms

   B. inflections

   C. phonetics

   D. etymology

72. The Elizabethans wrote in (Skill 2.2 Easy)

   A. Celtic

   B. Old English

   C. Middle English

   D. Modern English

73. **Which event triggered the beginning of Modern English? (Skill 2.2, Average Rigor)**

    A. Conquest of England by the Normans in 1066

    B. Introduction of the printing press to the British Isles

    C. Publication of Samuel Johnson's lexicon.

    D. American Revolution

74. **Which of the following is not true about the English language? (Skill 2.2, Average Rigor)**

    A. English is the easiest language to learn.

    B. English is the least inflected language.

    C. English has the most extensive vocabulary of any language.

    D. English originated as a Germanic tongue.

75. **Which word in the following sentence is a bound morpheme: "The quick brown fox jumped over the lazy dog"? (Skill 2.2, Rigorous)**

    A. The

    B. fox

    C. lazy

    D. jumped

76. **What was responsible for the standardizing of dialects across America in the 20th century? (Skill 2.2, Rigorous)**

    A. With the immigrant influx, American became a melting pot of languages and cultures.

    B. Trains enabled people to meet other people of different languages and cultures.

    C. Radio, and later, television, used actors and announcers who spoke without pronounced dialects.

    D. Newspapers and libraries developed programs to teach people to speak English with an agreed-upon common dialect.

77. Latin words that entered the English language during the Elizabethan age include (Skill 2.2, Rigorous)

    A. allusion, education, and esteem

    B. vogue and mustache

    C. canoe and cannibal

    D. alligator, cocoa, and armadillo

78. Which of the following sentences is properly punctuated? (Skill 2.3, Easy)

    A. The more you eat; the more you want.

    B. The authors—John Steinbeck, Ernest Hemingway, and William Faulkner—are staples of modern writing in American literature textbooks.

    C. Handling a wild horse, takes a great deal of skill and patience.

    D. The man, who replaced our teacher, is a comedian.

79. Which sentence below best minimizes the impact of bad news? (Skill 2.3, Rigorous)

    A. We have denied you permission to attend the event.

    B. Although permission to attend the event cannot be given, you are encouraged to buy the video.

    C. Although you cannot attend the event, we encourage you to buy the video.

    D. Although attending the event is not possible, watching the video is an option.

80. The arrangement and relationship of words in sentences or sentence structures best describes (Skill 2.3, Rigorous)

    A. style.

    B. discourse.

    C. thesis.

    D. syntax.

81. The substitution of *went to his rest* for *died* is an example of a/an (Skill 2.4, Easy)

    A. bowdlerism.

    B. jargon.

    C. euphemism.

    D. malapropism.

82. If students use slang and expletives, what is the best course of action to take in order to improve their formal communication skills? (Skill 2.4, Average Rigor)

    A. Ask the students to paraphrase their writing, that is, translate it into language appropriate for the school principal to read.

    B. Refuse to read the students' papers until they conform to a more literate style.

    C. Ask the students to read their work aloud to the class for peer evaluation.

    D. Rewrite the flagrant passages to show the students the right form of expression.

83. Which level of meaning is the hardest aspect of a language to master? (Skill 2.4, Rigorous)

    A. Denotation

    B. Jargon

    C. Connotation

    D. Slang

84. Reading a piece of student writing to assess the overall impression of the product is (Skill 3.1, Easy)

    A. holistic evaluation.

    B. portfolio assessment.

    C. analytical evaluation.

    D. using a performance system.

85. **What is not one of the advantages of collaborative or cooperative learning? (Skill 3.1, Easy)**

    A. Students that work together in groups or teams develop their skills in organizing, leadership, research, communication, and problem solving.

    B. Working in teams can help students overcome anxiety in distance learning courses and contribute a sense of community and belonging for the students.

    C. Students tend to learn more material being taught and retain the information longer than when the same information is taught using different methods.

    D. Teachers reduce their workload and the time spent on individuals the assignments, and grading.

86. **Writing ideas quickly without interruption of the flow of thoughts or attention to conventions is called (Skill 3.1, Easy)**

    A. brainstorming.

    B. mapping.

    C. listing.

    D. free writing.

87. **Which of the following should not be included in the opening paragraph of an informative essay? (Skill 3.1, Easy)**

    A. Thesis sentence

    B. Details and examples supporting the main idea

    C. Broad general introduction to the topic

    D. A style and tone that grabs the reader's attention

88. In the paragraph below, which sentence does not contribute to the overall task of supporting the main idea? (Skill 3.1 Easy)

   1) The Springfield City Council met Friday to discuss new zoning restrictions for the land to be developed south of the city. 2) Residents who opposed the new restrictions were granted 15 minutes to present their case. 3) Their argument focused on the dangers that increased traffic would bring to the area. 4) It seemed to me that the Mayor Simpson listened intently. 5) The council agreed to table the new zoning until studies would be performed.

   A. Sentence 2

   B. Sentence 3

   C. Sentence 4

   D. Sentence 5

89. In preparing your high school freshmen to write a research paper about a social problem, what recommendation can you make so they can determine the credibility of their information? (Skill 3.1, Average Rigor)

   A. Assure them that information on the Internet has been peer-reviewed and verified for accuracy.

   B. Find one solid source and use that exclusively.

   C. Use only primary sources.

   D. Cross check your information with another credible source.

90. Modeling is a practice that requires students to (Skill 3.1, Average Rigor)

   A. create a style unique to their own language capabilities.

   B. emulate the writing of professionals.

   C. paraphrase passages from good literature.

   D. peer evaluate the writings of other students.

91. Which of the following are secondary research materials? (Skill 3.1, Average Rigor)

   A. The conclusions and inferences of other historians.

   B. Literature and nonverbal materials, novels, stories, poetry and essays from the period, as well as coins, archaeological artifacts, and art produced during the period.

   C. Interviews and surveys conducted by the researcher.

   D. Statistics gathered as the result of the research's experiments.

92. Which of the following is the least effective procedure for promoting consciousness of audience? (Skill 3.1, Average Rigor)

   A. Pairing students during the writing process

   B. Reading all rough drafts before the students write the final copies

   C. Having students compose stories or articles for publication in school literary magazines or newspapers

   D. Writing letters to friends or relatives

93. In general, the most serious drawback of using a computer in writing is that (Skill 3.1, Average Rigor)

   A. the copy looks so good that students tend to overlook major mistakes.

   B. the spell check and grammar programs discourage students from learning proper spelling and mechanics.

   C. the speed with which corrections can be made detracts from the exploration and contemplation of composing.

   D. the writer loses focus by concentrating on the final product rather than the details.

94. The new teaching intern is developing a unit on creative writing and is trying to encourage her freshman high school students to write poetry. Which of the following would not be an effective technique? (Skill 3.1, Average Rigor)

   A. In groups, students will draw pictures to illustrate "The Love Song of J. Alfred Prufrock" by T.S. Eliot.

   B. Either individually or in groups, students will compose a song, writing lyrics that try to use poetic devices.

   C. Students will bring to class the lyrics of a popular song and discuss the imagery and figurative language.

   D. Students will read aloud their favorite poems and share their opinions of and responses to the poems.

95. In this paragraph from a student essay, identify the sentence that provides a detail. (Skill 3.1 Rigorous)

   (1) The poem concerns two different personality types and the human relation between them. (2) Their approach to life is totally different. (3) The neighbor is a very conservative person who follows routines. (4) He follows the traditional wisdom of his father and his father's father. (5) The purpose in fixing the wall and keeping their relationship separate is only because it is all he knows.

   A. Sentence 1

   B. Sentence 3

   C. Sentence 4

   D. Sentence 5

96. To determine the credibility of information, researchers should do all of the following except (Skill 3.1, Rigorous)

   A. establish the authority of the document.

   B. disregard documents with bias.

   C. evaluate the currency and reputation of the source.

   D. use a variety of research sources and methods.

97. Which of the following situations is not an ethical violation of intellectual property? (Skill 3.1, Rigorous)

   A. A student visits ten different websites and writes a report to compare the costs of downloading music. He uses the names of the websites without their permission.

   B. A student copies and pastes a chart verbatim from the Internet but does not document it because it is available on a public site.

   C. From an online article found in a subscription database, a student paraphrases a section on the problems of music piracy. She includes the source in her Works Cited but does not provide an in-text citation.

   D. A student uses a comment from M. Night Shyamalan without attribution claiming the information is common knowledge.

98. Students have been asked to write a research paper on automobiles and have brainstormed a number of questions they will answer based on their research findings. Which of the following is not an interpretive question to guide research? (Skill 3.1, Rigorous)

   A. Who were the first ten automotive manufacturers in the United States?

   B. What types of vehicles will be used fifty years from now?

   C. How do automobiles manufactured in the United States compare and contrast with each other?

   D. What do you think is the best solution for the fuel shortage?

99. In preparing a speech for a contest, your student has encountered problems with gender specific language. Not wishing to offend either women or men, she seeks your guidance. Which of the following is not an effective strategy? (Skill 3.1, Rigorous)

   A. Use the generic "he" and explain that people will understand and accept the male pronoun as all-inclusive.

   B. Switch to plural nouns and use "they" as the gender-neutral pronoun.

   C. Use passive voice so that the subject is not required.

   D. Use male pronouns for one part of the speech and then use female pronouns for the other part of the speech.

100.
100. For their research paper on the effects of the Civil War on American literature, students have brainstormed a list of potential online sources and are seeking your authorization. Which of these represent the strongest source? (Skill 3.1, Rigorous)

   A. http://www.wikipedia.org/

   B. http://www.google.com

   C. http://www.nytimes.com

   D. http://docsouth.unc.edu/southlit/civilwar.html

101. A formative evaluation of student writing (Skill 3.1, Rigorous)

   A. requires thorough markings of mechanical errors with a pencil or pen.

   B. making comments on the appropriateness of the student's interpretation of the prompt and the degree to which the objective was met.

   C. should require that the student hand in all the materials produced during the process of writing.

   D. several careful readings of the text for content, mechanics, spelling, and usage.

102. In preparing a report about William Shakespeare, students are asked to develop a set of interpretive questions to guide their research. Which of the following would not be classified as an interpretive question? (Skill 3.1, Rigorous)

   A. What would be different today if Shakespeare had not written his plays?

   B. How will the plays of Shakespeare affect future generations?

   C. How does the Shakespeare view nature in *A Midsummer's Night Dream* and *Much Ado About Nothing*?

   D. During the Elizabethan age, what roles did young boys take in dramatizing Shakespeare's plays?

103. In writing a report, Hector has to explain where acid rain comes from and what it has done to the environment. What is the most likely form of organizational structure? (Skill 3.2, Easy)

   A. Cause and effect

   B. Problem and solution

   C. Exposition

   D. Definition

104.

104. Explanatory or informative discourse is (Skill 3.2, Easy)

   A. exposition.

   B. narration.

   C. persuasion.

   D. description.

105. Which of the following is not a technique of prewriting? (Skill 3.2, Easy)

   A. Clustering

   B. Listing

   C. Brainstorming

   D. Proofreading

106. The following passage is written from which point of view? (Skill 3.2, Easy)

> As she mused the pitiful vision of her mother's life laid its spell on the very quick of her being —that life of commonplace sacrifices closing in final craziness. She trembled as she heard again her mother's voice saying constantly with foolish insistence: *Dearevaun Seraun! Dearevaun Seraun!**
>
> * "The end of pleasure is pain!" (Gaelic)

A. First person, narrator

B. Second person, direct address

C. Third person, omniscient

D. First person, omniscient

107. Which of the following is most true of expository writing? (Skill 3.2, Easy)

A. It is mutually exclusive of other forms of discourse.

B. It can incorporate other forms of discourse in the process of providing supporting details.

C. It should never employ informal expression.

D. It should only be scored with a summative evaluation.

108. 1Which of the following is not correct? (Skill 3.2, Easy)

A. Because most students have wide access to media, teachers should refrain from using it in their classrooms to diminish the overload.

B. Students can use CD-ROMs to explore information using a virtual reality experience.

C. Teacher can make their instruction more powerful by using educational media.

D. The Internet enables students to connect with people across cultures and to share interests.

109. Which of the following should students use to improve coherence of ideas within an argument? (Skill 3.2, Easy)

A. Transitional words or phrases to show relationship of ideas.

B. Conjunctions like "and" to join ideas together.

C. Use direct quotes extensively to improve credibility.

D. Adjectives and adverbs to provide stronger detail.

110. Which transition word would show contrast between these two ideas? (Skill 3.2, Average Rigor)

   We are confident in our skills to teach English. We welcome new ideas on this subject.

   A. We are confident in our skills to teach English, and we welcome new ideas on this subject.

   B. Because we are confident in our skills to teach English, we welcome new ideas on the subject.

   C. When we are confident in our skills to teach English, we welcome new ideas on the subject.

   D. We are confident in our skills to teach English; however, we welcome new ideas on the subject.

111. In preparing students for their oral presentations, the instructor provided all of these guidelines, except one. Which is not an effective guideline? (Skill 3.2, Average Rigor)

   A. Even if you are using a lectern, feel free to move about. This will connect you to the audience.

   B. Your posture should be natural, not stiff. Keep your shoulders toward the audience.

   C. Gestures can help communicate as long as you don't overuse them or make them distracting.

   D. You can avoid eye contact if you focus on your notes. This will make you appear more knowledgeable.

112. Which of the following statements indicates an instructional goal for using multimedia in the classroom? (Skill 3.2, Average Rigor)

   A. Audio messages invite the listener to form mental images consistent with the topic of the audio.

   B. Print messages appeal almost exclusively to the mind and push students to read with more thought.

   C. Listening to an audio message is more passive than reading a print message.

   D. Teachers who develop activities to foster a critical perspective on audiovisual presentation will decrease passivity.

113. What is the main form of discourse in this passage? (Skill 3.2, Average Rigor)

   It would have been hard to find a passer-by more wretched in appearance. He was a man of middle height, stout and hardy, in the strength of maturity; he might have been forty-six or seven. A slouched leather cap hid half his face, bronzed by the sun and wind, and dripping with sweat.

   A. Description

   B. Narration

   C. Exposition

   D. Persuasion

114. In literature, evoking feelings of pity or compassion is to create (Skill 3.2, Average Rigor)

   A. colloquy.

   B. irony.

   C. pathos.

   D. paradox

115. Which of the following would not be a major concern in an oral presentation? (Skill 3.2, Average Rigor)

   A. Establishing the purpose of the presentation

   B. Evaluating the audience's demographics and psychographics.

   C. Creating a PowerPoint slide for each point.

   D. Developing the content to fit the occasion.

116. Mr. Ledbetter has instructed his students to prepare a slide presentation that illustrates an event in history. Students are to include pictures, graphics, media clips and links to resources. What competencies will students exhibit at the completion of this project? (Skill 3.2, Rigorous)

   A. Analyze the impact of society on media.

   B. Recognize the media's strategies to inform and persuade.

   C. Demonstrate strategies and creative techniques to prepare presentations using a variety of media.

   D. Identify the aesthetic effects of a media presentation.

117.

117. In the following excerpt from "Civil Disobedience," what type of reasoning does Henry David Thoreau use? (Skill 3.2, Rigorous)

   Unjust laws exist; shall we be content to obey them, or shall we endeavor to amend them, and obey them until we have succeeded, or shall we transgress them at once? Men generally, under such a government as this, think that they ought to wait until they have persuaded the majority to alter them. They think that, if they should resist, the remedy would be worse than the evil. But it is the fault of the government itself that the remedy *is* worse than the evil. ... Why does it always crucify Christ, and excommunicate Copernicus and Luther, and pronounce Washington and Franklin rebels?
   --"Civil Disobedience" by Henry David Thoreau

   A. Ethical reasoning

   B. Inductive reasoning

   C. Deductive reasoning

   D. Intellectual reasoning

118. Which of the following is not a fallacy in logic? (Skill 3.2, Rigorous)

   A. All students in Ms. Suarez's fourth period class are bilingual.
      Beth is in Ms. Suarez's fourth period.
      Beth is bilingual.

   B. All bilingual students are in Ms. Suarez's class.
      Beth is in Ms. Suarez's fourth period.
      Beth is bilingual.

   C. Beth is bilingual.
      Beth is in Ms. Suarez's fourth period.
      All students in Ms. Suarez's fourth period are bilingual.

   D. If Beth is bilingual, then she speaks Spanish.
      Beth speaks French.
      Beth is not bilingual.

119. Which of the following is an example of the post hoc fallacy? (Skill 3.2, Rigorous)

   A. When the new principal was hired, student-reading scores improved; therefore, the principal caused the increase in scores.

   B. Why are we spending money on the space program when our students don't have current textbooks?

   C. You can't give your class a 10-minute break. Once you do that, we'll all have to give our students a 10-minute break.

   D. You can never believe anything he says because he's not from the same country as we are.

120. Identify the type of appeal used by Molly Ivins's in this excerpt from her essay "Get a Knife, Get a Dog, But Get Rid of Guns." (Skill 3.2, Rigorous)

> As a civil libertarian, I, of course, support the Second Amendment. And I believe it means exactly what it says: *A well regulated militia being necessary to the security of a free state, the right of the people to keep and bear arms shall not be infringed.*

A. Ethical

B. Emotional

C. Rational

D. Literary

121. What is the common advertising technique used by these advertising slogans? (Skill 3.2, Rigorous)

> "It's everywhere you want to be." - Visa
> "Have it your way." - Burger King
> "When you care enough to send the very best" - Hallmark
> "Be all you can be" – U.S. Army

A. Peer Approval

B. Rebel

C. Individuality

D. Escape

122. In presenting a report to peers about the effects of Hurricane Katrina on New Orleans, the students wanted to use various media in their argument to persuade their peers that more needed to be done. Which of these would be the most effective? (Skill 3.2, Rigorous)

A. A PowerPoint presentation showing the blueprints of the levees before the flood and redesigned now for current construction..

B. A collection of music clips made by the street performers in the French Quarter before and after the flood.

C. A recent video showing the areas devastated by the floods and the current state of rebuilding.

D. A collection of recordings of interviews made by the various government officials and local citizens affected by the flooding.

123. Based on the excerpt below from Kate Chopin's short story "The Story of an Hour," what can students infer about the main character? (Skill 3.2, Rigorous)

> She did not stop to ask if it were or were not a monstrous joy that held her. A clear and exalted perception enabled her to dismiss the suggestion as trivial. She knew that she would weep again when she saw the kind, tender hands folded in death; the face that had never looked save with love upon her, fixed and gray and dead. But she saw beyond that bitter moment a long procession of years to come that would belong to her absolutely. And she opened and spread her arms out to them in welcome.

A. She dreaded her life as a widow.

B. Although she loved her husband, she was glad that he was dead for he had never loved her.

C. She worried that she was too indifferent to her husband's death.

D. Although they had both loved each other, she was beginning to appreciate that opportunities had opened because of his death.

124. Which part of a classical argument is illustrated in this excerpt from the essay "What Should Be Done About Rock Lyrics?" (Skill 3.2, Rigorous)

> But violence against women is greeted by silence. It shouldn't be.
>
> This does not mean censorship, or book (or record) burning. In a society that protects free expression, we understand a lot of stuff will float up out of the sewer. Usually, we recognize the ugly stuff that advocates violence against any group as the garbage it is, and we consider its purveyors as moral lepers. We hold our nose and tolerate it, but we speak out against the values it proffers.
> "What Should Be Done About Rock Lyrics?" Caryl Rivers

A. Narration

B. Confirmation

C. Refutation and concession

D. Summation

125. Using the selection below from Edgar Alan Poe's "The Tell-Tale Heart," what form of literary criticism would you introduce to high school students? (Skill 4.1, Average Rigor)

> And have I not told you that what you mistake for madness is but over-acuteness of the sense? -- now, I say, there came to my ears a low, dull, quick sound, such as a watch makes when enveloped in cotton. I knew that sound well, too. It was the beating of the old man's heart. It increased my fury, as the beating of a drum stimulates the soldier into courage.

A. Marxist

B. Feminist

C. Psychoanalytic

D. Classic

Answer Key

1	C	26	A	51	A	76	C	101	B
2	C	27	C	52	D	77	A	102	D
3	C	28	B	53	A	78	B	103	A
4	A	29	A	54	A	79	B	104	A
5	D	30	C	55	D	80	D	105	D
6	A	31	D	56	D	81	C	106	C
7	B	32	D	57	C	82	A	107	B
8	D	33	D	58	B	83	C	108	A
9	D	34	D	59	A	84	A	109	B
10	C	35	A	60	A	85	D	110	D
11	D	36	A	61	D	86	D	111	D
12	D	37	B	62	C	87	B	112	D
13	A	38	B	63	A	88	C	113	A
14	A	39	A	64	C	89	D	114	C
15	B	40	B	65	A	90	B	115	C
16	D	41	A	66	C	91	A	116	B
17	A	42	A	67	A	92	C	117	C
18	C	43	D	68	C	93	B	118	A
19	D	44	C	69	B	94	A	119	A
20	B	45	D	70	A	95	C	120	A
21	D	46	B	71	D	96	B	121	C
22	C	47	D	72	D	97	A	122	C
23	D	48	D	73	B	98	A	123	D
24	A	49	C	74	A	99	A	124	C
25	B	50	C	75	D	100	D	125	C

Rigor Table

	Easy 20%	Average Rigor 40%	Rigorous 40%
Question	1, 9, 13, 22, 23, 28, 29, 30, 31, 71, 72, 78, 81, 84, 85, 86, 87, 88, 103, 104, 105, 106, 107, 108, 109,	2, 3, 4, 10, 11, 12, 14, 15, 16, 17, 18, 32, 33, 34, 35, 36, 37, 38, 39, 40, 41, 51, 52, 55, 56, 57, 58, 59, 60, 61, 62, 67, 68, 69, 73, 74, 82, 89, 90, 91, 92, 93, 94, 110, 111, 112, 113, 114, 115, 125	5, 6, 7, 8, 19, 20, 21, 24, 25, 26 17, 42, 43, 44, 45, 46, 47, 48, 49, 50, 53, 54, 63, 64, 65, 66, 70, 75, 76, 77, 79, 80, 83, 95 96, 97, 98, 99, 100, 101, 102, 116, 117, 118, 119, 120, 121, 122, 123, 124

TEACHER CERTIFICATION STUDY GUIDE

Rationales with Sample Questions

Explanation of Rigor

Easy: The majority of test takers would get this question correct. It is a simple understanding of the facts and/or the subject matter is part of the basics of an education for teaching English.

Average Rigor: This question represents a test item that most people would pass. It requires a level of analysis or reasoning and/or the subject matter exceeds the basics of an education for teaching English.

Rigorous: The majority of test takers would have difficulty answering this question. It involves critical thinking skills such as a very high level of abstract thought, analysis or reasoning, and it would require a very deep and broad education for teaching English.

Part A

Each underlined portion of sentences 1-10 contains one or more errors in grammar, usage, mechanics, or sentence structure. Circle the choice which best corrects the error without changing the meaning of the original sentence.

1. Joe <u>didn't hardly know his cousin Fred</u> who'd had a rhinoplasty. (Skill 2.3, Easy)

    A. hardly did know his cousin Fred

    B. didn't know his cousin Fred hardly

    C. hardly knew his cousin Fred

    D. didn't know his cousin Fred

    E. didn't hardly know his cousin Fred

The answer is C: using the adverb "hardly" to modify the verb creates a negative, and adding "not" creates the dreaded double negative.

2. **Mixing the batter for cookies**, the cat licked the Crisco from the cookie sheet. (Skill 2.3, Average Rigor)

    A. While mixing the batter for cookies

    B. While the batter for cookies was mixing

    C. While I mixed the batter for cookies

    D. While I mixed the cookies

    E. Mixing the batter for cookies

The answer is C. Answers A and E give the impression that the cat was mixing the batter (it is a dangling modifier.), Answer B that the batter was mixing itself, and Answer D lacks precision: it is the batter that was being mixed, not the cookies themselves.

3. Mr. Smith **respectfully submitted his resignation and had** a new job. (Skill 2.3, Average Rigor)

    A. respectfully submitted his resignation and has

    B. respectfully submitted his resignation before accepting

    C. respectfully submitted his resignation because of

    D. respectfully submitted his resignation and had

The answer is C. Answer A eliminates any relationship of causality between submitting the resignation and having the new job. Answer B just changes the sentence and, by omission, does not indicate the fact that Mr. Smith had a new job before submitting his resignation. Answer D means that Mr. Smith first submitted his resignation, and then got a new job.

4. Wally **groaned, "Why do I have to do an oral interpretation of "The Raven."** (Skill 2.3, Average Rigor)

   A. groaned "Why... of 'The Raven'?"

   B. groaned "Why... of "The Raven"?

   C. groaned ", Why... of "The Raven?"

   D. groaned, "Why... of "The Raven."

The answer is A. The question mark in a quotation that is an interrogation should be within the quotation marks. Also, when quoting a work of literature within another quotation, one should use single quotation marks ('...') for the title of this work, and they should close before the final quotation mark.

5. **The coach offered her assistance but the athletes wanted to practice on their own.** (Skill 2.3, Rigorous)

   A. The coach offered her assistance, however, the athletes wanted to practice on their own.

   B. The coach offered her assistance: furthermore, the athletes wanted to practice on their own.

   C. Having offered her assistance, the athletes wanted to practice on their own.

   D. The coach offered her assistance; however, the athletes wanted to practice on their own.

   E. The coach offered her assistance, and the athletes wanted to practice on their own.

The answer is D. A semicolon precedes a transitional adverb that introduces an independent clause. Answer A is a comma splice. In Answer B, the colon is used incorrectly since the second clause does not explain the first. In Answer C, the opening clause confuses the meaning of the sentence. In Answer E, the conjunction "and" is weak since the two ideas show contrast rather than an additional thought.

TEACHER CERTIFICATION STUDY GUIDE

6. **The Taj Mahal has been designated one of the Seven Wonders of the World, and people know it for its unique architecture. (Skill 2.3, Rigorous)**

    A. The Taj Mahal has been designated one of the Seven Wonders of the World, and it is known for its unique architecture.

    B. People know the Taj Mahal for its unique architecture, and it has been designated one of the Seven Wonders of the World.

    C. People have known the Taj Mahal for its unique architecture, and it has been designated of the Seven Wonders of the World.

    D. The Taj Mahal has designated itself one of the Seven Wonders of the World.

The answer is A. In the original sentence, the first clause is passive voice and the second clause is active voice, causing a voice shift. Answer B merely switches the clauses but does not correct the voice shift. In Answer C, only the verb tense in the first clause has been changed but it still active voice. Answer D changes the meaning. In Answer A, both clauses are passive voice.

7. **Walt Whitman was famous for his composition, *Leaves* of Grass, serving as a nurse during the Civil War, and a devoted son (Skill 2.3, Rigorous)**

    A. *Leaves of Grass*, his service as a nurse during the Civil War, and a devoted son

    B. composing *Leaves of Grass*, serving as a nurse during the Civil War, and being a devoted son

    C. his composition, *Leaves of Grass*, his nursing during the Civil War, and his devotion as a son

    D. his composition *Leaves of Grass,* serving as a nurse during the Civil War and a devoted son

    E. his composition *Leaves of Grass*, serving as a nurse during the Civil War. and a devoted son

The answer is B: In order to be parallel, the sentence needs three gerunds. The other sentences use both gerunds and nouns, which is a lack of parallelism.

TEACHER CERTIFICATION STUDY GUIDE

8. A teacher <u>must know not only her subject matter</u> but also the strategies of content teaching. (Skill 2.3, Rigorous)

    A. must not only know her subject matter but also the strategies of content teaching

    B. not only must know her subject matter but also the strategies of content teaching

    C. must not know only her subject matter but also the strategies of content teaching

    D. must know not only her subject matter but also the strategies of content teaching

The answer is D: the correlative conjunction "not only" must come directly after "know" because the intent is to create the clearest meaning link with the "but also" predicate section later in the sentence.

9. There were <u>fewer pieces</u> of evidence presented during the second trial. (Skill 2.4, Easy)

    A. fewer peaces

    B. less peaces

    C. less pieces

    D. fewer pieces

The answer is D. Use "fewer" for countable items; use "less" for amounts and quantities, such as fewer minutes but less time "Peace" is the opposite of war, not a "piece" of evidence.

ENG. LANGUAGE LIT. & COMP.

10. **The teacher implied from our angry words that there was conflict between you and me.** (Skill 2.4, Average Rigor)

    A. Implied… between you and I

    B. Inferred… between you and I

    C. Inferred… between you and me

    D. Implied… between you and me

The answer is C: the difference between the verb "to imply" and the verb "to infer" is that implying is directing an interpretation toward other people; to infer is to deduce an interpretation from someone else's discourse. Moreover, "between you and I" is grammatically incorrect: after the preposition "between," the object (or 'disjunctive' with this particular preposition) pronoun form, "me," is needed.

Part B

Directions: Select the best answer in each group of multiple choices.

11. Sometimes readers can be asked to demonstrate their understanding of a text. This might include all of the following except   (Skill 1.1, Average Rigor)

    A. role playing.

    B. paraphrasing.

    C. storyboarding a part of the story with dialogue bubbles.

    D. reading the story aloud

The answer is D. Reading the text aloud may help readers understand the text but it won't demonstrate their understanding of it. By role playing, paraphrasing, or storyboarding, they will convey their understanding of the purpose and main ideas of the text.

12. Which of the following reading strategies calls for higher order cognitive skills? (Skill 1.1, Average Rigor)

    A. Making predictions

    B. Summarizing

    C. Monitoring

    D. Making inferences

The answer is D. Making inferences from a reading text involves using other reading skills such as making predictions, skimming, scanning, summarizing, then coming to conclusions or making inferences which are not directly stated in the text.

13. Which definition is the best for defining diction? (Skill 1.2, Easy)

    A. The specific word choices of an author to create a particular mood or feeling in the reader.

    B. Writing which explains something thoroughly.

    C. The background, or exposition, for a short story or drama.

    D. Word choices that help teach a truth or moral.

The answer is A. Diction refers to an author's choice of words, expressions and style to convey his/her meaning.

14. In the following quotation, addressing the dead body of Caesar as though he were still a living being is to employ an (Skill 1.2, Average Rigor)

    > O, pardon me, though
    > Bleeding piece of earth
    > That I am meek and gentle with
    > These butchers.
    >   -Marc Antony from *Julius Caesar*

    A. apostrophe

    B. allusion

    C. antithesis

    D. anachronism

The answer is A. This rhetorical figure addresses personified things, absent people or gods. An allusion, on the other hand, is a quick reference to a character or event known to the public. An antithesis is a contrast between two opposing viewpoints, ideas, or presentation of characters. An anachronism is the placing of an object or person out of its time with the time of the text. The best-known example is the clock in Shakespeare's *Julius Caesar*.

TEACHER CERTIFICATION STUDY GUIDE

15. **The literary device of personification is used in which example below? (Skill 1.2, Average Rigor)**

    A. "Beg me no beggary by soul or parents, whining dog!"

    B. "Happiness sped through the halls cajoling as it went."

    C. "O wind thy horn, thou proud fellow."

    D. "And that one talent which is death to hide."

    The answer is B. "Happiness," an abstract concept, is described as if it were a person with the words "sped" and "cajoling."

16. **An extended metaphor comparing two very dissimilar things (one lofty one lowly) is a definition of a/an (Skill 1.2, Average Rigor)**

    A. antithesis.

    B. aphorism.

    C. apostrophe.

    D. conceit.

    The answer is D. A conceit is an unusually far-fetched metaphor in which an object, person or situation is presented in a parallel and simpler analogue between two apparently very different things or feelings, one very sophisticated and one very ordinary, usually taken either from nature or a well known every day concept, familiar to both reader and author alike. The conceit was first developed by Petrarch and spread to England in the sixteenth century.

17. **Which of the following is a characteristic of blank verse? (Skill 1.2, Average Rigor)**

    A. Meter in iambic pentameter

    B. Clearly specified rhyme scheme

    C. Lack of figurative language

    D. Unspecified rhythm

The answer is A. An iamb is a metrical unit of verse having one unstressed syllable followed by one stressed syllable. This is the most commonly used metrical verse in English and American poetry. An iambic pentameter is a ten-syllable verse made of five of these metrical units, either rhymed as in sonnets, or unrhymed as in free, or blank, verse.

18. **Which is the best definition of free verse, or *vers libre*? (Skill 1.2, Average Rigor)**

    A. Poetry, which consists of an unaccented syllable followed by an unaccented sound.

    B. Short lyrical poetry written to entertain but with an instructive purpose.

    C. Poetry, which does not have a uniform pattern of rhythm.

    D. A poem which tells the story and has a plot

The answer is C. Free verse has lines of irregular length (but it does not run on like prose).

TEACHER CERTIFICATION STUDY GUIDE

19. **Which term best describes the form of the following poetic excerpt? (Skill 1.2, Rigorous)**

	And more to lulle him in his slumber soft,
	A trickling streake from high rock tumbling downe,
	And ever-drizzling raine upon the loft.
	Mixt with a murmuring winde, much like a swowne
	No other noyse, nor peoples troubles cryes.
	As still we wont t'annoy the walle'd towne,
	Might there be heard: but careless Quiet lyes,
	Wrapt in eternall silence farre from enemyes.

	A. Ballad

	B. Elegy

	C. Spenserian stanza

	D. *Octava rima*

The answer is D. The *octava rima* is a specific eight-line stanza whose rhyme scheme is abababcc. A ballad is a narrative poem. An elegy is a form of lyric poetry typically used to mourn someone who has died. A form of the English sonnet created by Edmond Spenser combines the English form and the Italian. The Spenserian sonnet follows the English quatrain and couplet pattern but resembles the Italian in its rhyme scheme, which is linked: abab bcbc cdcd ee.

20. In the phrase "The Cabinet conferred with the President," Cabinet is an example of a/an (Skill 1.2, Rigorous)

    A. metonym

    B. synecdoche

    C. metaphor

    D. allusion

The answer is B. In a synecdoche, a whole is referred to by naming a part of it. Also, a synecdoche can stand for a whole of which it is a part: for example, the Cabinet for the Government. Metonymy is the substitution of a word for a related word. For example, "hit the books" means "to study." A metaphor is a comparison such as "a cat burglar." An allusion is a reference to someone or something in history. To say that 'she met her Waterloo and was fired" alludes to Napoleon's defeat.

21. What syntactic device is most evident from Abraham Lincoln's "Gettysburg Address"? (Skill 1.2, Rigorous)

    > It is rather for us to be here dedicated to the great task remaining before us -- that from these honored dead we take increased devotion to that cause for which they gave the last full measure of devotion—that we here highly resolve that these dead shall not have died in vain -- that this nation, under God, shall have a new birth of freedom—and that government of the people, by the people, for the people, shall not perish from the earth.

    A. Affective connotation

    B. Informative denotations

    C. Allusion

    D. Parallelism

The answer is D. Parallelism is the repetition of grammatical structure. In speeches such as this as well as speeches of Martin Luther King, Jr., parallel structure creates a rhythm and balance of related ideas. Lincoln's repetition of clauses beginning with "that" ties four examples back "to the great task." Connotation is the emotional attachment of words; denotation is the literal meaning of words. Allusion is a reference to a historic event, person, or place.

TEACHER CERTIFICATION STUDY GUIDE

22. A traditional, anonymous story, ostensibly having a historical basis, usually explaining some phenomenon of nature or aspect of creation, defines a/an (Skill 1.3, Easy)

    A. proverb.

    B. idyll.

    C. myth.

    D. epic.

The answer is C. A myth is usually traditional and anonymous and explains natural and supernatural phenomena. Myths are usually about creation, divinity, the significance of life and death, and natural phenomena. A proverb is a saying or adage. An idyll is a short, pastoral poem. In its simplest form, an epic is a narrative poem.

23. Which of the following is not a characteristic of a fable? (Skill 1.3, Easy)

    A. Animals that feel and talk like humans.

    B. Happy solutions to human dilemmas.

    C. Teaches a moral or standard for behavior.

    D. Illustrates specific people or groups without directly naming them.

The answer is D. A fable is a short tale with animals, humans, gods, or even inanimate objects as characters. Fables often conclude with a moral, delivered in the form of an epigram (a short, witty, and ingenious statement in verse). Fables are among the oldest forms of writing in human history: it appears in Egyptian papyri of c 1500 BC. The most famous fables are those of Aesop, a Greek slave living in about 600 BC. In India, the *Pantchatantra* appeared in the third century. The most famous modern fables are those of seventeenth century French poet Jean de La Fontaine.

24. **Which poem is typified as a villanelle? (Skill 1.3, Rigorous)**

    A. "Do not go gentle into that good night"

    B. "Dover Beach"

    C. *Sir Gawain and the Green Knight*

    D. *Pilgrim's Progress*

The answer is A. This poem by Dylan Thomas typifies the villanelle because it was written as such. A villanelle is a form that was invented in France in the sixteenth century, and used mostly for pastoral songs. It has an uneven number (usually five) of tercets rhyming aba, with a final quatrain rhyming abaa. This poem is the most famous villanelle written in English. "Dover Beach" by Matthew Arnold is not a villanelle, while *Sir Gawain and the Green Knight* was written in alliterative verse by an unknown author usually referred to as The Pearl Poet around 1370. *Pilgrim's Progress* is a prose allegory by John Bunyan.

25. **In classic tragedy, a protagonist's defeat is brought about by a tragic flaw which is called (Skill 1.3, Rigorous)**

    A. hubris

    B. hamartia

    C. catharsis

    D. the skene

The answer is B. Hubris is excessive pride, a type of tragic flaw. Catharsis is an emotional purging the character feels. *Skene* is the Greek word for scene. All of these terms come from Greek drama.

TEACHER CERTIFICATION STUDY GUIDE

26. Which sonnet form describes the following? (Skill 1.3, Rigorous)

>My galley charg'd with forgetfulness,
>Through sharp seas, in winter night doth pass
>'Tween rock and rock; and eke mine enemy, alas,
>That is my lord steereth with, cruelness.
>And every oar a thought with readiness,
>As though that death were light in such a case.
>An endless wind doth tear the sail apace
>Or forc'ed sighs and trusty fearfulness.
>A rain of tears, a cloud of dark disdain,
>Hath done the wearied cords great hinderance,
>Wreathed with error and eke with ignorance.
>The stars be hid that led me to this pain
>Drowned is reason that should me consort,
>And I remain despairing of the poet

A. Petrarchan or Italian sonnet

B. Shakespearian or Elizabethan sonnet

C. Romantic sonnet

D. Spenserian sonnet

The answer is A. The Petrarchan sonnet, also known as Italian sonnet, is named after the Italian poet Petrarch (1304-74). It is divided into an octave rhyming abbaabba and a sestet normally rhyming cdecde.

27. **What is the salient literary feature of this excerpt from an epic? (Skill 1.3, Rigorous)**

>Hither the heroes and the nymphs resorts,
>To taste awhile the pleasures of a court;
>In various talk th'instructive hours they passed,
>Who gave the ball, or paid the visit last;
>One speaks the glory of the English Queen,
>And another describes a charming Indian screen;
>A third interprets motion, looks, and eyes;
>At every word a reputation dies.

A. Sprung rhythm

B. Onomatopoeia

C. Heroic couplets

D. Motif

The answer is C. A couplet is a pair of rhyming verse lines, usually of the same length. It is one of the most widely used verse-forms in European poetry. Chaucer established the use of couplets in English, notably in the *Canterbury Tales,* using rhymed iambic pentameters (a metrical unit of verse having one unstressed syllable followed by one stressed syllable) later known as heroic couplets. Other authors who used heroic couplets include Ben Jonson, Dryden, and especially Alexander Pope, who became the master of them.

28. **The tendency to emphasize and value the qualities and peculiarities of life in a particular geographic area exemplifies (Skill 1.4, Easy)**

    A. pragmatism.

    B. regionalism.

    C. pantheism.

    D. abstractionism.

The answer is B. Pragmatism is a philosophical doctrine according to which there is no absolute truth. All truths change their trueness as their practical utility increases or decreases. The main representative of this movement is William James who in 1907 published *Pragmatism: A New Way for Some Old Ways of Thinking*. Pantheism is a philosophy according to which God is omnipresent in the world, everything is God and God is everything. The great representative of this sensibility is Spinoza. Also, the works of writers such as Wordsworth, Shelly and Emerson illustrate this doctrine. Abstract Expressionism is one of the most important movements in American art. It began in the 1940's with artists such as Willem de Kooning, Mark Rothko and Arshile Gorky. The paintings are usually large and non-representational.

29. **Charles Dickens, Robert Browning, and Robert Louis Stevenson were (Skill 1.4, Easy)**

    A. Victorians.

    B. Medievalists.

    C. Elizabethans.

    D. Absurdists.

The answer is A. The Victorian Period is remarkable for the diversity and quality of its literature. Robert Browning wrote chilling monologues such as "My Last Duchess," and long poetic narratives such as *The Pied Piper of Hamlin*. Robert Louis Stevenson wrote his works partly for young adults, whose imaginations were quite taken by his *Treasure Island* and *The Case of Dr. Jekyll and Mr. Hyde*. Charles Dickens tells of the misery of the time and the complexities of Victorian society in novels such as *Oliver Twist* or *Great Expectations*.

30. **Among junior-high school students of low-to-average readability levels, which work would most likely stir reading interest?** (Skill 1.4, Easy)

    A. *Elmer Gantry*, Sinclair Lewis

    B. *Smiley's People*, John Le Carre

    C. *The Outsiders*, S.E. Hinton

    D. *And Then There Were None*, Agatha Christie.

The answer is C. The students can easily identify with the characters and the gangs in the book. S.E. Hinton has actually said about this book: "*The Outsiders* is definitely my best-selling book; but what I like most about it is how it has taught a lot of kids to enjoy reading." The other three novels have more mature subject matter, more complex characters, and higher reading levels. Lewis' novel satirizes hypocrisy in the character of a debauched evangelist. Le Carre's novel is the third part of a spy novel trilogy. Christie's mystery has a wide cast of characters who are murdered one by one.

31. **What is considered the first work of English literature because it was written in the vernacular of the day?** (Skill 1.4, Easy)

    A. *Beowulf*

    B. *Le Morte d'Arthur*

    C. *The Faerie Queene*

    D. *Canterbury Tales*

The answer is D. Chaucer wrote the *Canterbury Tales* in the street language of medieval England. *Beowulf* was written during the Anglo-Saxon period and is a Teutonic saga. *Le Morte d'Arthur*, by Thomas Malory was written after Chaucer. Sir Edmund Spencer's *The Faerie Queene* was written during the Renaissance under the reign of Queen Elizabeth I.

32. Considered one of the first feminist plays, this Ibsen drama ends with a door slamming symbolizing the lead character's emancipation from traditional societal norms. (Skill 1.4, Average Rigor)

    A. *The Wild Duck*

    B. *Hedda Gabler*

    C. *Ghosts*

    D. *The Doll's House*

The answer is D. Nora in *The Doll's House* leaves her husband and her children when she realizes her husband is not the man she thought he was. Hedda Gabler, another feminist icon, shoots herself. *The Wild Duck* deals with the conflict between idealism and family secrets. *Ghosts,* considered one of Ibsen's most controversial plays, deals with many social ills, some of which include alcoholism, incest, and religious hypocrisy.

33. Which of the following titles is known for its scathingly condemning tone? (Skill 1.4, Average Rigor)

    A. Boris Pasternak's *Dr Zhivago*

    B. Albert Camus' *The Stranger*

    C. Henry David Thoreau's "On the Duty of Civil Disobedience"

    D. Benjamin Franklin's "Rules by Which a Great Empire May Be Reduced to a Small One"

The answer is D. In this work, Benjamin Franklin adopts a scathingly ironic tone to warn the British about the probable outcome in their colonies if they persist with their policies. These are discussed one by one in the text, and the absurdity of each is condemned.

34. American colonial writers were primarily (Skill 1.4, Average Rigor)

A. Romanticists.

B. Naturalists.

C. Realists.

D. Neo-classicists.

The answer is D. The early colonists had been schooled in England, and even though their writing became quite American in content, their emphasis on clarity and balance in their language remained British. This literature reflects the lives of the early colonists, such as William Bradford's excerpts from "The Mayflower Compact," Anne Bradstreet's poetry and William Byrd's journal, *A History of the Dividing Line*.

35. Arthur Miller wrote *The Crucible* as a parallel to what twentieth century event? (Skill 1.4, Average Rigor)

A. Sen. McCarthy's House un-American Activities Committee Hearing

B. The Cold War

C. The fall of the Berlin wall

D. The Persian Gulf War

The answer is A. The episode of the seventeenth century witch-hunt in Salem, Mass., gave Miller a storyline that was very comparable to what was happening to persons suspected of communist beliefs in the 1950s.

TEACHER CERTIFICATION STUDY GUIDE

36. Which of the writers below is a renowned Black poet? (Skill 1.4, Average Rigor)

    A. Maya Angelou

    B. Sandra Cisneros

    C. Richard Wilbur

    D. Richard Wright

The answer is A. Among her most famous work are *I Know Why the Caged Bird Sings* (1970), *And Still I Rise* (1978), and *All God's Children Need Traveling Shoes* (1986). Richard Wilbur is a poet and a translator of French dramatists Racine and Moliere, but he is not African American. Richard Wright is a very important African American author of novels such as *Native Son* and *Black Boy*. However, he was not a poet. Sandra Cisneros is a Latina author who is very important in developing Latina Women's literature.

37. Which of the following is not a theme of Native American writing? (Skill 1.4, Average Rigor)

    A. Emphasis on the hardiness of the human body and soul

    B. The strength of multi-cultural assimilation

    C. Contrition for the genocide of native peoples

    D. Remorse for the love of the Indian way of life

The answer is B. Native American literature was first a vast body of oral traditions from as early as before the fifteenth century. The characteristics include reverence for and awe of nature and the interconnectedness of the elements in the life cycle. The themes often reflect the hardiness of body and soul, remorse for the destruction of the Native American way of life, and the genocide of many tribes by the encroaching settlements of European Americans. These themes are still present in today's contemporary Native American literature, such as in the works of Duane Niatum, Gunn Allen, Louise Erdrich and N. Scott Momaday.

38. The writing of Russian naturalists is (Skill 1.4, Average Rigor)

    A. optimistic.

    B. pessimistic.

    C. satirical.

    D. whimsical.

The answer is B. Although the movement, which originated with the critic Vissarion Belinsky, was particularly strong in the 1840's, it can be said that the works of Dostoevsky, Tolstoy, Chekov, Turgenev and Pushkin owe much to it. These authors' works are among the best in international literature, yet are shrouded in stark pessimism. Tolstoy's *Anna Karenina* or Dostoevsky's *Crime and Punishment* are good examples of this dark outlook.

39. **Most children's literature prior to the development of popular literature was intended to be didactic. Which of the following would not be considered didactic? (Skill 1.4, Average Rigor)**

    A. "A Visit from St. Nicholas" by Clement Moore

    B. *McGuffy's Reader*

    C. Any version of Cinderella

    D. Parables from the Bible

The answer is A. "A Visit from St. Nicholas" is a cheery, non-threatening child's view of "The Night before Christmas." Didactic means intended to teach some lesson.

40. Written on the sixth grade reading level, most of S. E. Hinton's novels (for instance, *The Outsiders*) have the greatest reader appeal with (Skill 1.4, Average Rigor)

    A. sixth graders.

    B. ninth graders.

    C. twelfth graders.

    D. adults.

The answer is B. Adolescents are concerned with their changing bodies, their relationships with each other and adults, and their place in society. Reading *The Outsiders* makes them confront different problems that they are only now beginning to experience as teenagers, such as gangs and social identity. The book is universal in its appeal to adolescents.

41. Children's literature became established in the (Skill 1.4, Average Rigor)

    A. seventeenth century

    B. eighteenth century

    C. nineteenth century

    D. twentieth century

The answer is A. In the seventeenth Century, authors such as Jean de La Fontaine and his fables, Pierre Perreault's tales, Mme d'Aulnoye's novels based on old folktales and Mme de Beaumont's *Beauty and the Beast* all created a children's literature genre. In England, Perreault was translated and a work allegedly written by Oliver Smith, *The Renowned History of Little Goody Two Shoes,* also helped to establish children's literature in England.

42. After watching a movie of a train derailment, a child exclaims, "Wow, look how many cars fell off the tracks. There's junk everywhere. The engineer must have really been asleep." Using the facts that the child is impressed by the wreckage and assigns blame to the engineer, a follower of Piaget's theories would estimate the child to be about (Skill 1.4, Rigorous)

   A. ten years old.

   B. twelve years old.

   C. fourteen years old.

   D. sixteen years old.

The answer is A. According to Piaget's theory, children seven-to-eleven years old begin to apply logic to concrete things and experiences. They can combine performance and reasoning to solve problems. They have internalized moral values and are willing to confront rules and adult authority.

43. **The most significant drawback to applying learning theory research to classroom practice is that (Skill 1.4, Rigorous)**

    A. today's students do not acquire reading skills with the same alacrity as when greater emphasis was placed on reading classical literature.

    B. development rates are complicated by geographical and cultural In analyzing literature and in looking for ways to bring a work to life for an audience, the use of comparable themes and ideas from other pieces of literature and from one's own life experiences, including from reading the daily newspaper, is very important and useful.

    C. homogeneous grouping has contributed to faster development of some age groups.

    D. social and environmental conditions have contributed to an escalated maturity level than research done twenty of more years ago would seem to indicate.

The answer is D. Because of the rapid social changes, topics that were not interesting to younger readers are now topics of books for even younger readers. Many books dealing with difficult topics, and it is difficult for the teacher to steer students toward books that they are ready for and to try to keep them away from books whose content, although well written, are not yet appropriate for their level of cognitive and social development. There is a fine line between this and censorship.

44. **Which of the following is the best definition of existentialism? (Skill 1.4, Rigorous)**

    A. The philosophical doctrine that matter is the only reality and that everything in the world, including thought, will and feeling, can be explained only in terms of matter.

    B. Philosophy that views things as they should be or as one would wish them to be.

    C. A philosophical and literary movement, variously religious and atheistic, stemming from Kierkegaard and represented by Sartre.

    D. The belief that all events are determined by fate and are hence inevitable.

The answer is C. Even though there are other very important thinkers in the movement known as Existentialism, such as Camus and Merleau-Ponty, Sartre remains the main figure in this movement.

45. The following lines from Robert Browning's poem "My Last Duchess" come from an example of what form of dramatic literature? (Skill 1.4, Rigorous)

> That's my last Duchess painted on the wall,
> Looking as if she were alive. I call
> That piece a wonder
> now: Frà Pandolf's hands
> Worked busily a day
> and there she stands.
> Will 't please you sit and look at her?

   A. Tragedy

   B. Comic opera

   C. Dramatis personae

   D. Dramatic monologue

The answer is D. A dramatic monologue is a speech given by a character or narrator that reveals characteristics of the character or narrator. This form was first made popular by Robert Browning, a Victorian poet. Tragedy is a form of literature in which the protagonist is overwhelmed by opposing forces. Comic opera is a form of sung music based on a light or happy plot. Dramatis personae is the Latin phrase for the cast of a play.

46. "Every one must pass through Vanity Fair to get to the celestial city" is an allusion from a (Skill 1.4, Rigorous)

   A. Chinese folk tale.

   B. British allegory.

   C. Norse sage.

   D. German fairy tale.

The answer is B. This is a reference to John Bunyan's *Pilgrim's Progress* from *This World to That Which Is to Come* (Part I, 1678; Part II, 1684), in which the hero, Christian, flees the City of Destruction and must undergo different trials and tests to get to the Celestial City.

TEACHER CERTIFICATION STUDY GUIDE

47. Which author did not write satire? (Skill 1.4, Rigorous)

    A. Joseph Addison

    B. Richard Steele

    C. Alexander Pope

    D. John Bunyan

The answer is D. John Bunyan was a religious writer, known for his autobiography, *Grace Abounding to the Chief of Sinners,* as well as other books, all religious in their inspiration, such as *The Holy City, or the New Jerusalem* (1665), *A Confession of My Faith,* and *A Reason of My Practice* (1672), or *The Holy War* (1682).

48. What were two major characteristics of the first American literature? (Skill 1.4, Rigorous)

    A. Vengefulness and arrogance

    B. Bellicosity and derision

    C. Oral delivery and reverence for the land

    D. Maudlin and self-pitying egocentricism

The answer is D. This characteristic can be seen in Captain John Smith's work, as well as William Bradford's and Michael Wigglesworth's works.

49. Hoping to take advantage of the popularity of the Harry Potter series, a teacher develops a unit on mythology comparing the story and characters of Greek and Roman myths with the story and characters of the Harry Potter books. Which of these is a commonality that would link classical literature to popular fiction? (Skill 1.4, Rigorous)

    A. The characters are gods in human form with human-like characteristics.

    B. The settings are realistic places in the world where the characters interact as humans would.

    C. The themes center on the universal truths of love and hate and fear.

    D. The heroes in the stories are young males and only they can overcome the opposing forces.

The answer is C. Although the gods in Greek and Roman myths take human form, they are immortal as gods must be. The characters in Harry Potter may be wizards, but they are not immortal. Although the settings in these stories have familiar associations, their worlds are vastly different from those inhabited by mortals and Muggles. While male heroes may dominate the action, the females (Hera, Dianna, Hermione) are powerful as well.

50. In the following poem, what literary movement is reflected? (Skill 1.4, Rigorous)

"My Heart Leaps Up" by William Wordsworth

My heart leaps up when I behold
  A rainbow in the sky:
So was it when my life began;
So is it now I am a man;
So be it when I shall grow old,
  Or let me die!
The Child is father of the Man;
And I could wish my days to be
Bound each to each by natural piety

A. Neo-classicism

B. Victorian literature

C. Romanticism

D. Naturalism

The answer is C. The Romantic period of the 19th century is known for its emphasis on feelings, emotions, and passions. William Wordsworth and William Blake were two notable poets from this period. In the neoclassicism of the previous period, the literature echoed the classical ideals of proportion, common sense, and reason over raw emotion and imagination, and the purpose was more didactic than celebratory. The Victorian period of the late 19th century exerted more restraint on emotions and feelings. In naturalistic writing, authors depict the world more harshly and more objectively.

51. In preparing a unit on 20th century immigration you prepare a list of books for students to read. Which book would not be appropriate for this topic? (Skill 1.5, Average Rigor)

    A. The Things They Carried by Tim O'Brien

    B. Exodus by Leon Uris

    C. The Joy Luck Club by Amy Tan

    D. Tortilla Flats by John Steinbeck

The answer is A. O'Brien's book centers on American soldiers serving in Viet Nam. Uris' book details the founding of Israel after World War II. Tan's novel contrasts her family's life in China and in the United States. Steinbeck's novel illustrates the plight of Mexican migrant workers.

52. To explore the relationship of literature to modern life, which of these activities would not enable students to explore comparable themes? (Skill 1.5, Average Rigor)

    A. After studying various world events, such as the Palestinian-Israeli conflict, students write an updated version of *Romeo and Juliet* using modern characters and settings.

    B. Before studying *Romeo and Juliet,* students watch *West Side Story*.

    C. Students research the major themes of *Romeo and Juliet* by studying news stories and finding modern counterparts for the story.

    D. Students would explore compare the romantic themes of *Romeo and Juliet* and *The Taming of the Shrew*.

The answer is D. By comparing the two plays by Shakespeare, students will be focusing on the culture of the period in which the plays were written. In Answer A, students should be able to recognize modern parallels with current culture clashes. By comparing the *Romeo and Juliet* to the 1950's update of *West Side Story,* students can study how themes are similar in two completely different historical periods. In Answer C, students can study local, national, and international news for comparable stories and themes.

53. Mr. Phillips is creating a unit to study *To Kill a Mockingbird* and wants to familiarize his high school freshmen with the attitudes and issues of the historical period. Which activity would familiarize students with the attitudes and issues of the Depression-era South? (Skill 1.5, Rigorous)

> A. Create a detailed timeline of 15-20 social, cultural, and political events that focus on race relations in the 1930s.
>
> B. Research and report on the life of its author Harper Lee. Compare her background with the events in the book.
>
> C. Watch the movie version and note language and dress.
>
> D. Write a research report on the stock market crash of 1929 and its effects.

The answer is A. By identifying the social, cultural, and political events of the 1930s, students will better understand the attitudes and values of America during the time of the novel. While researching the author's life could add depth to their understanding of the novel, it is unnecessary to the appreciation of the novel by itself. The movie version is an accurate depiction of the novel's setting but it focuses on the events in the novel, not the external factors that fostered the conflict. The stock market crash and the subsequent Great Depression would be important to note on the timeline but students would be distracted from themes of the book by narrowing their focus to only these two events.

54. Which choice below best defines naturalism? (Skill 1.5, Rigorous)

A. A belief that the writer or artist should apply scientific objectivity in his/her observation and treatment of life without imposing value judgments.

B. The doctrine that teaches that the existing world is the best to be hoped for.

C. The doctrine that teaches that God is not a personality, but that all laws, forces and manifestations of the universe are God-related.

D. A philosophical doctrine that professes that the truth of all knowledge must always be in question.

The answer is A. Naturalism is a movement that was started by French writers Jules and Edmond de Goncourt with their novel *Germinie Lacerteux* (1865), but its real leader is Emile Zola, who wanted to bring "a slice of life" to his readers. His saga, *Les Rougon Macquart,* consists in twenty-two novels depicting various aspects of social life. English writing authors representative of this movement include George Moore and George Gissing in England, but the most important naturalist novel in English is Theodore Dreiser's *Sister Carrie*.

55. The students in Mrs. Cline's seventh grade language arts class were invited to attend a performance of *Romeo and Juliet* presented by the drama class at the high school. To best prepare, they should (Skill 1.6, Average Rigor)

A. read the play as a homework exercise.

B. read a synopsis of the plot and a biographical sketch of the author.

C. examine a few main selections from the play to become familiar with the language and style of the author.

D. read a condensed version of the story and practice attentive listening skills.

The answer is D. By reading a condensed version of the story, students will know the plot and therefore be able to follow the play on stage. It is also important for them to practice listening techniques such as one one-to-one tutoring and peer-assisted reading.

TEACHER CERTIFICATION STUDY GUIDE

56. **What is the best course of action when a child refuses to complete a reading/ literature assignment on the grounds that it is morally objectionable? (Skill 1.6, Average Rigor)**

    A. Speak with the parents and explain the necessity of studying this work

    B. Encourage the child to sample some of the text before making a judgment

    C. Place the child in another teacher's class where they are studying an acceptable work

    D. Provide the student with alternative selections that cover the same performance standards that the rest of the class is learning.

    The answer is D. In the case of a student finding a reading offensive, it is the responsibility of the teacher to assign another title. As a general rule, it is always advisable to notify parents if a particularly sensitive piece is to be studied.

57. **The English department is developing strategies to encourage all students to become a community of readers. From the list of suggestions below, which would be the least effective way for teachers to foster independent reading? (Skill 1.6, Average Rigor)**

    A. Each teacher will set aside a weekly 30-minute in-class reading session during which the teacher and students read a magazine or book for enjoyment.

    B. Teacher and students develop a list of favorite books to share with each other.

    C. The teacher assigns at least one book report each grading period to ensure that students are reading from the established class list.

    D. The students gather books for a classroom library so that books may be shared with each other.

    The answer is C. Teacher-directed assignments such as book reports appear routine and unexciting. Students will be more excited about reading when they can actively participate. In Answer A, the teacher is modeling reading behavior and providing students with a dedicated time during which time they can read independently and still be surrounded by a community of readers. In Answers B and D, students share and make available their reading choices.

58. **Which of the following responses to literature typically give middle school students the most problems? (Skill 1.6, Average Rigor)**

    A. Interpretive

    B. Evaluative

    C. Critical

    D. Emotional

The answer is B. Middle school readers will exhibit both emotional and interpretive responses. In middle/junior high school, organized study models enable students to identify main ideas and supporting details, to recognize sequential order, to distinguish fact from opinion, and to determine cause/effect relationships. Also, a child's being able to say why a particular book was boring or why a particular poem made him/her sad evidences critical reactions on a fundamental level. It is a bit early for evaluative responses, however. These depend on the reader's consideration of how the piece represents its genre, how well it reflects the social/ethical mores of a given society, and how well the author has approached the subject for freshness and slant. Evaluative responses are made only by a few advanced high school students.

59. **Which of the following is a formal reading-level assessment? (Skill 1.6, Average Rigor)**

    A. A standardized reading test

    B. A teacher-made reading test

    C. An interview

    D. A reading diary

The answer is A. If assessment is standardized, it has to be objective whereas Answers B, C and D are all subjective assessments.

60. Which of the following would be the most significant factor in teaching Homer's *Iliad* and *Odyssey* to any particular group of students? (Skill 1.6, Average Rigor)

    A. Identifying a translation on the appropriate reading level

    B. Determining the students' interest level

    C. Selecting an appropriate evaluative technique

    D. Determining the scope and delivery methods of background study

The answer is A. Students will learn the importance of these two works if the translation reflects both the vocabulary that they know and their reading level. Greece will always be foremost in literary assessments due to Homer's works. Homer is the most often cited author, next to Shakespeare. Greece is the cradle of both democracy and literature. This is why it is so crucial that Homer be included in the works assigned.

61. Which of the following definitions best describes a parable? (Skill 1.6, Average Rigor)

    A. A short entertaining account of some happening, usually using talking animals as characters.

    B. A slow, sad song or poem, or prose work expressing lamentation.

    C. An extensive narrative work expressing universal truths concerning domestic life.

    D. A short, simple story of an occurrence of a familiar kind, from which a moral or religious lesson may be drawn.

The answer is D. A parable is usually brief, and should be interpreted as an allegory teaching a moral lesson. Jesus' forty parables are the model of the genre, but modern, secular examples exist such as Wilfred Owen's "The Parable of The Young Man" and "The Young" (1920), or John Steinbeck's prose work *The Pearl* (1948).

62. Which teaching method would best engage underachievers in the required senior English class? (Skill 1.6, Average Rigor)

   A. Assign use of glossary work and extensively footnoted excerpts of great works.

   B. Have students take turns reading aloud the anthology selection

   C. Let students choose which readings they'll study and write about.

   D. Use a chronologically arranged, traditional text, but assigning group work, panel presentations, and portfolio management

The answer is C. It will encourage students to react honestly to literature. Students should take notes on what they're reading so they will be able to discuss the material. They should not only react to literature, but also experience it. Small-group work is a good way to encourage them. The other answers are not fit for junior-high or high school students. They should be encouraged, however, to read critics of works in order to understand criteria work.

63. **How will literature help students in a science class able understand the following passage? (Skill 1.6, Rigorous)**

   > Just as was the case more than three decades ago, we are still sailing between the Scylla of deferring surgery for too long and risking irreversible left ventricular damage and sudden death, and the Charibdas of operating too early and subjecting the patient to the early risks of operation and the later risks resulting from prosthetic valves.
   > --E. Braunwald, *European Heart Journal,* July 2000

   A. They will recognize the allusion to Scylla and Charibdas from Greek mythology and understand that the medical community has to select one of two unfavorable choices.

   B. They will recognize the allusion to sailing and understand its analogy to doctors as sailors navigating unknown waters.

   C. They will recognize that the allusion to Scylla and Charibdas refers to the two islands in Norse mythology where sailors would find themselves shipwrecked and understand how the doctors feel isolated by their choices.

   D. They will recognize the metaphor of the heart and relate it to Eros, the character in Greek mythology who represents love. Eros was the love child of Scylla and Charibdas.

The answer is A. Scylla and Charibdas were two sea monsters guarding a narrow channel of water. Sailors trying to elude one side would face danger by sailing too close to the other side. The allusion indicates two equally undesirable choices.

64. **Which is not a Biblical allusion? (Skill 1.6, Rigorous)**

    A. The patience of Job

    B. Thirty pieces of silver

    C. "Man proposes; God disposes"

    D. "Suffer not yourself to be betrayed by a kiss"

The answer is C. This saying is attributed to Thomas à Kempis (1379-1471) in his *Imitation of Christ,* Book 1, chapter 19. Anyone who exhibits the patience of Job is being compared to the Old Testament biblical figure who retained his faith despite being beset by a series of misfortunes. "Thirty pieces of silver" refers to the amount of money paid to Judas to identify Jesus. Used by Patrick Henry, the quote in D is a biblical reference to Judas' betrayal of Judas by a kiss.

65. **Before reading a passage, a teacher gives her students an anticipation guide with a list of statements related to the topic they are about to cover in the reading material. She asks the students to indicate their agreement or disagreement with each statement on the guide. This activity is intended to (Skill 1.6, Rigorous)**

    A. elicit students' prior knowledge of the topic and set a purpose for reading.

    B. help students to identify the main ideas and supporting details in the text.

    C. help students to synthesize information from the text.

    D. help students to visualize the concepts and terms in the text.

The correct answer is A. Establishing a purpose for reading, the foundation for a reading unit or activity, is intimately connected to activating the students' prior knowledge in strategic ways. When the reason for reading is developed in the context of the students' experiences, they are far better prepared to succeed because they can make connections from a base they thoroughly understand. This influences motivation, and with proper motivation, students are more enthused and put forward more effort to understand the text. The other choices are only indirectly supported by this activity and are more specific in focus.

TEACHER CERTIFICATION STUDY GUIDE

66. Recognizing empathy in literature is mostly a/an (Skill 1.6, Rigorous)

    A. emotional response.

    B. interpretive response.

    C. critical response.

    D. evaluative response.

The answer is C. In critical responses, students make value judgments about the quality and atmosphere of a text. Through class discussion and written assignments, students react to and assimilate a writer's style and language.

67. If a student has a poor vocabulary, the teacher should recommend first that (Skill 2.1, Average Rigor)

    A. the student read newspapers, magazines and books on a regular basis.

    B. the student enroll in a Latin class.

    C. the student write the words repetitively after looking them up in the dictionary.

    D. the student use a thesaurus to locate synonyms and incorporate them into his/her vocabulary

The answer is A. The teacher can personally influence what the student chooses as reading material, but the student must be able to choose independently where to search for the reading pleasure indispensable for enriching vocabulary.

TEACHER CERTIFICATION STUDY GUIDE

68. Which of the following sentences contains a subject-verb agreement error? (Skill 2.1, Average Rigor)

   A. Both mother and her two sisters were married in a triple ceremony.

   B. Neither the hen nor the rooster is likely to be served for dinner.

   C. My boss, as well as the company's two personnel directors, have been to Spain.

   D. Amanda and the twins are late again.

The answer is C. The reason for this is that the true subject of the verb is "My boss," not "two personnel directors."

69. The synonyms *gyro, hero,* and *submarine* reflect which influence on language usage? (Skill 2.1, Average Rigor)

   A. Social

   B. Geographical

   C. Historical

   D. Personal

The answer is B. They are interchangeable but their use depends on the region of the United States, not on the social class of the speaker. Nor is there any historical context around any of them. The usage can be personal but will most often vary with the region.

70. **Which aspect of language is innate? (Skill 2.1, Rigorous)**

    A. Biological capability to articulate sounds understood by other humans

    B. Cognitive ability to create syntactical structures

    C. Capacity for using semantics to convey meaning in a social environment

    D. Ability to vary inflections and accents

The answer is A. Language ability is innate and the biological capability to produce sounds lets children learn semantics and syntactical structures through trial and error. Linguists agree that language is first a vocal system of word symbols that enable a human to communicate his/her feelings, thoughts, and desires to other human beings.

71. **To understand the origins of a word, one must study the (Skill 2.2, Easy)**

    A. synonyms

    B. inflections

    C. phonetics

    D. etymology

The answer is D. Etymology is the study of word origins. A synonym is an equivalent of another word and can substitute for it in certain contexts. Inflection is a modification of words according to their grammatical functions, usually by employing variant word-endings to indicate such qualities as tense, gender, case, and number. Phonetics is the science devoted to the physical analysis of the sounds of human speech, including their production, transmission, and perception.

72. **The Elizabethans wrote in (Skill 2.2 Easy)**

    A. Celtic

    B. Old English

    C. Middle English

    D. Modern English

The answer is D. There is no document written in Celtic in England, and a work such as Beowulf is representative of Old English in the eighth century. It is also the earliest Teutonic written document. Before the fourteenth century, little literature is known to have appeared in Middle English, which had absorbed many words from the Norman French spoken by the ruling class, but at the end of the fourteenth century there appeared the works of Chaucer, John Gower, and the novel *Sir Gawain and the Green Knight*. The Elizabethans wrote in modern English and their legacy is very important: they imported the Petrarchan, or Italian, sonnet, which Sir Thomas Wyatt and Sir Philip Sydney illustrated in their works. Sir Edmund Spencer invented his own version of the Italian sonnet and wrote *The Faerie Queene*. Other literature of the time includes the hugely important works of Shakespeare and Marlowe.

73. **Which event triggered the beginning of Modern English? (Skill 2.2, Average Rigor)**

    A. Conquest of England by the Normans in 1066

    B. Introduction of the printing press to the British Isles

    C. Publication of Samuel Johnson's lexicon.

    D. American Revolution

The answer is B. With the arrival of the written word, reading matter became mass-produced, so the public tended to adopt the speech and writing habits printed in books and the language became more stable.

TEACHER CERTIFICATION STUDY GUIDE

74. Which of the following is not true about the English language? (Skill 2.2, Average Rigor)

    A. English is the easiest language to learn.

    B. English is the least inflected language.

    C. English has the most extensive vocabulary of any language.

    D. English originated as a Germanic tongue.

The answer is A. Just like any other language, English has inherent difficulties which make it difficult to learn, even though English has no declensions such as those found in Latin, Greek, or contemporary Russian, or a tonal system such Chinese.

75. Which word in the following sentence is a bound morpheme: "The quick brown fox jumped over the lazy dog"? (Skill 2.2, Rigorous)

    A. The

    B. fox

    C. lazy

    D. jumped

The answer is D. The suffix "-ed" is an affix that cannot stand alone as a unit of meaning. Thus it is bound to the free morpheme "jump." "The" is always an unbound morpheme since no suffix or prefix can alter its meaning. As written, "fox" and "lazy" are unbound but their meaning is changed with affixes, such as "foxes" or "laziness."

76. **What was responsible for the standardizing of dialects across America in the 20th century? (Skill 2.2, Rigorous)**

    A. With the immigrant influx, American became a melting pot of languages and cultures.

    B. Trains enabled people to meet other people of different languages and cultures.

    C. Radio, and later, television, used actors and announcers who spoke without pronounced dialects.

    D. Newspapers and libraries developed programs to teach people to speak English with an agreed-upon common dialect.

    The answer is C. The growth of immigration in the early part of the 20th century created pockets of language throughout the country. Coupled with regional differences already in place, the number of dialects grew. Transportation enabled people to move to different regions where languages and dialects continued to merge. With the growth of radio and television, however, people were introduced to a standardized dialect through actors and announcers who spoke so that anyone across American could understand them. Newspapers and libraries never developed programs to standardize spoken English.

77. **Latin words that entered the English language during the Elizabethan age include (Skill 2.2, Rigorous)**

    A. allusion, education, and esteem

    B. vogue and mustache

    C. canoe and cannibal

    D. alligator, cocoa, and armadillo

    The answer is A. These words reflect the Renaissance interest in the classical world and the study of ideas. The words in Answer B are French derivation, and the words in Answers C and D are more modern with younger etymologies.

TEACHER CERTIFICATION STUDY GUIDE

78. Which of the following sentences is properly punctuated? (Skill 2.3, Easy)

    A. The more you eat; the more you want.

    B. The authors—John Steinbeck, Ernest Hemingway, and William Faulkner—are staples of modern writing in American literature textbooks.

    C. Handling a wild horse, takes a great deal of skill and patience.

    D. The man, who replaced our teacher, is a comedian.

The answer is B. Dashes should be used instead of commas when commas are used elsewhere in the sentence for amplification or explanation —here within the dashes.

79. Which sentence below best minimizes the impact of bad news? (Skill 2.3, Rigorous)

    A. We have denied you permission to attend the event.

    B. Although permission to attend the event cannot be given, you are encouraged to buy the video.

    C. Although you cannot attend the event, we encourage you to buy the video.

    D. Although attending the event is not possible, watching the video is an option.

The answer is B. Subordinating the bad news and using passive voice minimizes the impact of the bad news. In Answer A, the sentence is active voice and thus too direct. The word *denied* sets a negative tone. In Answer C, the bad news is subordinated but it is still active voice with negative wording. In Answer D, the sentence is too unclear.

80. The arrangement and relationship of words in sentences or sentence structures best describes (Skill 2.3, Rigorous)

   A. style.

   B. discourse.

   C. thesis.

   D. syntax.

The answer is D. Syntax is the grammatical structure of sentences. Style is the manner of expression of writing or speaking. Discourse is an extended expression of thought through either oral or written communication. A thesis is the unifying main idea that can be either explicit or implicit.

81. The substitution of *went to his rest* for *died* is an example of a/an (Skill 2.4, Easy)

   A. bowdlerism.

   B. jargon.

   C. euphemism.

   D. malapropism.

The answer is C. A euphemism replaces an unpleasant or offensive word or expression by a more agreeable one. It also alludes to distasteful things in a pleasant manner, and it can even paraphrase offensive texts. Bowdlerism is named after Thomas Bowdler who excised from Shakespeare what he considered vulgar and offensive. Jargon is a specialized language used by a particular group. What was groovy to one generation has become awesome to another. Named after Mrs. Malaprop, a character in a play by Richard Sheridan, a malapropism is a misuse of words, often to comical effect. Mrs. Malaprop once said "...she's as headstrong as an allegory on the banks of Nile" misusing allegory for alligator.

82. If students use slang and expletives, what is the best course of action to take in order to improve their formal communication skills? (Skill 2.4, Average Rigor)

    A. Ask the students to paraphrase their writing, that is, translate it into language appropriate for the school principal to read.

    B. Refuse to read the students' papers until they conform to a more literate style.

    C. Ask the students to read their work aloud to the class for peer evaluation.

    D. Rewrite the flagrant passages to show the students the right form of expression.

The answer is A. Asking the students to write for a specific audience will help them become more involved in their writing. If they continue writing to the same audience—the teacher—they will continue seeing writing as just another assignment, and they will not apply grammar, vocabulary and syntax the way they should be. By rephrasing their own writing, they will learn to write for a different public.

83. Which level of meaning is the hardest aspect of a language to master? (Skill 2.4, Rigorous)

    A. Denotation

    B. Jargon

    C. Connotation

    D. Slang

The answer is C. Connotation refers to the meanings suggested by a word, rather than the dictionary definition. For example, the word "slim" means thin, and it is usually used with a positive connotation, to compliment of admire someone's figure. The word "skinny" also means thin, but its connotations are not as flattering as those of the word "slim." The connotative aspect of language is more difficult to master than the denotation (dictionary definition), as the former requires a mastery of the social aspect of language, not just the linguistic rules.

84. Reading a piece of student writing to assess the overall impression of the product is (Skill 3.1, Easy)

    A. holistic evaluation.

    B. portfolio assessment.

    C. analytical evaluation.

    D. using a performance system.

The answer is A. Holistic scoring assesses a piece of writing as a whole. Usually a paper is read quickly through once to get a general impression. The writing is graded according to the impression of the whole work rather than the sum of its parts. Often holistic scoring uses a rubric that establishes the overall criteria for a certain score to evaluate each paper.

85. What is not one of the advantages of collaborative or cooperative learning? (Skill 3.1, Easy)

    A. Students that work together in groups or teams develop their skills in organizing, leadership, research, communication, and problem solving.

    B. Working in teams can help students overcome anxiety in distance learning courses and contribute a sense of community and belonging for the students.

    C. Students tend to learn more material being taught and retain the information longer than when the same information is taught using different methods.

    D. Teachers reduce their workload and the time spent on individuals the assignments, and grading.

The answer is D. Teacher continue to expend time in planning, monitoring and evaluating the students, their groups, and their activities.

86. Writing ideas quickly without interruption of the flow of thoughts or attention to conventions is called (Skill 3.1, Easy)

    A. brainstorming.

    B. mapping.

    C. listing.

    D. free writing.

The answer is D. Free writing for ten or fifteen minutes allows students to write out their thoughts about a subject. This technique allows the students to develop ideas that they are conscious of, but it also helps them to develop ideas that are lurking in the subconscious. It is important to let the flow of ideas run through the hand. If the students get stuck, they can write the last sentence over again until inspiration returns.

87. Which of the following should not be included in the opening paragraph of an informative essay? (Skill 3.1, Easy)

    A. Thesis sentence

    B. Details and examples supporting the main idea

    C. Broad general introduction to the topic

    D. A style and tone that grabs the reader's attention

The answer is B. The introductory paragraph should introduce the topic, capture the reader's interest, state the thesis and prepare the reader for the main points in the essay. Details and examples, however, should be given in the second part of the essay, so as to help develop the thesis presented at the end of the introductory paragraph, following the inverted triangle method consisting of a broad general statement followed by some information, and then the thesis at the end of the paragraph.

TEACHER CERTIFICATION STUDY GUIDE

88. In the paragraph below, which sentence does not contribute to the overall task of supporting the main idea? (Skill 3.1 Easy)

    1) The Springfield City Council met Friday to discuss new zoning restrictions for the land to be developed south of the city. 2) Residents who opposed the new restrictions were granted 15 minutes to present their case. 3) Their argument focused on the dangers that increased traffic would bring to the area. 4) It seemed to me that the Mayor Simpson listened intently. 5) The council agreed to table the new zoning until studies would be performed.

    A. Sentence 2

    B. Sentence 3

    C. Sentence 4

    D. Sentence 5

The answer is C. The other sentences provide detail to the main idea of the new zoning restrictions. Because sentence 4 provides no example or relevant detail, it should be omitted.

89. In preparing your high school freshmen to write a research paper about a social problem, what recommendation can you make so they can determine the credibility of their information? (Skill 3.1, Average Rigor)

    A. Assure them that information on the Internet has been peer-reviewed and verified for accuracy.

    B. Find one solid source and use that exclusively.

    C. Use only primary sources.

    D. Cross check your information with another credible source.

The answer is D. When researchers find the same information in multiple reputable sources, the information is considered credible. Using the Internet for research requires strong critical evaluation of the source. Nothing from the Internet should be taken without careful scrutiny of the source. To rely on only one source is dangerous and short-sighted. Most high school freshmen would have limited skills to conduct primary research for a paper about a social problem.

TEACHER CERTIFICATION STUDY GUIDE

90. Modeling is a practice that requires students to (Skill 3.1, Average Rigor)

   A. create a style unique to their own language capabilities.

   B. emulate the writing of professionals.

   C. paraphrase passages from good literature.

   D. peer evaluate the writings of other students.

The answer is B. Modeling has students analyze the writing of a professional writer and try to reach the same level of syntactical, grammatical and stylistic mastery as the author whom they are studying.

91. Which of the following are secondary research materials? (Skill 3.1, Average Rigor)

   A. The conclusions and inferences of other historians.

   B. Literature and nonverbal materials, novels, stories, poetry and essays from the period, as well as coins, archaeological artifacts, and art produced during the period.

   C. Interviews and surveys conducted by the researcher.

   D. Statistics gathered as the result of the research's experiments.

The answer is A. Secondary sources are works written significantly after the period being studied and based upon primary sources. In this case, historians have studied artifacts of the time and drawn their conclusion and inferences. Primary sources are the basic materials that provide raw data and information. Students or researchers may use literature and other data they have collected to draw their own conclusions or inferences.

92. In general, the most serious drawback of using a computer in writing is that (Skill 3.1, Average Rigor)

   A. the copy looks so good that students tend to overlook major mistakes.

   B. the spell check and grammar programs discourage students from learning proper spelling and mechanics.

   C. the speed with which corrections can be made detracts from the exploration and contemplation of composing.

   D. the writer loses focus by concentrating on the final product rather than the details.

The answer is C. Because the process of revising is very quick with the computer, it can discourage contemplation, exploring, and examination, which are very important in the writing process.

93. Which of the following is the least effective procedure for promoting consciousness of audience? (Skill 3.1, Average Rigor)

   A. Pairing students during the writing process

   B. Reading all rough drafts before the students write the final copies

   C. Having students compose stories or articles for publication in school literary magazines or newspapers

   D. Writing letters to friends or relatives

The answer is B. Reading all rough drafts will not encourage the students to take control of their text and might even inhibit their creativity. On the contrary, pairing students will foster their sense of responsibility, and having them compose stories for literary magazines will boost their self-esteem as well as their organization skills.

94. The new teaching intern is developing a unit on creative writing and is trying to encourage her freshman high school students to write poetry. Which of the following would not be an effective technique? (Skill 3.1, Average Rigor)

    A. In groups, students will draw pictures to illustrate "The Love Song of J. Alfred Prufrock" by T.S. Eliot.

    B. Either individually or in groups, students will compose a song, writing lyrics that try to use poetic devices.

    C. Students will bring to class the lyrics of a popular song and discuss the imagery and figurative language.

    D. Students will read aloud their favorite poems and share their opinions of and responses to the poems.

The answer is A. While drawing is creative, it will not accomplish as much as the other activities to encourage students to write their own poetry. Furthermore, "The Love Song of J. Alfred Prufrock" is not a freshman-level poem. The other activities involve students in music and their own favorites, which will be more appealing.

95. In this paragraph from a student essay, identify the sentence that provides a detail. (Skill 3.1 Rigorous)

    (1) The poem concerns two different personality types and the human relation between them. (2) Their approach to life is totally different. (3) The neighbor is a very conservative person who follows routines. (4) He follows the traditional wisdom of his father and his father's father. (5) The purpose in fixing the wall and keeping their relationship separate is only because it is all he knows.

    A. Sentence 1

    B. Sentence 3

    C. Sentence 4

    D. Sentence 5

The answer is C. Sentence 4 provides a detail to sentence 3 by explaining how the neighbor follows routine. Sentence 1 is the thesis sentence, which is the main idea of the paragraph. Sentence 3 provides an example to develop that thesis. Sentence 4 is a reason that explains why.

96. To determine the credibility of information, researchers should do all of the following except (Skill 3.1, Rigorous)

    A. establish the authority of the document.

    B. disregard documents with bias.

    C. evaluate the currency and reputation of the source.

    D. use a variety of research sources and methods.

The answer is B. Keep an open mind. Researchers should examine the assertions, facts, and reliability of the information.

97. Which of the following situations is not an ethical violation of intellectual property? (Skill 3.1, Rigorous)

    A. A student visits ten different websites and writes a report to compare the costs of downloading music. He uses the names of the websites without their permission.

    B. A student copies and pastes a chart verbatim from the Internet but does not document it because it is available on a public site.

    C. From an online article found in a subscription database, a student paraphrases a section on the problems of music piracy. She includes the source in her Works Cited but does not provide an in-text citation.

    D. A student uses a comment from M. Night Shyamalan without attribution claiming the information is common knowledge.

The answer is A. In this scenario, the student is conducting primary research by gathering the data and using it for his own purposes. He is not violating any principle by using the names of the websites. In Answer B, students who copy and paste from the Internet without documenting the sources of their information are committing plagiarism, a serious violation of intellectual property. Even when a student puts information in her own words by paraphrasing or summarizing as in Answer C, the information is still secondary and must be documented. While dedicated movie buffs might consider anything that M. Night Shyamalan says to be common knowledge in Answer D, his comments are not necessarily known in numerous places or known by a lot of people.

98. **Students have been asked to write a research paper on automobiles and have brainstormed a number of questions they will answer based on their research findings. Which of the following is not an interpretive question to guide research? (Skill 3.1, Rigorous)**

    A. Who were the first ten automotive manufacturers in the United States?

    B. What types of vehicles will be used fifty years from now?

    C. How do automobiles manufactured in the United States compare and contrast with each other?

    D. What do you think is the best solution for the fuel shortage?

The answer is A. The question asks for objective facts. Answer B is a prediction that asks how something will look or be in the future, based on the way it is now. Answer C asks for similarities and differences, which is a higher-level research activity that requires analysis. Answer D is a judgment question that requires informed opinion.

99. **In preparing a speech for a contest, your student has encountered problems with gender specific language. Not wishing to offend either women or men, she seeks your guidance. Which of the following is not an effective strategy? (Skill 3.1, Rigorous)**

    A. Use the generic "he" and explain that people will understand and accept the male pronoun as all-inclusive.

    B. Switch to plural nouns and use "they" as the gender-neutral pronoun.

    C. Use passive voice so that the subject is not required.

    D. Use male pronouns for one part of the speech and then use female pronouns for the other part of the speech.

The answer is A. No longer is the male pronoun considered the universal pronoun. Speakers and writers should choose gender-neutral words and avoid nouns and pronouns that inaccurately exclude one gender or another.

100. **For their research paper on the effects of the Civil War on American literature, students have brainstormed a list of potential online sources and are seeking your authorization. Which of these represent the strongest source? (Skill 3.1, Rigorous)**

    A. http://www.wikipedia.org/

    B. http://www.google.com

    C. http://www.nytimes.com

    D. http://docsouth.unc.edu/southlit/civilwar.html

The answer is D. Sites with an "edu" domain are associated with educational institutions and tend to be more trustworthy for research information. Wikipedia has an "org" domain, which means it is a nonprofit. While Wikipedia may be appropriate for background reading, its credibility as a research site is questionable. Both Google and the New York Times are "com" sites, which are for profit. Even though this does not discredit their information, each site is problematic for researchers. With Google, students will get overwhelmed with hits and may not choose the most reputable sites for their information. As a newspaper, the New York Times would not be a strong source for historical information.

101. **A formative evaluation of student writing (Skill 3.1, Rigorous)**

    A. requires thorough markings of mechanical errors with a pencil or pen.

    B. making comments on the appropriateness of the student's interpretation of the prompt and the degree to which the objective was met.

    C. should require that the student hand in all the materials produced during the process of writing.

    D. several careful readings of the text for content, mechanics, spelling, and usage.

The answer is B. It is important to give students numerous experiences with formative evaluation (evaluation as the student writes the piece). Formative evaluation will assign points to every step of the writing process, even though it is not graded. The criteria for the writing task should be very clear, and the teacher should read each step twice. Responses should be non critical and supportive, and the teacher should involve students in the process of defining criteria, and make it clear that formative and summative evaluations are two distinct processes.

102. In preparing a report about William Shakespeare, students are asked to develop a set of interpretive questions to guide their research. Which of the following would not be classified as an interpretive question? (Skill 3.1, Rigorous)

    A. What would be different today if Shakespeare had not written his plays?

    B. How will the plays of Shakespeare affect future generations?

    C. How does the Shakespeare view nature in *A Midsummer's Night Dream* and *Much Ado About Nothing*?

    D. During the Elizabethan age, what roles did young boys take in dramatizing Shakespeare's plays?

The answer is D. This question requires research into the historical facts; Shakespeare in Love notwithstanding, women did not act In Shakespeare's plays, and their parts were taken by young boys. Answers A and B are hypothetical questions requiring students to provide original thinking and interpretation. Answer C requires comparison and contrast, which are interpretive skills.

103. In writing a report, Hector has to explain where acid rain comes from and what it has done to the environment. What is the most likely form of organizational structure? (Skill 3.2, Easy)

    A. Cause and effect

    B. Problem and solution

    C. Exposition

    D. Definition

The answer is A. This report would discuss what has caused acid rain and what effects acid rain has had on the environment. Although it could offer a solution, the report questions do not focus on that. Most report writing is expository because it provided information and an explanation. While a definition might be an important detail, it would not be the major organizational structure.

104. Explanatory or informative discourse is (Skill 3.2, Easy)

    A. exposition.

    B. narration.

    C. persuasion.

    D. description.

The answer is A. Exposition sets forth a systematic explanation of any subject. It can also introduce the characters of a literary work, and their situations in the story. Narration relates a sequence of events (the story) told through a process of narration (discourse), in which events are recounted in a certain order (the plot). Persuasion strives to convince either a character in the story or the reader.

105. Which of the following is not a technique of prewriting? (Skill 3.2, Easy)

    A. Clustering

    B. Listing

    C. Brainstorming

    D. Proofreading

The answer is D. Proofreading cannot be a method of prewriting, since it is done on already written texts only. Clustering, listing, and brainstorming are all prewriting strategies.

TEACHER CERTIFICATION STUDY GUIDE

106. The following passage is written from which point of view? (Skill 3.2, Easy)

> As she mused the pitiful vision of her mother's life laid its spell on the very quick of her being —that life of commonplace sacrifices closing in final craziness. She trembled as she heard again her mother's voice saying constantly with foolish insistence: *Dearevaun Seraun! Dearevaun Seraun!**
>
> * "The end of pleasure is pain!" (Gaelic)

   A. First person, narrator

   B. Second person, direct address

   C. Third person, omniscient

   D. First person, omniscient

The answer is C. The passage is clearly in the third person (the subject is "she"), and it is omniscient since it gives the characters' inner thoughts.

107. Which of the following is most true of expository writing? (Skill 3.2, Easy)

   A. It is mutually exclusive of other forms of discourse.

   B. It can incorporate other forms of discourse in the process of providing supporting details.

   C. It should never employ informal expression.

   D. It should only be scored with a summative evaluation.

The answer is B. Expository writing sets forth an explanation or an argument about any subject and can use distinct or combined forms of discourse, a sign of academic literacy. This directly contradicts Answer A. Writing can use formal and informal language and can be evaluated in many subjective and objective ways.

TEACHER CERTIFICATION STUDY GUIDE

108. Which of the following is not correct? (Skill 3.2, Easy)

    A. Because most students have wide access to media, teachers should refrain from using it in their classrooms to diminish the overload.

    B. Students can use CD-ROMs to explore information using a virtual reality experience.

    C. Teacher can make their instruction more powerful by using educational media.

    D. The Internet enables students to connect with people across cultures and to share interests.

The answer is A. Teachers can use media in productive ways to enrich instruction. Rather than ignoring it, educators should use a wide assortment of media for the benefit of their students.

109. Which of the following should students use to improve coherence of ideas within an argument? (Skill 3.2, Easy)

    A. Transitional words or phrases to show relationship of ideas.

    B. Conjunctions like "and" to join ideas together.

    C. Use direct quotes extensively to improve credibility.

    D. Adjectives and adverbs to provide stronger detail.

The answer is B. Transitional words and phrases are two-way indicators that connect the previous idea to the following idea. Sophisticated writers use transitional devices to clarify text (for example), to show contrast (despite), to show sequence (first, next), to show cause (because).

110. **Which transition word would show contrast between these two ideas? (Skill 3.2, Average Rigor)**

>We are confident in our skills to teach English. We welcome new ideas on this subject.

- A. We are confident in our skills to teach English, and we welcome new ideas on this subject.

- B. Because we are confident in our skills to teach English, we welcome new ideas on the subject.

- C. When we are confident in our skills to teach English, we welcome new ideas on the subject.

- D. We are confident in our skills to teach English; however, we welcome new ideas on the subject.

The answer is D. Transitional words, phrases and sentences help clarify meanings. In A, the transition word "and" introduces another equal idea. In Answer B, the transition word "because" indicates cause and effect. In Answer C, the transition word "when" indicates order or chronology. In Answer D, "however," shows that these two ideas contrast with each other.

111. **In preparing students for their oral presentations, the instructor provided all of these guidelines, except one. Which is not an effective guideline? (Skill 3.2, Average Rigor)**

- A. Even if you are using a lectern, feel free to move about. This will connect you to the audience.

- B. Your posture should be natural, not stiff. Keep your shoulders toward the audience.

- C. Gestures can help communicate as long as you don't overuse them or make them distracting.

- D. You can avoid eye contact if you focus on your notes. This will make you appear more knowledgeable.

The answer is D. Although many people are nervous about making eye contact, they should focus on two or three people at a time. Body language, such as movement, posture, and gestures, helps the speaker connect to the audience.

112. Which of the following statements indicates an instructional goal for using multimedia in the classroom? (Skill 3.2, Average Rigor)

    A. Audio messages invite the listener to form mental images consistent with the topic of the audio.

    B. Print messages appeal almost exclusively to the mind and push students to read with more thought.

    C. Listening to an audio message is more passive than reading a print message.

    D. Teachers who develop activities to foster a critical perspective on audiovisual presentation will decrease passivity.

The answer is D. Each of the statements is true but only the last one establishes a goal for using multimedia in the classroom.

113. What is the main form of discourse in this passage? (Skill 3.2, Average Rigor)

    It would have been hard to find a passer-by more wretched in appearance. He was a man of middle height, stout and hardy, in the strength of maturity; he might have been forty-six or seven. A slouched leather cap hid half his face, bronzed by the sun and wind, and dripping with sweat.

    A. Description

    B. Narration

    C. Exposition

    D. Persuasion

The answer is A. A description presents a thing or a person in detail, and tells the reader about the appearance of whatever it is presenting. Narration relates a sequence of events (the story) told through a process of narration (discourse), in which events are recounted in a certain order (the plot). Exposition is an explanation or an argument within the narration. It can also be the introduction to a play or a story. Persuasion strives to convince either a character in the story or the reader.

TEACHER CERTIFICATION STUDY GUIDE

114. **In literature, evoking feelings of pity or compassion is to create (Skill 3.2, Average Rigor)**

    A. colloquy.

    B. irony.

    C. pathos.

    D. paradox

The answer is C. A very well known example of pathos is Desdemona's death in *Othello*, but there are many other examples of pathos. In *King Lear*, Cordelia accepts defeat with this line: "We are not the first / Who with best meaning have incurred the worst." A colloquy is a formal conversation. Irony is a discrepancy between what is expected and what occurs. A paradox is a contradictory statement.

115. **Which of the following would not be a major concern in an oral presentation? (Skill 3.2, Average Rigor)**

    A. Establishing the purpose of the presentation

    B. Evaluating the audience's demographics and psychographics.

    C. Creating a PowerPoint slide for each point.

    D. Developing the content to fit the occasion.

The answer is C. PowerPoint slides should be kept to a minimum of one slide per minute and should not overwhelm the presentation. The slides should be a supplement so that the speaker can accomplish the purpose. To reach that goal, the speaker should understand the makeup of the audience: demographics, such as age, education level or other quantifiable characteristic; and, psychographics, such as attitudes or values. Knowing the purpose and the audience will enable the speaker to develop the content to fit the occasion.

TEACHER CERTIFICATION STUDY GUIDE

116. Mr. Ledbetter has instructed his students to prepare a slide presentation that illustrates an event in history. Students are to include pictures, graphics, media clips and links to resources. What competencies will students exhibit at the completion of this project? (Skill 3.2, Rigorous)

    A. Analyze the impact of society on media.

    B. Recognize the media's strategies to inform and persuade.

    C. Demonstrate strategies and creative techniques to prepare presentations using a variety of media.

    D. Identify the aesthetic effects of a media presentation.

The answer is B. Students will have learned how to use various media to convey a unified message.

117. In the following excerpt from "Civil Disobedience," what type of reasoning does Henry David Thoreau use? (Skill 3.2, Rigorous)

    > Unjust laws exist; shall we be content to obey them, or shall we endeavor to amend them, and obey them until we have succeeded, or shall we transgress them at once? Men generally, under such a government as this, think that they ought to wait until they have persuaded the majority to alter them. They think that, if they should resist, the remedy would be worse than the evil. But it is the fault of the government itself that the remedy *is* worse than the evil. ... Why does it always crucify Christ, and excommunicate Copernicus and Luther, and pronounce Washington and Franklin rebels?
    > --"Civil Disobedience" by Henry David Thoreau

    A. Ethical reasoning

    B. Inductive reasoning

    C. Deductive reasoning

    D. Intellectual reasoning

The answer is C. Deductive reasoning begins with a general statement that leads to the particulars. In this essay, Thoreau begins with the general question about what should be done about unjust laws. His argument leads to the government's role in suppressing dissent.

ENG. LANGUAGE LIT. & COMP.

118. Which of the following is not a fallacy in logic? (Skill 3.2, Rigorous)

A. All students in Ms. Suarez's fourth period class are bilingual.
Beth is in Ms. Suarez's fourth period.
Beth is bilingual.

B. All bilingual students are in Ms. Suarez's class.
Beth is in Ms. Suarez's fourth period.
Beth is bilingual.

C. Beth is bilingual.
Beth is in Ms. Suarez's fourth period.
All students in Ms. Suarez's fourth period are bilingual.

D. If Beth is bilingual, then she speaks Spanish.
Beth speaks French.
Beth is not bilingual.

The correct answer is A. The second statement, or premise, is tested against the first premise. Both premises are valid and the conclusion is logical. In Answer B, the conclusion is invalid because the first premise does not exclude other students. In Answer C, the conclusion cannot be logically drawn from the preceding premises—you cannot conclude that all students are bilingual based on one example. In Answer D, the conclusion is invalid because the first premise is faulty.

119. **Which of the following is an example of the post hoc fallacy? (Skill 3.2, Rigorous)**

    A. When the new principal was hired, student-reading scores improved; therefore, the principal caused the increase in scores.

    B. Why are we spending money on the space program when our students don't have current textbooks?

    C. You can't give your class a 10-minute break. Once you do that, we'll all have to give our students a 10-minute break.

    D. You can never believe anything he says because he's not from the same country as we are.

The correct answer is A. A post hoc fallacy assumes that because one event preceded another, the first event caused the second event. In this case, student scores could have increased for other reasons. Answer B is a red herring fallacy in which one raises an irrelevant topic to side track from the first topic. In this case, the space budget and the textbook budget have little effect on each other. Answer C is an example of a slippery slope, in which one event is followed precipitously by another event. Answer D is an ad hominem ("to the man") fallacy in which a person is attacked rather than the concept or interpretation.

120. **Identify the type of appeal used by Molly Ivins's in this excerpt from her essay "Get a Knife, Get a Dog, But Get Rid of Guns." (Skill 3.2, Rigorous)**

    As a civil libertarian, I, of course, support the Second Amendment. And I believe it means exactly what it says:
    A well regulated militia being necessary to the security of a free state, the right of the people to keep and bear arms shall not be infringed.

    A. Ethical

    B. Emotional

    C. Rational

    D. Literary

The answer is A. An ethical appeal is using the credentials of a reliable and trustworthy authority. In this case, Ivins cites the Constitution. Pathos is an emotional appeal and logos is a rational appeal. Literature might appeal to you but it's not a rhetorical appeal.

121. **What is the common advertising technique used by these advertising slogans? (Skill 3.2, Rigorous)**

>"It's everywhere you want to be." - Visa
>"Have it your way." - Burger King
>"When you care enough to send the very best" - Hallmark
>"Be all you can be" – U.S. Army

    A. Peer Approval

    B. Rebel

    C. Individuality

    D. Escape

The answer is C. All of these ads associate products with people who can think and act for themselves. Products are linked to individual decision making. With peer approval, the ads would associate their products with friends and acceptance. For rebelling, the ads would associates products with behaviors or lifestyles that oppose society's norms. Escape would suggest the appeal of getting away from it all.

122. In presenting a report to peers about the effects of Hurricane Katrina on New Orleans, the students wanted to use various media in their argument to persuade their peers that more needed to be done. Which of these would be the most effective? (Skill 3.2, Rigorous)

    A. A PowerPoint presentation showing the blueprints of the levees before the flood and redesigned now for current construction..

    B. A collection of music clips made by the street performers in the French Quarter before and after the flood.

    C. A recent video showing the areas devastated by the floods and the current state of rebuilding.

    D. A collection of recordings of interviews made by the various government officials and local citizens affected by the flooding.

The answer is C. For maximum impact, a video would offer dramatic scenes of the devastated areas. A video by its very nature is more dynamic than a static PowerPoint presentation. Further, the condition of the levees would not provide as much impetus for change as seeing the devastated areas. Oral messages such as music clips and interviews provide another way of supplementing the message but, again, they are not as dynamic as video.

123. **Based on the excerpt below from Kate Chopin's short story "The Story of an Hour," what can students infer about the main character? (Skill 3.2, Rigorous)**

> She did not stop to ask if it were or were not a monstrous joy that held her. A clear and exalted perception enabled her to dismiss the suggestion as trivial. She knew that she would weep again when she saw the kind, tender hands folded in death; the face that had never looked save with love upon her, fixed and gray and dead. But she saw beyond that bitter moment a long procession of years to come that would belong to her absolutely. And she opened and spread her arms out to them in welcome.

A. She dreaded her life as a widow.

B. Although she loved her husband, she was glad that he was dead for he had never loved her.

C. She worried that she was too indifferent to her husband's death.

D. Although they had both loved each other, she was beginning to appreciate that opportunities had opened because of his death.

The answer is D. Dismissing her feeling of "monstrous joy" as insignificant, the young woman realizes that she will mourn her husband who had been good to her and had loved her. But that "long procession of years" does not frighten her; instead she recognizes that this new life belongs to her alone and she welcomes it with open arms.

124. **Which part of a classical argument is illustrated in this excerpt from the essay "What Should Be Done About Rock Lyrics?" (Skill 3.2, Rigorous)**

> But violence against women is greeted by silence. It shouldn't be.
>
> This does not mean censorship, or book (or record) burning. In a society that protects free expression, we understand a lot of stuff will float up out of the sewer. Usually, we recognize the ugly stuff that advocates violence against any group as the garbage it is, and we consider its purveyors as moral lepers. We hold our nose and tolerate it, but we speak out against the values it proffers.
> --"What Should Be Done About Rock Lyrics?" Caryl Rivers

A. Narration

B. Confirmation

C. Refutation and concession

D. Summation

The answer is C. The author acknowledges refutes the idea of censorship and concedes that society tolerates offensive lyrics as part of our freedom of speech. Narration provides background material to produce an argument. In confirmation, the author details the argument with claims that support the thesis. In summation, the author concludes the argument by offering the strongest solution.

125. **Using the selection below from Edgar Alan Poe's "The Tell-Tale Heart," what form of literary criticism would you introduce to high school students? (Skill 4.1, Average Rigor)**

> And have I not told you that what you mistake for madness is but over-acuteness of the sense? --now, I say, there came to my ears a low, dull, quick sound, such as a watch makes when enveloped in cotton. I knew that sound well, too. It was the beating of the old man's heart. It increased my fury, as the beating of a drum stimulates the soldier into courage.

   A. Marxist

   B. Feminist

   C. Psychoanalytic

   D. Classic

The answer is C. Poe's writings focus on the workings of the human mind and would provide a clear introduction of Freudian literary analysis. Marxist criticism focuses on class conflict and the exploitation of the workers, which is not evident in this short story. Feminist criticism focuses on gender roles, which is also not obvious in this short story. Classic criticism is not a recognized type of literary criticism; however, this story could be analyzed according to the New Criticism where the story would be studied as a work of literature.

XAMonline, INC. 21 Orient Ave. Melrose, MA 02176

Toll Free number 800-509-4128

TO ORDER Fax 781-662-9268 OR www.XAMonline.com

WEST SERIES

PO#　　　　　　　Store/School:

Address 1:

Address 2 (Ship to other):

City, State Zip

Credit card number＿＿＿-＿＿＿-＿＿＿-＿＿＿　　expiration＿＿＿

EMAIL ＿＿＿＿＿＿＿＿＿＿＿＿＿＿＿＿

PHONE　　　　　　　　**FAX**

ISBN	TITLE	Qty	Retail	Total
978-1-58197-638-0	WEST-B Basic Skills			
978-1-58197-609-0	WEST-E Biology 0235			
978-1-58197-565-9	WEST-E Chemistry 0245			
978-1-58197-566-6	WEST-E Designated World Language: French Sample Test 0173			
978-1-58197-557-4	WEST-E Designated World Language: Spanish 0191			
978-1-58197-614-4	WEST-E Elementary Education 0014			
978-1-58197-636-6	WEST-E English Language Arts 0041			
978-1-58197-634-2	WEST-E General Science 0435			
978-1-58197-637-3	WEST-E Health & Fitness 0856			
978-1-58197-635-9	WEST-E Library Media 0310			
978-1-58197-674-8	WEST-E Mathematics 0061			
978-1-58197-556-7	WEST-E Middle Level Humanities 0049, 0089			
978-1-58197-568-0	WEST-E Physics 0265			
978-1-58197-563-5	WEST-E Reading/Literacy 0300			
978-1-58197-552-9	WEST-E Social Studies 0081			
978-1-58197-639-7	WEST-E Special Education 0353			
978-1-58197-633-5	WEST-E Visual Arts Sample Test 0133			
	SUBTOTAL		Ship	$8.25
	FOR PRODUCT PRICES VISIT WWW.XAMONLINE.COM		TOTAL	

www.ingramcontent.com/pod-product-compliance
Lightning Source LLC
Chambersburg PA
CBHW080535300426
44111CB00017B/2737